TAXATION IN SIX CONCEPTS

A STUDENT'S GUIDE

For Lily,

With admiration and friendship.

Warmly,
Anne

ANNE L. ALSTOTT

JACQUIN D. BIERMAN PROFESSOR IN TAXATION
YALE LAW SCHOOL

Wolters Kluwer

EDITORIAL STAFF
Editor: Barbara L. Post, Esq.
Production: Diana Roozeboom
Cover Design: Laila Gaidulis
Interior Design: Laila Gaidulis

ISBN: 978-0-8080-4298-3

4025 W. Peterson Ave.
Chicago, IL 60646-6085
800 248 3248
CCHGroup.com

Printed in the United States of America

Introduction

Tax law has an undeserved reputation. Each generation of students hears the same rumors: tax is dry and corporate. It involves thousands of pages of incomprehensible rules. Even worse, tax uses—sharp intake of breath here—*math*. The stories persist into law practice: tax is dangerous terrain that only a specialist can navigate.

So it's no wonder that my students edge into tax class on the first day of the semester with tense expressions and venti espressos. Despite the occasional positive word on tax that filters down from 3Ls who have taken the class, most students are sure, absolutely certain, that they're about to sacrifice thirteen weeks to frustration and boredom.

But tax doesn't merit its reputation. Tax law isn't hard to understand once you know that tax doctrines rest on a handful of concepts—just six, in fact. Armed with six concepts, you can decipher the law. Even better, tax is—I mean it, no irony, no scare quotes—fascinating. In the United States, more so than in any other developed country, the tax law hosts many of the government's most important social and economic policies. If you care about health care, housing, financial markets, education, or poverty, you should care about tax. In short, tax turns out to host many of the interesting and pressing public policy problems that may have enticed you to law school in the first place. In this book, I introduce the six concepts and use them to unpack leading cases and real-world transactions. The six are *valuation, net income, realization, tax deferral, substance over form* and *income-shifting*. The cases I discuss are the ones covered by the leading casebooks, and I show you how one (or two) of the six concepts reveal what each case is really about. This book also looks beyond the classroom. At every step, I include real-world transactions to show how tax planning harks back to the six concepts.

Of course, tax law, like all law, is full of ambiguity and contradiction. Sometimes there is no single right answer. Courts reach conflicting decisions and use inconsistent reasoning. But the six concepts reveal the conflicts within the law that give rise to ambiguity and uncertainty.

This short book has its limitations. It is an introduction to income taxation, and not a treatise, so while it covers the major cases, it doesn't attempt to explain every doctrine. There are excellent treatises out there, and I encourage you to consult them. (Open secret: that is what tax lawyers do when they confront a new doctrine in tax law. Sure, we read the Code, but we also grab a reliable treatise and read what we need.)

This book also doesn't cover the specialized topics of corporate, partnership, and international tax. But the six concepts take you a long way in understanding common tax-planning techniques, and the book explains common financial and real estate transactions. I've included a glossary of tax and business jargon, so you have a quick reference when a judicial opinion (or a client) invokes "accelerated depreciation" or "nonrecourse debt."

In fact, the six concepts bring something to the table for the tax specialist too. The best tax lawyers can explain issues in conceptual terms to other lawyers and to clients. No business client appreciates a string of jargon punctuated by section numbers. But clients understand—and appreciate—an explanation couched in concepts. Try it. Would you rather hear that "section 265(a)(2) prohibits tax arbitrage subject to the 163 regulations and Rev. Proc. 72-18"—or that "the tax law gives no relief for your costs when you borrow to buy tax-favored assets"?

Before we get started, I have to make one concession to the tax rumor mill. Tax law does involve math. I admit it. But if you made it through the fourth grade and can add, subtract, multiply, and divide, you'll be fine. Tax law requires logical thinking, but there's no higher mathematics involved. We don't even use algebra, except for one footnote in one chapter, and you can even ignore that if algebra just doesn't speak to you.

About the Author

Anne L. Alstott is the Jacquin D. Bierman Professor in Taxation at the Yale Law School. She has held the Bierman chair from 2004-2008 and again beginning in 2011. From 2008-2011, Professor Alstott was the Manley O. Hudson Professor at the Harvard Law School.

Professor Alstott has taught tax law, tax policy, and social welfare policy at Yale, Harvard, and Columbia since 1992. She has won the annual teaching award at Yale Law School three times (in 2012, 2004, and 1998) and at Columbia Law School once (in 1995). The Yale Law School graduating class of 2013 elected her to speak at Commencement.

Professor Alstott's books include *A New Deal for Old Age* (2016, Harvard University Press), *No Exit: What Parents Owe Their Children and What Society Owes Parents* (2004, Oxford University Press) and *The Stakeholder Society* (1999, Yale University Press) (with Bruce Ackerman). Her scholarly articles have been published in the Harvard Law Review, the Columbia Law Review, and the Tax Law Review, as well as in many other journals and in books.

Professor Alstott was born in Indianapolis. Her parents are Dr. David F. Alstott and the late Dr. Rosemary Lester Alstott.

How to Use This Book

This book explains and then uses six concepts that recur throughout the income tax law to illuminate classic cases and real-world transactions. It's probably easiest to read straight through the book. If you're already in practice, the book includes an abundance of examples drawn from the real-world transactions that you see every day. If you're still in law school, you'll find that the book's organization mirrors the layout of most casebooks. But just in case your particular casebook follows a different plan, I've included (at the back of the book in Appendix C) a section called "Roadmaps to Major Casebooks," which cross-references the contents of this book to leading casebooks used in law schools.

I've also included (in Appendix A) a glossary of tax and business terminology. Students without a business background may find it especially useful to have a straightforward guide to non-intuitive concepts like stocks, bonds, and options.

Finally, law students may want to look at Appendix B, which is a guide to writing an issue-spotter exam. These exams recur in almost every class, but they differ from the kinds of essay exams you took in college. The appendix offers a short primer on what to do—and what not to do—when you're asked to spot legal issues.

Contents

Introduction . . . iii

About the Author . . . v

How to Use This Book . . . vii

CHAPTER 1 The Six Concepts: An Overview . . . 1

¶100 Introduction . . . 1
¶101 Valuation . . . 2
¶102 Net Income . . . 3
¶103 Realization . . . 4
¶104 Tax Deferral . . . 5
¶105 Substance Over Form . . . 5
¶106 Income Shifting . . . 6

CHAPTER 2 Salary and Fringe Benefits . . . 9

¶200 Introduction . . . 9
¶201 Valuation and the Problem of Measuring Income . . . 10
¶202 Real-World Transactions: Company Stock and Stock Options . . . 12
¶203 Fringe Benefits . . . 13
¶204 Real-World Transactions: Employer-Provided Health Insurance . . . 19
¶205 Code Section 132 . . . 21
Appendix 2-1: Valuation and Fringe Benefits . . . 24

CHAPTER 3 Gifts and Bequests . . . 27

¶300 Introduction . . . 27
¶301 Income Shifting and Code Section 102 . . . 28
¶302 *Duberstein* . . . 29
¶303 Real-World Transactions: Bonuses, Tips, and Business Gifts . . . 34

CHAPTER 4 Marginal and Average Tax Rates . . . 37

¶400 Introduction . . . 37
¶401 Two Tax Rates . . . 37
¶402 Real-World Transactions: The Value of Tax Breaks for Real Estate and Education . . . 40
¶403 Distribution and the Average Tax Rate . . . 43
¶404 *Old Colony* and Substance Over Form . . . 44
¶405 Real-World Transactions: Signing Bonuses and the Gross Up for Taxes . . . 47

CHAPTER 5 Gains and Losses . . . 49

¶500 Introduction . . . 49
¶501 The Concept of Basis . . . 50
¶502 Real-World Transactions: Corporate Acquisitions . . . 52
¶503 When is Basis Recovered? *Hort v. Commissioner* . . . 54
¶504 Allocating Basis and *Inaja Land Co. v. Commissioner* . . . 58
¶505 Basis Rules for Gifts and Bequests . . . 60
¶506 Real-World Transactions: Estate Planning and the Income Tax . . . 62
¶507 Basis and Pre-Nuptial Agreements: *Farid-Es-Sultaneh v. Commissioner* . . . 64

CHAPTER 6 The Realization Requirement . . . 67

¶600 Introduction . . . 67
¶601 Valuation, Realization and Tax Deferral . . . 67
¶602 Realization and Windfalls . . . 69
¶603 Defining Realization: *Eisner v. Macomber* . . . 71
¶604 What is a "Sale or Other Disposition"? *Cottage Savings Association v. Commissioner* . . . 73
¶605 Real-World Transactions: Year-End Stock Trading . . . 76
¶606 Real-World Transactions: Real Estate Swaps . . . 78

CHAPTER 7 Borrowed Funds . . . 81

¶700 Introduction . . . 81
¶701 Valuation and the Exclusion of Borrowed Funds . . . 81
¶702 Cancellation of Indebtedness: *U.S. v. Kirby Lumber Co.* . . . 83
¶703 *Zarin v. Commissioner* and Code Section 108(e)(5) . . . 85
¶704 *Commissioner v. Tufts* and Nonrecourse Debt . . . 87
¶705 Real-World Transactions: Tax Planning for Bankruptcy and Insolvency . . . 90
¶706 Borrowing and the Time Value of Money . . . 91

CHAPTER 8 Business Deductions in General . . . 93

¶800 Introduction . . . 93
¶801 Net Income, Deductions, and Exclusions . . . 94
¶802 *Welch v. Helvering* . . . 95
¶803 *Exacto Spring Corporation v. Commissioner* . . . 97
¶804 Real-World Transactions: Disguised Dividends and Disguised Gifts . . . 99

CHAPTER 9 Deductions for Business Meals, Commuting, Clothing and Child Care . . 101

¶900 Introduction . . . 101
¶901 Business Meals and *Moss v. Commissioner* . . . 102
¶902 *Commissioner v. Flowers* and the Problem of Commuting . . . 104
¶903 Real-World Transactions: Tax Lobbying and the Restaurant Industry . . . 106
¶904 Work Clothing and *Pevsner v. Commissioner* . . . 107
¶905 Child Care and *Smith v. Commissioner* . . . 108

CHAPTER 10 Capitalization and Depreciation 111

¶1000 Introduction 111
¶1001 The Value of Tax Deferral 112
¶1002 Capital Expenditures and *Indopco, Inc. v. Commissioner* 114
¶1003 Depreciation and *Simon v. Commissioner* 116
¶1004 Real World Transactions: Bonus Depreciation and the Great Recession 119

CHAPTER 11 Losses and the Interest Deduction 121

¶1100 Introduction 121
¶1101 The Interest Deduction 121
¶1102 Tax Arbitrage and *Knetsch v. U.S.* 122
¶1103 Hobby Losses, *Storey v. Commissioner*, and *Nickerson v. Commissioner* 126
¶1104 Real-World Transactions: Wash Sales and Repos 129
¶1105 Selective Loss Realization and *Fender v. United States* 131

CHAPTER 12 Whose Income Is It? 135

¶1200 Introduction 135
¶1201 Marriage and *Druker v. Commissioner* 136
¶1202 Real-World Transaction: Dividing Property and Income at Divorce 138
¶1203 Assignments of Earned Income: *Lucas v. Earl* 141
¶1204 Assignments of Income Using Entities 142
¶1205 Assignments of Income from Property: *Blair v. Commissioner* and *Helvering v. Horst* 144

CHAPTER 13 Capital Gains and Losses 149

¶1300 Introduction 149
¶1301 The Preferential Rate 150
¶1302 The Capital Loss Limitation 154
¶1303 Real-World Transactions: Sale of a Closely-Held Business 156
¶1304 What Is a Capital Asset? 157
¶1305 Real-World Transaction: Stocks and Bonds 160
¶1306 Conversion and *Bramblett v. Commissioner* 162

CHAPTER 14 Tax Shelters 165

¶1400 Introduction 165
¶1401 *Estate of Franklin* 165
¶1402 *Frank Lyon Co. v. U.S.* 168
¶1403 *ACM Partnership v. Commissioner* 172

APPENDIX A A Glossary of Tax and Business Jargon 179

APPENDIX B How to Answer an Issue-Spotter Exam Question 187

APPENDIX C Roadmaps to Major Casebooks 193

Case Table 197

Table of Code, Regulations and Rulings 199

Index 201

CHAPTER 1

The Six Concepts: An Overview

Introduction .... ¶100
Valuation .... ¶101
Net Income .... ¶102
Realization .... ¶103
Tax Deferral .... ¶104
Substance Over Form .... ¶105
Income Shifting .... ¶106

¶100 INTRODUCTION

The income tax is familiar to nearly everyone in the United States. Our employers withhold part of our wages and send them to Uncle Sam. Every April, most everyone grumbles about filling out their tax returns.

The income tax, in this everyday sense, isn't so different from other taxes we pay. Employers must also withhold FICA (the Social Security payroll tax). Homeowners must write annual checks for local property taxes. We pay sales taxes at the cash register when we shop.

But while the sales tax targets your spending and the property tax targets the value of your house, the income tax targets, well, income. And it turns out that 99% of the complexity of the Tax Code arises because of the difficulty in defining income.

Intuitively, income measures how much richer you've become during a year. If you've earned $75,000 from your job, you're $75,000 better off than you were last year. Income also helps us compare the situation of different individuals. If you earned $75,000 last year, and I earned $50,000, then you are $25,000 better off than I am.

Clearly, income provides a powerful tool for public policy. Looking at income from year to year tells us how much (more) money a person has this year and whether she can meet her basic needs. Examining the income of different people also helps us tell whether some people (or groups) are doing particularly well or badly. The income tax, then, represents our collective political judgment that people should contribute to the costs of government based on how well they're doing in a particular year.

So far, so good. Income is an intuitive measure of how well someone is doing, and it's a valuable tool for policy. Easy enough.

But, just as in other bodies of law, complications arise. Torts is the law of accidents, as we know. But it isn't always clear what counts as an accident and who is at fault. Lawyers can make arguments on both sides of most issues, and judges reach conflicting conclusions.

The same kind of legal ambiguity arises in tax: it isn't always clear what counts as income or whose income it is. If my boss pays me a bonus of $5,000 at the end of the year, it's pretty intuitive that I have $5,000 of extra income. But what if my boss sends me to a $5,000 tax conference in Hawaii instead? You could argue that the trip should count as income: after all, Hawaii in December is a pretty nice perk. Or you could argue that a business trip isn't really income—after all, maybe I hate the beach and would much rather stay home. In that case, it's less clear that I'm better off by $5,000.

Luckily, the complexities and ambiguities of tax center around a handful of concepts. Six, in fact. And by an amazing coincidence, these are the six concepts that recur throughout this book. As we progress from hypotheticals about Hawaiian trips to complex transactions among Fortune 500 companies, we will see that the six concepts underlie even the trickiest and most complex tax planning.

In the remaining pages of this chapter, I introduce the six concepts. The following chapters deploy these concepts to analyze major cases and real-world transactions.

¶101 VALUATION

To measure how much better off an individual has become during the year, an income tax has to assign a money value to the economic resources that the individual has gained. Sometimes, valuation is so easy that it's nearly automatic, and we don't have to think very hard. If my employer pays me $100 cash, I'm clearly better off by $100. Not much ambiguity there.

But *valuation poses a problem when the law faces uncertainty in measuring an individual's gain in well-being*. Consider the all-expenses-paid tax conference in Hawaii. Depending on my personal preferences and my situation, that trip might be the vacation of a lifetime—or worse than staying home. If I love the beach, love to travel, and don't mind a few business meetings, the trip will feel a lot like a free $5,000 holiday. If I sunburn easily, hate to fly, and dislike meetings, then I won't feel better off by anything like $5,000.

The puzzle, then, is one of *valuation*. The item in question—the Hawaii trip—doesn't change. But its perceived value changes depending on the tastes and situation of the recipient. Perhaps the law should respond by inquiring into individuals' unique situations: Anne hates beaches, while Brent loves to surf. Or perhaps the law should treat a $5,000 trip as objectively worth $5,000, no matter what. The law, it turns out, takes both approaches, depending on the item in question and the circumstances.

We will see that *valuation* uncertainties permeate the tax law far beyond business trips and other fringe benefits (that is, employer-provided perks). For instance, when a big company like Apple Computer sells intellectual property to its wholly-owned subsidiary located in a tax haven, it may be making use of the uncertainties of *valuation* to help reduce its total worldwide tax bill.

¶102 NET INCOME

We've already said that the income tax aims to measure how much better off an individual has become during the year. Intuitively, the law should only count money that a person earns free and clear—not money that she has tied up in her business and can't spend on herself.

To see why, imagine that you have started a small business—a wine store, say. Every year, customers plunk down a good amount of money at the cash register, perhaps as much as $100,000. But the law would clearly be off base if it recorded your income as $100,000. You had to spend a good chunk of that money buying and storing the wine, renting the building, and paying your employees. If the costs of running the store amount to $70,000, then your *net income* or profit is just $30,000.

Put another way, you, the wine-store owner, aren't as well off as a lawyer whose salary is $100,000. You have, at most, $30,000 to spend on your own food, rent, clothing, and entertainment. Your lawyer friend who earns $100,000 has way more, since her law firm provides her with an office, a computer, and anything else she needs to do her job. The government would be taking a distorted snapshot of reality if it treated the two of you as equally well-off in terms of your income.

So *net income* is the amount a taxpayer can spend on herself after paying the costs of running her business. That's pretty straightforward.

But—wait for it—*net income* isn't always such a clear concept. *Net income issues arise when the law cannot easily measure how much spending is truly required for a taxpayer's business.*

Now imagine a wine store owner who spends $15,000 on an Armani wardrobe. We can view her purchase in either of two lights. On the one hand, fancy clothes just don't seem related to the wine business. She could go for minimalist chic with simple black clothing from the Gap for around $150, for heaven's sake! On the other hand, maybe she is courting a high-end clientele that expects their wine merchant to dress like a peer. Maybe, just maybe, the Armani investment will pay off in bigger sales.

We will see that the Armani wardrobe stands in for a host of similar problems in deciding whether spending is tied up in the business. Business travel, commuting, and business meals represent big money to American business, and yet the law has a surprisingly hard time distinguishing business spending from personal spending.

Even big-dollar corporate tax planning can center on *net income* issues. When a company pays its CEO $10 million per year, the tax law has to sort out what is really going on. Maybe the CEO is worth $10 million, and so paying his salary is necessary to the business. But if the CEO is also the company's largest stockholder, part of that $10 million may be something very different— disguised payment of profits, or a disguised dividend. The tax law has to tackle the task of sorting out whether the CEO is worth his big paycheck.[1]

¶103 REALIZATION

When the law tries to measure income, it runs smack up against a problem of timing. To see why, imagine that you own stock[2] in Apple. You bought the stock for $1,000, and today, *The Wall Street Journal* informs you, the stock is worth $1,250.

Yay! You made $250 of income, right? You are definitely better off than your friend, who bought stock in Microsoft for $1,000 that is still worth just $1,000.

But maybe you don't feel $250 richer just yet. After all, the $250 exists only on paper. By the time you sell the Apple stock, it might be worth less than $1,250. You won't really know how the investment has turned out until you sell.

Once again, the law could adopt one of two points of view. On the one hand, the law could tax you on your economic profit of $250 today. After all, you could sell and claim your $250. On the other hand, taxing you on paper profits might seem harsh. If you don't sell, you may not have the cash to pay the tax, and it might be bad for the economy to force people to sell their investments just to pay Uncle Sam.

Realization is the tax concept that responds to the problem of paper profits: the tax law generally waits until the taxpayer sells to measure her income on an investment.

Thanks to the *realization* requirement, you don't have to report $250 of income on your tax return now. In fact, you won't report any income until the day you sell your stock. Whew! Problem solved.

But not so fast. This simple solution opens up new puzzles for the law. For instance, suppose you sell your Apple stock but then immediately reinvest the proceeds in Dell stock. Is that transaction a "sale," because you had cash for one millisecond—or not a sale, because you don't have any cash now, after buying the Dell stock?

Taxpayers and their advocates have shown endless ingenuity in taking advantage of the *realization* requirement to reduce their taxes. We'll see one case in which the savings and loan industry colluded with federal banking regulators to engineer an unintended payout from the IRS. And the Supreme Court held that the gambit worked![3]

From a tax policy perspective, *realization* is a problem, because it creates a huge incentive for people to hold, not sell, assets, and to engage in barter

---

1 Exacto Spring v. Commissioner, 196 F.3d 833 (7th Cir. 1999), discussed in Chapter 3, *infra*.

2 Corporate stock represents an ownership interest in a corporation.

3 Cottage Savings Association v. Commissioner, 499 U.S. 554 (1991). In Chapter 8, we'll consider whether the banking regulators' action was justified. (*Hint:* you can argue the point both ways.)

instead of cash sales. Tax policy wonks worry that these incentives are bad for the economy, and we'll see that the Congress has responded with rules that—you guessed it—make the Tax Code more complex.

¶104 TAX DEFERRAL

The *realization* requirement stars in many tax-reduction strategies because it permits *tax deferral, which allows taxpayers to put off paying their taxes. Tax deferral*, it turns out, is great for taxpayers but costs the Treasury a bundle. To see why, imagine you have a $1,000 credit card bill from MasterCard. Now suppose you have a choice: you can pay the bill now or in 15 years without interest or penalties. If you're like most people, you would love to put off paying (and the flip side is that MasterCard wouldn't like it much). *Tax deferral*, we will see, describes just the same situation—when taxpayers can use tax planning to delay paying taxes without interest or penalties.

Realization creates one major source of *tax deferral.* For instance, suppose your client has invested $50 million in a downtown office building. A buyer comes along and offers $60 million. That's a pretty good deal, but it would be an even better deal from a tax perspective if the client could defer income tax on his $10 million profit. So, instead of a cash deal, parties in this situation will often swap properties instead, because the Code doesn't treat the swap of real property as an occasion for *realization* of gain.[4] Your client receives a $60 million uptown building he had his eye on, and he pays nothing in taxes—until later, perhaps much later—when he sells his new building, this time for cash.

But even beyond *realization*, the tax law is rife with opportunities for *tax deferral.* Sometimes Congress uses *tax deferral* as a carrot to induce investors to behave in certain ways. For instance, Congress adopted something called "bonus depreciation," which provides *tax deferral* for investors in plant and equipment in an effort to help the nation spend its way out of the Great Recession.[5]

Sometimes, though, *tax deferral* is the unintended consequence of the Code's complex rules. We will see a host of audacious tax shelters that attempted to twist the Code's words to permit extreme *tax deferral.* And we'll see that the courts turned to something called the *substance over form* doctrine to stem the tide.[6]

¶105 SUBSTANCE OVER FORM

In the popular imagination, the IRS is an all-powerful agency, staffed with humorless, dark-suited agents who can detect even the smallest cadge on your tax return. But, in reality, the IRS is outmanned by the private bar. To even the

---

[4] *See* Code Section 1031.

[5] *See* Chapter 10, *infra*.

[6] *See* Chapters 11 and 14, *infra*.

playing field, judges have created the *substance over form doctrine, which allows the IRS to challenge taxpayers who go too far in their tax planning.*

As the name suggests, the *substance over form* doctrine lets the IRS argue that what a taxpayer really did is different from what the taxpayer says she did. For example, suppose your employer offers you a year-end bonus of $25,000. That's a nice perk, but you now know that the income tax will take a bite out of a cash bonus. You're a law-abiding taxpayer, but if there's any way to save on taxes legally, you'd be open to it.

Ha! A bright idea strikes. You ask your employer to send the $25,000 to your landlord, prepaying your rent for a year. Your employer is fine with the plan; it doesn't cost her anything extra. And you now have no bonus to report on your tax return. Right?

Well, no. The *substance over form* doctrine will knock this tax plan out of the box. The key question is: *What's really going on here?* The answer, of course, is that your employer is paying you $25,000 as a bonus. Whether she gives you the check or sends it to a third party to pay your bills, it's still—in substance—your money. Accordingly, the tax law will treat you as having $25,000 of income.

The *substance over form* doctrine is a powerful tool in the hands of the IRS—too powerful, some lawyers say. Armed with *substance over form,* the IRS can challenge nearly any tax plan, creating massive uncertainty in the law. We shall see that the legal record on *substance over form* is mixed: the IRS often prevails, but on occasion, judges turn back the IRS, finding the agency to be over-zealous in its efforts to deter tax abuses.

¶106 INCOME SHIFTING

Like many countries, the United States has a progressive income tax, which imposes higher tax rates as income rises. Very low-income people (under about $10,000 for a single individual) pay no federal income tax at all—they have a zero rate. Very high-income people face a federal income tax rate of nearly 40% when they earn extra money.[7] Progressive rates also apply to businesses. Very profitable businesses pay taxes at high rates, while less profitable ones may pay low or zero tax rates. Tax-exempt entities pay a zero tax rate: these include universities, charities, and governments.

Progressive rates are politically controversial. Progressives tend to think that it's fair to tax higher incomes at higher rates, while conservatives think it isn't fair to ask people who earn more to pay disproportionately more. Some people worry that progressive taxes may dampen economic activity, while others respond that fairness is more important than economic growth.

But set aside the policy debate for a moment, and take a look at what progressive rates mean for tax planning. Progressive tax rates create an opening for

---

[7] *See* the discussion of marginal and average tax rates in Chapter 2, *infra*.

income shifting—that is, the opportunity for taxpayers to lower their total tax bill by having money taxed at a low rate instead of at a high rate.

Income shifting works like this. Suppose that Andy and Bill, a committed couple, happen to work together in a law firm. If both have the same tax rate, then they won't much care whether clients send their fees to Andy or to Bill. But suppose that Andy works full time, while Bill works part-time. Bill earns less, so his tax rate is low—say, 10% instead of 40%. All of a sudden, the Andy-Bill law firm has a tax incentive to tell clients to send their next few payments to Bill. Think about it: if the couple can choose their tax rate, they'll choose Bill's low tax rate over Andy's high tax rate every time.

What makes *income shifting* work is that the tax system (in this hypothetical) treats Andy and Bill as separate taxpayers with separate tax rates—even though Andy and Bill actually share their money. If the tax system, instead, treated Andy and Bill as one taxpayer, then they'd have the same tax rate, defeating *income shifting*.

We will see that the tax law responds to the prospect of *income shifting* in various ways. If Andy and Bill are married, the law treats them as a single taxpayer with a single tax rate, and so they cannot shift income. But if Andy and Bill are unmarried, the tax law ignores their relationship, and they can often shift income rather easily.

Income shifting also occurs in corporate transactions. For instance, suppose that Donald Trump enters into a joint venture with the city of New York to build a new skyscraper. Donald, let's suppose, has a high tax rate, while the city (as a governmental entity) pays zero income tax. If the project will generate taxable income (from rents, say), the parties have an incentive to claim that the income belongs to ...

The city, of course. If the parties can label joint venture income "tax-exempt," then the venture as a whole will save on its taxes, leaving more money for the two parties to divvy up. The Donald won't mind a bit, as long as he gets his fair share of actual profits from the deal.

Income shifting represents a challenge for the income tax whenever parties join forces. Personal relationships and business relationships pose constant opportunities for the taxpayer—and threats to the tax base. We shall see that the texture of the law is uneven: depending on the situation, *income shifting* can be perfectly legal—or absolutely prohibited.[8]

---

[8] *See* Chapters 3 and 12, *infra*.

CHAPTER 2

Salary and Fringe Benefits

Introduction . . . ¶200
Valuation and the Problem of Measuring Income . . . ¶201
Real-World Transactions: Company Stock and Stock Options . . . ¶202
Fringe Benefits . . . ¶203
Real-World Transactions: Employer-Provided Health Insurance . . . ¶204
Code Section 132 . . . ¶205
Valuation and Fringe Benefits . . . Appendix 2-1

¶200 INTRODUCTION

The intuition behind the income tax, as we've seen, is that individuals (and companies) should share in the cost of funding the government based on how much richer they've become during the year. So, if Cara earns $100,000 from her job and Derek earns $40,000 from his, then Cara should pay more, all else equal.

But whenever anyone says, "all else equal," you should immediately ask what happens when all else isn't equal. In the income tax, all else is rarely equal because people and their situations are so different. Suppose Cara spends every penny to live in a cramped walk-up in high-priced Manhattan, while Derek rents a comfortable house in suburban Boise. And suppose Derek's company pays him only $40,000 in cash salary but also gives him stock worth 10% of the company. Now it isn't so clear that Cara is better off.

These are, of course, *valuation* problems, which arise when the law faces uncertainty in measuring an individual's gain in well-being. The income tax law seeks to measure how much richer an individual is this year. But there are, legitimately, a number of different answers, depending on how you understand value. The law could take Cara's income at face value—or it could take note of the sky-high rents in New York City. The law could cut Derek a break, taxing him only on his cash income. Or, in analyzing his ownership interest, the law might inquire whether Derek's company is a tiny startup or a social media giant like Facebook or Twitter.

But once the law begins to take notice of individuals' unique situations, the possibilities stretch to infinity. One person may earn a good living in advertising but is miserable because she dreamed of being a writer. Another may live the Zen life on Wal*Mart wages. We could make a serious philosophical argument that the Zen guy is richer in a meaningful sense, but is that really the kind of well-being the income tax is about?

In this chapter, we will see that the law cuts off arguments about *valuation* with doctrines that often ignore the details of an individual's situation.

¶201 VALUATION AND THE PROBLEM OF MEASURING INCOME

Since the tax law cannot look inside individuals' heads, it cannot feasibly measure subjective well-being. So the tax law doesn't ask people how they feel. (Any income tax that asked people, "Do you feel richer this year?" probably wouldn't raise much revenue.) Instead, the law adopts three conventions, or rules of thumb, that allow the IRS to measure income in objective terms, using limited information about people's circumstances.

The first convention is that the law infers value from market transactions in dollars. If your employer pays you $100, then you have $100 of income. If you sublet your apartment for $1,500, then you have $1,500 of income. (Yes, you have to report that!)

Measuring transactions in dollars is certainly practical. The IRS can verify dollar transactions far more easily than it can ascertain how people feel. But is that fair? Suppose you earn $100 from your job, and, in a fit of enthusiasm, you spend it on a sweater in an unfortunate shade of green. You wear that sweater once, hate how you look, and throw it in your closet, never to see the light of day again. The whole thing was a nightmare.

But the income tax will still record your income from your job at $100. The IRS latches onto the objective fact that you had $100 in your hand, paid to you by your employer. The IRS doesn't want to hear the saga of the sweater, how you wish you could get your money back but didn't save the receipt. The relevant transaction, for the IRS, is the market exchange: you did the work and your employer paid you $100. Period. If you spent the money on a hideous sweater, don't ask Uncle Sam to share the pain.

Once you think about it, taxing dollars received is not just practical; it also has a firm foundation in economics. If you have $100 in your hand, and you use it to buy a sweater, then, at that moment, you must have valued the sweater at $100. Otherwise, you wouldn't have bought it. The IRS basically doesn't want to hear us whine about our bad purchases: it assumes a value-for-value exchange.

The law also adopts a second convention that helps sidestep *valuation* problems: the law identifies income based on categories, types of market transactions that typically generate income. For instance, Code Section 61 provides that income includes salaries, dividends, interest, rents, and royalties. These categories offer a crisp way to cut off argument: if your boss pays you $100,000 in salary, that's income. Period. No arguing about whether your particular relationship with that particular employer actually rendered you better off by that amount or whether, really, the psychic damage from that job left you reeling.

The categories used in Code Section 61 represent a *sources* approach to defining income, and they may feel familiar. Form 1040, the federal income tax return, uses the same categories, listing income on lines for wages, interest, dividends and so on. The strength of the sources approach is that it produces predictable results and does not permit individuals to engage in special pleading.

But the simplicity of the sources approach is also its downside. Precisely because it ignores differences among individuals, it can badly mismeasure income. For example, imagine two roommates who each earn $50,000 from their jobs. The sources approach would treat them as having the same income. Reasonable enough, until you learn that Aaron never travels, while Brett is on the road three days a week—and pays for his business travel out of his own salary. Last year, Brett spent $10,000 on planes, trains, and hotel bills just so he could do his job.

In this scenario, Brett probably doesn't feel as if he has $50,000 in income because $10,000 is eaten up in travel costs. But the sources view can't detect the difference.

To address this kind of problem, the tax law makes use of a third convention, the *uses* approach to defining income. The uses view takes advantage of a neat proposition borrowed from economics. When you think about it, people can do just two things with their income: save it or spend it. If you earn $75 in interest on your bank account, you can withdraw that money and take some friends out to dinner. Or, you can leave it in the bank account. The first option (dinner) is spending; the second option (leaving it in the bank) is saving. (There really isn't a third option: even if you go crazy and just burn the money, an economist would say that your act of defiance is just a form of personal consumption—you used up the money by burning it.)

The uses view is, well, useful, because it solves the problem of Brett, the traveling sales rep. He has $50,000 in salary, but with $10,000 in business travel costs, Brett only has $40,000 to spend as he chooses.[1] So the uses view incorporates more information about the individual in order to measure what really matters: the resources individuals have available to spend or save, as they choose.

We can summarize the point this way: the uses view shows us that *income does not include money that must be spent on business inputs; it includes only money that is spent on personal consumption (or that is saved and can later be spent for personal consumption).* Two economists—Haig and Simons—translated the uses view of income into a handy formula, which we will use from time to time (and which your casebook probably contains as well):

$$Y = C + \Delta S$$

Y is income, C is consumption, and S is savings. So the formula means that income equals the sum of what you spend during the year (consumption)

---

[1] Mechanically, the law accomplishes this result by including all $50,000 in income and then permitting a *deduction* (or subtraction) of $10,000. We will study deductions in detail in Chapter 8, but, for now, the point is that the uses view of income justifies the deduction.

plus what you've added to your savings (Δ is the Greek symbol used in math to indicate change).

You won't see this formula on the Form 1040, thank goodness. But you will see that tax policy makers and judges invoke Haig-Simons as a way of thinking about income in hard cases. And because law school focuses on the hard cases, we'll consult Haig-Simons a fair bit.

¶202 REAL-WORLD TRANSACTIONS: COMPANY STOCK AND STOCK OPTIONS

The three conventions—dollar measurement, categories of income, and the Haig-Simons definition of income—combine to solve some significant real-world *valuation* problems. Return to the example of Derek, who earns $40,000 in cash salary plus stock representing ownership of 10% of the company he works for. The puzzle is whether his income is $40,000 or something more than that, taking into account the value of the stock.

Derek, of course, would like to pay tax only on his cash earnings. But the law, for obvious reasons, doesn't let people ignore non-cash compensation. Imagine the consequences if people could avoid paying tax on income received in kind: we'd devolve into a barter economy pretty quickly. So Code Section 61 includes in income the dollar value of all "compensation," whether received in cash or in kind. Thus, if Derek's stock could be sold in the stock market for $50,000, then the Code will treat him as if he has total income of $90,000 ($40,000 cash salary plus $50,000 stock).

This result (taxing Derek on the full value of his company stock) makes sense from a sources perspective: salary is one of the typical sources of income. It makes sense from a uses (Haig-Simons) perspective too. After all, the stock gives Derek choices. He can sell the stock for $50,000 and either spend it or reinvest it in some other investment. Even if he holds onto the stock, he's exercised a choice: in effect, he has chosen to invest his $50,000 in his company's stock. Choice, once again, is the key to income.

But wait just a minute. How much choice does Derek really have? Company stock (and stock options) often are restricted. Companies want their employees to stay around and hold a stake in the firm's success—not sell out and retire to Tahiti. Very often, companies restrict the sale of employee stock or provide that the stock is forfeited if the employee leaves the company within a certain period.

Restricted choice is significant if we take the Haig-Simons view: if Derek has no choice about spending the $50,000 or saving it, then arguably he has no income. The tax law recognizes that point in Code Section 83, which applies to company stock received by employees. The rule is that the fair market value of Derek's stock is included in his income at the time he can transfer the stock or at the time there is no longer a substantial risk of having to forfeit the stock.[2] So if Derek receives $50,000 worth of stock, but he has to work for five more years before ownership vests, then he won't be taxed until the waiting period has expired.

The Section 83 rules are not the end of the story when it comes to the taxation of stock and stock options. The Code contains special rules that govern certain employee stock and stock options. But the rules illustrate one application of the Haig-Simons view of income.

¶203 FRINGE BENEFITS

To this point, we've seen that not all cash receipts are income for tax purposes. Instead, as Haig and Simons helpfully tell us, income includes only money that is (1) spent now on personal consumption or (2) saved to be spent later on personal consumption.

Understanding this point has a legal payoff when it comes to the tax treatment of fringe benefits, or valuable items provided to workers by their employers. Haig-Simons gives us a ready principle: when fringe benefits amount to personal consumption, they should be included in income at fair market value.

For example, a few New York City law firms used to provide summer associates with free "dream nights" on the town. Summer associates were given a firm credit card and could charge restaurant meals, Broadway tickets, and drinks. Those dream nights were clearly salary in disguise: the firms, in effect, paid the summer associates extra as a recruiting gambit.

From an income tax perspective, the dream nights are an easy call. Eating in restaurants, attending a show of your choice, and drinking till midnight all constitute personal consumption. The result is that a summer associate who racked up, say, a $1,000 dream night tab should have $1,000 added to her income.

You might wonder whether there is a *valuation* problem here. Perhaps the summer associate protests that the firm didn't give her the choice to take $1,000 in cash and that she really only enjoyed the night out to the tune of, oh, $400 or so. Or perhaps the restaurant was mediocre and the show was lame, so really it was pretty much less fun than a $20 movie and a bucket of popcorn. Right?

Well, no. As we have seen, this kind of special pleading based on subjective valuation is exactly the kind of *valuation* problem that the tax law has learned to sidestep by looking to dollar transactions. From the IRS's point of view, the associate received a benefit worth $1,000, and so she is taxable on that amount. If she didn't want to include the $1,000 in her income, she should've declined the dream night.

By contrast, many valuable items provided on the job are obviously not personal consumption. When a biology teacher uses tens of thousands of dollars of

---

[2] Code Section 83(a).

lab space and microscopes to teach students about microbes, she isn't engaged in personal consumption: she's simply doing her job. The lab space and microscopes are business inputs, not personal consumption.

The distinction between business inputs and personal consumption is one of the central concepts of the income tax. And the stakes are high. If the system imposes tax on business inputs (taxing, say, the value of the lab equipment to the bio teacher), then it is overtaxing those people. But if the system fails to tax personal consumption provided by employers (like the dream nights paid for by the law firms), then it is undertaxing others.

The problem is that it can be difficult to draw the line when employees make use of valuable resources that combine business inputs and personal consumption. *Benaglia v. Commissioner*[3] poses the classic puzzle.

Benaglia. Here's the story: In 1933, Arthur Benaglia worked as the live-in manager of the Royal Hawaiian Hotel in Honolulu. In return for living in the hotel and being on duty around the clock, the hotel paid Arthur about $10,000 in cash and provided him (and his wife) with a suite of rooms and all meals at no cost.

Arthur reported the $10,000 cash salary on his income tax return, but the IRS wanted more. The Commissioner claimed that he should also pay tax on the value of the free room and board he received. From the IRS perspective, the suite and meals were personal consumption, and the agency easily calculated the fair market value at $8,000, based on the hotel prices charged to customers. But Arthur pointed out that he wasn't a tourist. He couldn't lie on a chaise by the pool, sipping cocktails and reading a novel. Instead, he lived on-site and ate in the hotel dining room so that he could work (or be on call) 24-7. For Arthur, the room and meals were business inputs—tools that helped him do his job, much like the biology lab for the bio teacher.

The stakes in the case were high—on both sides. The $8,000 fair market value of the Benaglias' room and board doesn't sound like much today. But once we take inflation into account, the case involved a suite and meals worth, in 2013 dollars, a whopping $143,000.[4]

The problem for the tax law is that both the IRS and taxpayer positions capture a piece of the truth. On the one hand, Arthur is a little like the summer associate who goes out on a dream night. The Royal Hawaiian was (and apparently still is) a fabulous hotel, and it's hard to imagine that Mr. and Mrs. B. hated their filet mignon dinners and the privilege of daily maid service. Even if they preferred less luxurious quarters, the free room and board meant that the Benaglias didn't have to spend anything on rent and groceries.

On the other hand, Arthur didn't have much choice in the matter. Accepting the job meant accepting the obligation to be on call 24-7. He probably couldn't

---

[3] 36 BTA 838 (1937).

[4] The Bureau of Labor Statistics provides a handy inflation calculator here: http://www.bls.gov/data/inflation_calculator.htm.

finish breakfast without having to deal with guest complaints about the bacon or the waiters. He certainly didn't receive the peace and quiet a tourist would expect for shelling out market prices for the room and meals.

Viewed in that light, Arthur's position may seem the stronger one: after all, he had a whole lot less choice—and less fun—than the summer associate enjoying a dream night on the town. But the complication is that personal consumption in the tax law doesn't always involve *pleasant* choices. After all, most of us spend plenty on necessary items that aren't all that much fun. I don't enjoy spending $200 for a few bags of groceries at Stop & Shop, and you probably don't love paying your rent each month. And yet, the tax law doesn't excuse us from paying tax on the portion of our salaries we spend on food and rent. If you earn $100,000 at your job, it's all income, and you can't plead to the IRS that you had to spend $30,000 on ho-hum meals and a cramped city apartment.

The larger point is that *Benaglia* poses a *valuation* problem, because the law cannot easily determine the value of the personal consumption he received. In the end, the court sided with Arthur, finding that the meals and lodging were not compensation but were, in the now-famous phrase, for the "convenience of the employer." (The Congress later codified that result as it pertains to meals and lodging provided on an employer's premises in Code Section 119, which has some specific requirements that taxpayers must meet in order to exclude meals and lodging from income.)

In effect, the court solved the *valuation* problem by assigning a zero value to the personal consumption that the Benaglias received. The decision may seem innocuous enough: after all, there aren't all that many live-in hotel managers who can benefit from the tax break. But, in fact, the case created enormous mischief in the tax law, mischief that spread to all kinds of workers (and firms) eager to pay tax-free compensation to their workers. In effect, the *Benaglia* decision throws U.S. Treasury money at any worker (or firm) who can arrange a live-in position.

Think about it this way: when employers offer a worker an extra $1 in cash salary, the worker takes home a smaller amount after paying taxes. For instance, if the worker's marginal tax rate is 30%, then an extra dollar of cash salary is only 70 cents after the Treasury takes its share. (Chapter 4 discusses marginal tax rates at some length. For now, just think of it as the taxpayer's tax rate—that is, she pays 30 cents of every dollar to the government.)

But if the extra $1 is in the form of free meals or lodging "for the convenience of the employer," then the worker keeps the whole dollar, tax-free. The tax rate drops to zero! And the employer can likely capture some of that value. For instance, both parties come out ahead if the firm can pay 90 cents of tax-free compensation instead of $1 in taxable compensation. Thank you, Uncle Sam.

Far from being innocuous, *Benaglia* invites workers and employers to profit at the U.S. government's expense. And that invitation sets in motion some troubling dynamics. Workers now have a tax reason to prefer live-in jobs to live-out jobs, and firms have a tax incentive to offer such jobs. Of course, not all industries can plausibly offer live-in employment "for the convenience of the employer." Hotels can; auto dealerships cannot. Colleges can plausibly claim that students benefit if faculty live on campus,[5] but the Gap can't reasonably claim that customers need live-in salespeople.

As the logic of *Benaglia* filters through the economy, it produces perverse arrangements from the perspective of economic efficiency. Economists typically think that the economy works best when people take jobs or buy goods based on market prices. Workers should choose (and employers should offer) a live-in job or a live-out job based on market factors. When the tax law puts a thumb on the scale in favor of live-in jobs, the economy skews toward live-in jobs and toward the industries that have them. The result, in big-picture terms, is that the United States is spending tax dollars to subsidize live-in workers—the hotel industry and colleges—at the expense of live-out workers, law firms and clothing stores.

By this point, you might conclude that the right answer would be to reverse *Benaglia*. If we tax live-in managers on the full fair market value of their meals and lodging, then employers will no longer have a tax reason to create live-in jobs. Only companies that really need live-ins will hire them. And if the tax bill is burdensome to the workers (recall Arthur Benaglia's $143,000 income item), let the hotels and other employers raise wages to cover the taxes too. Problem solved.

But it's not quite that easy. Taxing live-in managers on the full fair market value of their room and board (as if they were tourists) would create a set of mirror-image problems: that approach would *overtax* live-in managers and their employers and discourage investment in the industries that rely on such arrangements.

To see why, let's set some plausible values in the Benaglia case (using 1933 dollars). Suppose that if Arthur had been a live-out manager, he would have spent $2,000 annually on meals and lodging in Honolulu. And suppose that's the value he placed on the free room and board he received at the Royal Hawaiian: the rooms and meals were nicer than what he'd buy, but the extra fun was (let's suppose) exactly offset by the extra hassle of being on-call. So Arthur, by hypothesis, felt as if he were paid a $12,000 salary—$10,000 in cash plus the free room and board's value to him.

Now you can see the problem. If the IRS nevertheless taxes Mr. B. on the full $8,000 fair market value to a tourist, it is overtaxing him by $6,000. Arthur (and other hotel managers) surely would turn to their employers to fund the higher tax bill. And perhaps the hotels would cough up some extra cash—otherwise, few managers would accept live-in jobs. But the extra tax bill would raise the hotel's wage costs for live-in (but not live-out) managers.

Overtaxing live-in managers sets in motion the parade of horribles we have already seen, but this time in reverse. Live-in managers will pay too much in taxes. Hotels will have a tax incentive to discontinue live-in jobs. And, overall,

---

5 *See* Code Section 119(d).

industries that rely on live-in managers (hotels, colleges, and so on) will find that their wage costs are too high. (If you're still skeptical about this point, see Appendix 2-1, where I offer a numerical example.)

Kowalski and Gotcher. The problem of mixed business and personal fringe benefits has perplexed the courts. The courts almost always opt for an all-or-nothing solution, either taxing the fringe at market value or excluding it entirely. But it's hard to predict which way a given case will go.

One of the most confounding situations involved police and firefighters, who often receive meals or meal allowances while on duty. In *Commissioner v. Kowalski*,[6] the Supreme Court considered the case of a New Jersey state trooper who received a cash meal allowance. The meal allowance, bargained for as part of the police union contract, funded one meal per shift. Robert Kowalski wasn't obligated to spend the allowance, however; he could bring a brown bag from home and eat in his cruiser.

Robert argued that the meal allowance was excludable from income under Code Section 119, as meals provided for the convenience of the employer on the business premises of the employer. He noted that the meal allowances served a business purpose by keeping state troopers in their patrol areas during meals. In effect, the troopers were on call and available even at mealtime.

But the Supreme Court disagreed. Ruling for the IRS, the Court found that Section 119 applies only to meals provided in-kind and not cash reimbursements for meals.

At first glance, the *Kowalski* holding seems sensible enough. Imagine two officers: A is paid $100 per shift and buys (or brings) her own meals, while B is paid $80 per shift plus a $20 cash meal allowance. Both A and B can spend $100 as they choose; either one can buy a restaurant meal or brown-bag it and save the difference. It's hard to justify a tax preference for B just because 1/5 of her compensation has a "meal allowance" label, especially since she can pocket the $20 if she brown-bags her lunch.

But a closer look reveals that Robert Kowalski isn't so different from Arthur Benaglia, minus the glamorous surroundings. A police officer working an eight-hour shift has to eat something, and her choices are constrained by the job. She can stop at one of the fast-food joints that line the highway, or she can eat a soggy sandwich out of a lunch box. Either way, she is still on the job and must be ready to go at a moment's notice.

The *valuation* problem is just the same for the police officer as for Benaglia. When Robert spends, say $20 on his lunch, he's buying two things: a meal and the ability to stay on the job as he eats. The meal has some personal value to him, of course, but the pure personal value may be far lower than the $20 he spends. (Imagine a health-conscious officer who would far rather eat a cheap, vegetarian dish freshly made at home than the $20 burger-and-fries available at the I-95

---

6 434 U.S. 77 (1977).

rest stop.) So the officer who eats on the job—just like the hotel manager who eats on the job—is consuming an item that has *mixed business and personal value*.

The red herring, it turns out, is the comparison between officers who do and do not receive a meal allowance. Once we see the *valuation* issue, we can see that A (who is paid $100) and B (who receives $80 plus a $20 meal allowance) actually are in the same situation. Both A and B are constrained in their choices; both A and B are mixing business and personal consumption. The better comparison would be with off-duty Officer C, who can dine on $2 worth of leftovers from her fridge while leafing through magazines on her couch. Only C is engaged in purely personal consumption.

But the implications of this conclusion are far-reaching. If, in fact, any worker who eats on the job resembles *Benaglia*, then the income tax faces a far bigger dilemma than the one posed by the live-in hotel manager. Imagine the stakes if every one of the hundreds of millions of workers in the United States could exclude the portion of her wages spent for meals eaten on the job. The cost to the Treasury would be high, and the cascade of consequences is predictable. Employers would compete to offer higher and higher "meal allowances." Workers would have a tax reason to eat more expensive meals, fattening the profits of restaurants (and possibly, the waistlines of America).

The Supreme Court likely didn't want to open up that Pandora's box. But in failing to recognize the very real *valuation* problem, the Court opted to overtax meals on the job, with equally predictable consequences: workers are overtaxed compared to nonworkers.

But not always. In a victory for Minnesota state troopers that post-dates *Kowalski*, the Eighth Circuit approved a deduction from income for meals eaten on the job.[7] The Minnesota troopers paid for their own meals, but the rules required them to eat in restaurants adjacent to the highway: they were not permitted to bring meals from home and eat in their patrol cars. These constraints persuaded the court that the troopers could deduct the amounts they spent on their meals, despite the IRS argument that the troopers faced "restrictions ... no different from those placed upon other taxpayers who have to work during meals and are subject to interruptions."

But permitting a full deduction for the meals goes too far in the opposite direction. The roadside meals eaten by the Minnesota officers were personal consumption to some degree, and so a full deduction is too much.

Another taxpayer prevailed on a similar *valuation* issue in *U.S. v. Gotcher*.[8] John and Lois Gotcher took an all-expense-paid, twelve-day trip to Germany to tour Volkswagen factories there. John argued that the free trip was a business trip. He was considering investing in VW, and so the value of the trip should be excluded from his income. The IRS countered that the trip was a free vacation

---

[7] Christey v. United States, 841 F.2d 809 (8th Cir. 1988).

[8] 401 F.2d 118 (5th Cir. 1968).

and represented taxable personal consumption. The Fifth Circuit ruled for the taxpayers, finding that the "dominant purpose of the trip" was business and that "the personal benefit to Gotcher was clearly subordinate to the concrete benefits to VW."

By this point, you can probably spot the *valuation* problem in your sleep. John's trip to Germany represented both a business input and personal consumption. He genuinely learned about VW—and one suspects he genuinely enjoyed sightseeing and evenings in the Biergarten with his hosts. But in *Gotcher*, just as in *Benaglia* and *Kowalski*, the court opted for an all-or-nothing solution, here ignoring the personal value of the trip.

And, by now, you can also spot the real-world consequences of the law's blunder: business trips represent one of the biggest tax goodies around, because they permit people to smuggle in tax-free personal consumption as long as they meet the dominant business purpose test. The result is that the tax law subsidizes vacations, as long as they are mixed with business trips. Uncle Sam basically throws tax dollars on the table for employers and workers who can arrange business trips to beautiful, faraway places. And, over time, the tax subsidy became entrenched: what do you suppose the hotel, airline, and restaurant industries would do if any administration proposed to reverse the rule in *Gotcher*?

¶204 REAL-WORLD TRANSACTIONS: EMPLOYER-PROVIDED HEALTH INSURANCE

Today, the exclusion of meals and lodging provided "for the convenience of the employer" costs the federal government about $3 billion in revenue per year.[9] And the holding of *Benaglia* has been extended, over time, to a wide array of fringe benefits. I suspect that $3 billion is only a fraction of the (unmeasured) revenue cost of the *Gotcher* rule, which permits tax-free vacations when combined with business trips.

But the truly big dollars lie elsewhere in the Code. The tax law (in Sections 105 and 106) permits employers to provide tax-free health insurance coverage to workers. So, if Acme, Inc. provides its workers with health insurance worth $10,000 per year, the workers can exclude from income the value of the health insurance and health care they receive.

Tax-free health insurance costs the federal Treasury about $160 billion every year[10]—more than twice the amount spent on the food stamp (SNAP) program.

[9] According to the Joint Committee on Taxation, the exclusion of meals and lodging under Code Section 119 cost about $10 billion from 2014-2017, and the exclusion of housing provided to ministers cost another $4 billion. (These estimates exclude the value of excludable military housing.) See https://www.jct.gov/publications.html?func=startdown&id=4503.

[10] According to the Joint Committee on Taxation, the exclusion of employer-provided health benefits added up to about $800 billion from 2014-2017. https://www.jct.gov/publications.html?func=startdown&id=4503.

The exclusion for employer-provided health care represents one piece of America's complicated health care system, and I won't attempt a full analysis here. But I want to show how the tax break for health care sets in motion the same kinds of dynamics we've spotted in the case of other tax-free fringe benefits.

Once upon a time, employer-provided health insurance was rare and not all that valuable, since medicine could do very little for even serious diseases. But advances in medical technology during the 1940s coincided with the imposition of war-time wage and price controls. Employers were not permitted to increase cash wages, but fringe benefits were—you guessed it!—exempt from wage controls and federal income tax as well. Workers began to bargain for health insurance, and employers were happy to oblige, since the tax exemption made it cheaper to pay workers in health insurance than in cash.[11]

Strikingly, health insurance doesn't pose the kind of *valuation* puzzle we saw in *Benaglia*, *Kowalski*, and *Gotcher*. Recall that personal consumption includes the cost of feeding, clothing, and caring for ourselves and our families. Health care is one of the most basic human needs, and so it counts as personal consumption—even if we'd rather spend our money on more amusing items.

Health care does enable workers to work, and in that sense, we could stretch and term it a business input. It is awfully hard to work with an untreated broken leg, after all. But that line of argument proves too much, because nearly all personal consumption contributes to workers' general fitness for work. You can't work unless you sleep, rest, and eat during your downtime. Vacations, novels, even a happy family life all help us bounce back, ready for another working day. But if the income tax law were to adopt that expansive view of business inputs, there would be nothing left of the income tax base: it's hard to think of anything we spend money on that doesn't in some indirect way improve our fitness for work.

We can imagine true borderline cases, where medical care directly supports business needs as well as personal health. For instance, an NFL quarterback might undergo extensive knee surgery and rehabilitation that go well beyond what he needs for basic health: he and the team are trying to restore a level of functioning that will get him back on the playing field.

All this makes the exclusion for employer-provided health insurance a stunning instance of tax subsidies for personal consumption. In essence, Uncle Sam has thrown cash on the table, and employers and workers have jumped at the chance for tax-free salary in the form of health insurance. Today, about 83 percent of workers are offered health insurance at work, and about two-thirds of those take up the offer.[12]

You might think that these effects are benign, because health care is important for individuals and good for society as a whole. But critics argue that the tax

---

[11] *See* Robert B. Helms, Tax Policy and the History of the Health Insurance Industry, http://www.taxpolicycenter.org/tpccontent/healthconference_helms.pdf.

[12] These data are provided by the Urban-Brookings Tax Policy Center at http://www.taxpolicycenter.org/briefing-book/key-elements/health-insurance/coverage.cfm.

exclusion represents a suboptimal way of subsidizing health care. For instance, critics argue that the tax rules have led to the over-provision of health insurance and have subsidized increases in health-care costs.[13] They also point out that the exclusion (like a deduction)[14] offers the greatest benefits to higher-income taxpayers.[15] A worker who is too poor to pay federal income taxes saves nothing when she receives tax-free health insurance at work. By contrast, a high-income worker who would pay 40% on a cash raise of $10,000 will save $4,000 if her employer offers health insurance instead.

For these reasons, some policy analysts advocate taxing all (or part) of the value of employer-provided health insurance; they argue that doing so would raise tax revenue and reduce the nation's spending on health care.[16]

But, so far, taxing employer-provided health insurance has (mostly) been a political non-starter. The Affordable Care Act takes employer-provided coverage as the norm, adding provisions to ensure that employers don't drop coverage, while also subsidizing individual coverage for uninsured, low-income Americans. The Act doesn't directly tax workers who receive health insurance through their jobs although it does impose a special 40% tax on high-cost "Cadillac" plans. [17]

¶205 CODE SECTION 132

The *valuation* problems we've discussed in this chapter underlie a number of cases and Code sections. We've seen that Section 119 codifies the result in *Benaglia*, permitting employees to exclude the value of meals and lodging provided for the convenience of the employer, if certain conditions are met.

Code Section 132 is a grab-bag provision that approves the exclusion of a range of fringe benefits, including transit passes, company cafeterias, and stand-by airline seats for airline workers. A closer look reveals that most of these exclusions are outright giveaways to favored industries rather than a considered response to difficult *valuation* problems. For instance, Section 132(a)(1) permits airline employees to exclude the value of flying free, as long as the airline requires them to fly on a stand-by basis (no reserved tickets).

Thanks to Section 132, an airline worker can exclude from her income the (considerable) value of free air travel. Imagine a flight attendant who travels from

---

[13] *See* Cato Institute at http://www.cato.org/sites/cato.org/files/serials/files/cato-handbook-policymakers/2009/9/hb111-14.pdf.

[14] *See* ¶205 and Chapter 8, *infra*.

[15] *See* Urban-Brookings Tax Policy Center, http://www.taxpolicycenter.org/briefing-book/key-elements/health-insurance/exclusion.cfm.

[16] *See, e.g.*, this proposal by the Robert Wood Johnson Foundation: http://www.rwjf.org/en/research-publications/find-rwjf-research/2013/05/limiting-the-tax-exclusion-of-employer-sponsored-health-insuranc.html.

[17] Code Sections 36B (refundable premium credit), 4980H (tax on employers not offering health insurance), 4980I (tax on high-cost employer-sponsored health coverage).

New York to Hawaii for vacation, taking her spouse, children, and parents along. The value of the air travel is, let's say, $10,000. There simply is no *valuation* problem of the *Benaglia* kind: the flight attendant (by hypothesis) isn't working or attending a conference. Her free trip is pure personal consumption.

So if *valuation* isn't the rationale for the Section 132 exclusion, what is? There's a technocratic explanation and a political explanation, and only the latter really holds up to scrutiny. The technocratic explanation is that the no-additional-cost fringe operates only when it doesn't cost the employer anything to provide the fringe. If an airline seat would otherwise go empty, the argument runs, why not offer it to airline employees for free? No harm, no foul.

The technocratic explanation provides a perfectly good argument for why the airlines ought to offer free stand-by tickets to workers. Free stand-by tickets allow the airlines to lower their wage costs at no additional cost: people who take jobs as flight attendants or gate agents will take a bit less in cash salary thanks to the value of stand-by flights. What the technocratic explanation *doesn't* do is explain why the tax law should subsidize the bargain by excluding the value of free flights from workers' incomes!

To see the point, imagine two flight attendants. Both earn $40,000 in cash salary, and both work similar hours with similar working conditions. But Kate works for American Airlines and takes an annual, free trip to Hawaii, treating her extended family to free flights. Her neighbor, Larry, works for a small regional airline that doesn't fly to any vacation destinations. It isn't a stretch to say that Kate's salary is higher than Larry's. There isn't a mixed business-personal problem of the *Benaglia* or *Gotcher* type in sight: Kate is going on a vacation, not a business trip, and while she's on the plane, she's a customer, not a worker.

To be sure, we might quibble about *exactly* how much Kate's trip is worth: there is some hassle factor in flying stand-by that would warrant some discount from Expedia prices for regular tickets. And perhaps, in an emergency, the airline would expect Kate to get up and help out. But the consumption value of the trip is still considerable.

The real reason for Section 132(a)(1), then, is political. Airlines have long treated employees to free flights, considering them to be tax-free fringes, lowering their wage bills at Uncle Sam's expense. Had Section 132 attempted to tax those benefits, you can envision the army of airline lobbyists that would have descended on Congress to express their disapproval.

Still, Section 132 does limit the value of some tax-free fringes, including employer-provided free parking at work, now capped at $175 per month (roughly $250 today, thanks to the inflation adjustment provided in the Code).[18] From an environmental-protection perspective, that's probably still too high a subsidy for driving to work. But the limitation ends the prior practice of permitting workers to exclude free parking whatever its value. (The limitation still has an uneven

[18] *See* Code Sections 132(a)(5), 132(f)(2)(B) and 132(f)(6).

geographic impact, since monthly parking is worth about $150 per month in Boise but at least $500 per month in Manhattan.)

Section 132 also attempts to clamp down on employers who take the position that tax-free fringes are too small to warrant taxation. Take, for instance, a department store that distributes $20 gift cards to salespeople who meet sales targets or receive a customer commendation for great service. Absent Section 132, it might be tempting for the firm (and its lawyers) to argue that the $20 gift cards aren't worth all that much and so shouldn't be taxed. But Section 132(e) provides that employees can exclude a fringe as *de minimis* only if the value is "so small as to make accounting for it unreasonable or administratively impracticable."[19] It is easy enough to track who receives the $20 gift cards and how much they are worth—and so the employer should report the $20 value as salary to the recipients. (You might be wondering whether the gift cards might be gifts, and if so, whether some tax loophole might render them nontaxable. The answers to these questions are no and no, as we will see in Chapter 4.)

So what *does* Section 132 apply to—what is left in the category of items that cannot feasibly be accounted for? Mostly aggregate items of small value: a pot of free coffee or a bowl of free candy. Meals at the company cafeteria, it turns out, must meet special rules. If the meals do not qualify under the "convenience of the employer" standard for exclusion in Section 119, the cafeteria must charge enough to cover operating costs and the meals must be available on equal terms to most workers (not just executives).[20]

Section 132 may seem ungenerous. After all, the $20 gift cards for department-store salespeople are a drop in the bucket compared to the luxurious (tax-free) lifestyle enjoyed by Arthur Benaglia and John Gotcher. The law, it seems, looks the other way when it comes to business travel and high-end service industries, while taking a stingier approach to the ordinary worker. Hold that thought: we will revisit the *valuation* problem posed by mixed business-personal spending again in Chapter 9. There, we will see that the tax law subsidizes expensive business meals and overnight business travel by highly-paid professionals but overtaxes ordinary workers' commuting and child-care costs.

---

[19] Code Section 132(e)(1).

[20] Code Section 132(e)(2).

APPENDIX 2-1
VALUATION AND FRINGE BENEFITS

Sometimes the proper tax rule for fringe benefits is obvious. When a summer associate receives an all-expenses-paid night on the town, that's personal consumption and, therefore, income. When a teacher uses chalk to write on the board during class, he isn't engaged in personal consumption, and the value of the chalk isn't income to him.

But when fringe benefits serve both personal and business purposes, the tax law confronts two unappealing choices: include the full fair market value of the fringe or exclude it entirely. For the most part, neither solution reaches the right answer in these hard cases. To see why, let's look at a stylized account of the problem of the live-in hotel manager in the *Benaglia* case.

Suppose that a hotel initially has 100 rooms, which rent for $1,000 per night (this is a seriously nice hotel!), and employs a live-out manager. Now the owners decide to take one room out of service and require the manager to live in.

Why would the owners give up $1,000 in nightly revenue? They must project that the value of doing so is greater than the cost, and there are two potential sources of value:

(1) To the extent the manager values free housing (call this amount h), the hotel can reduce her cash wages by up to h;
(2) To the extent customers value having a live-in manager, the hotel can increase revenue by raising room rates (call this added revenue r).

From the outside, then, any observer can tell that if the hotel switches to a live-in manager, then it must be true that:

$$h + r > \$1,000$$

But without looking into the manager's and owners' heads, the IRS cannot know what h is—the agency cannot observe the *compensation value of the free room.*

The impossibility of observing the value of h poses a deep dilemma for the income tax, because the mandate of Haig-Simons is to tax personal consumption but not business inputs (*i.e.*, costs of earning income). Further, an income tax with progressive rates demands that items of income be taxed to the correct person at her tax rate.

In principle, then, the income tax should tax h at the manager's tax rate but should not directly tax the rest of the revenue (r or $1,000 – h). Why not? Because the hotel will report the higher revenue as part of its normal business income when it is earned. There is no need (and indeed, no way) for the IRS to detect the revenue specially attributable to the change to a live-in manager.

The impossibility of valuing either *h* or *r*, then, explains why the income tax is left with two unsatisfying solutions. If the tax law ignores the value of *h*, then hotels can pay managers tax-free salary, which undertaxes them compared to workers in other businesses. If the tax law taxes the full fair market value of the hotel room ($1,000) to the manager, then live-in managers and the hotels that employ them will be overtaxed (assuming that *h* is less than $1,000). And over- or undertaxation can redistribute income and alter the allocation of resources in the economy, as we have seen.

CHAPTER 3

Gifts and Bequests

Introduction . . . . ¶300
Income Shifting and Code Section 102 . . . . ¶301
Duberstein . . . . ¶302
Real-World Transactions: Bonuses, Tips, and Business Gifts . . . . ¶303

¶300 INTRODUCTION

Gifts are among the most common of human interactions, and yet they pose intractable difficulties for the income tax, because the IRS can't see into the human heart. And, really, it shouldn't try. Imagine how futile—not to mention creepy—it would be for the IRS to audit our emotions. What *are* your true feelings toward your boss, your college roommate, your mother?

So scratch the idea that the IRS can or should inquire (much) into true motivations. But without that ability, the tax law has a hard time distinguishing between gifts from the heart and "gifts" with so many strings attached that they aren't really gifts at all. The result is that canny taxpayers have been able to use gifts to reduce their income tax bills, and the tax law has scrambled to catch up.

Begin with the simplest gift—a birthday present. Suppose that Mom and Dad give Emma a nice surprise, say, a $1,000 bracelet. Emma has wanted that bracelet for some time, and she's happy. Mom and Dad are happy too. But what's the income tax angle on all this well-being? Perhaps Emma should have to report her good fortune to the IRS. After all, she is $1,000 richer than she was yesterday. And perhaps Mom and Dad should be able to reduce their income by $1,000 (by deducting the $1,000). After all, their bank account is $1,000 smaller than it was yesterday.

If you're starting to worry that the IRS may come after *you* for all those off-the-grid birthdays, you can relax. The rule on gifts in Code Section 102 is that the recipient excludes them from income (and the donor may not deduct them).[1]

That's a relief. But the Section 102 exclusion should also strike you as odd. If the income tax is supposed to detect transactions that make people richer, then omitting gifts from income seems wrong-headed. After all, if Emma gets a $1,000 bracelet for her birthday, and her friend Fiona gets only hugs and kisses

[1] The nondeduction rule is implied by Code Section 262, which denies any deduction for "personal, living, or family expenses."

and a homemade cake from *her* parents, then Emma really is richer than Fiona in the dollar terms that matter for the income tax.

The IRS would certainly tax that difference if Emma *earned* $1,000 more than Fiona. So why shouldn't the income tax capture the economic value of a gift?

¶301 INCOME SHIFTING AND CODE SECTION 102

The answer, you will be shocked to learn, is not that the IRS has a soft heart when it comes to gifts. Quite the opposite: the Section 102 gift exclusion actually operates to prevent *income shifting*, the tax-avoidance technique that is one of our six core concepts. *Income shifting*, you'll recall, comes about because the income tax adopts progressive rates, creating the opportunity for taxpayers to cut their tax bill by having money taxed at a low rate instead of at a high rate.

To see how gifts can be used to shift income, imagine a tax system that treats gifts in the intuitive way, including gifts in the income of the recipient and permitting the donor to deduct them. In our hypothetical, lucky Emma would report $1,000 in income, and Mom and Dad would deduct the same amount. For a true gift, that's an appealing result, and it puts Emma in the same position as if she earned $1,000 from a job. Put another way, a true gift *properly shifts income from the donor to the recipient*; the $1,000 value of the bracelet represents personal consumption to Emma and not her parents.[2]

But *income shifting* is an attractive tax-avoidance strategy, and gifts offer easy abuse potential. A middle-aged Mom and Dad's income is (usually) taxable at a higher rate than their children's. If Mom and Dad are in the 40% income tax bracket, while Emma (without much income of her own, let's say) has a 0% tax rate, then the three of them could make money by pretending to make gifts. *You* wouldn't do that, of course, because it involves lying to the IRS, and that is tax fraud. But some crafty taxpayers might try it. The payoff is tempting: for every $100 that Mom and Dad give or pretend to give to Emma, they save $40 in taxes. That means that the three of them are richer by $40, courtesy of the U.S. Treasury.

Now, $40 in tax savings might not be enough to induce people to engage in illegal, fake gift-giving, but just add zeros, and the sum quickly becomes more interesting. If Emma's parents have two other children, also with zero income, they could easily shift about $10,000 to each child every year without putting the children into a positive marginal tax rate bracket.[3] If Mom and Dad can shift a total of $30,000 in income, they save $12,000 in taxes. And while (I repeat!) lying to the IRS is a crime, the family may figure that it will be hard for the IRS to untangle what's really going on.

---

[2] We could debate this point, and tax scholars have. After all, Emma's parents love her, and seeing her happy must be worth at least the $1,000 they spent. So there's a respectable case for including gifts in recipients' income while *not* permitting donors to deduct them.

[3] For the sticklers among you, this is because the standard deduction and personal exemption for a single person add up to about $10,000. So someone with income of less than that is, in effect, in a zero marginal tax rate bracket.

So *income shifting* arises because the tax law has a hard time doing two things: distinguishing close families from distant ones, and distinguishing real from fake gifts. One way to solve the income-shifting problem would be to have family members *all* file a single tax return. If the children are still young, and the family is close, then it might make sense to tax the whole family as a unit.

This is the approach the IRS takes until children are 18 (or age 24, if full-time students). Until that time, kids pay tax on investment income at their parents' marginal tax rate.[4] That approach prevents *income shifting*. But the difficulty is that families are very different. For every 22-year-old Emma who's out of college but still close to her parents, there's a 22-year-old Ethan who keeps his finances separate and maybe doesn't speak to his parents. The IRS can't look into people's hearts, and so it draws a bright line based on age.

But the tax advantages of *income shifting* don't evaporate when a child reaches adulthood. Close families could still reduce their tax bill by making "gifts" to their adult children. The boldest fraud would be to claim to make gifts that aren't made. A less-bold, but still fraudulent, transaction would be to give the adult child a gift but agree that she will either give it right back or spend it for the parents' benefit (paying their rent, say, or their credit card bills).

To forestall this all-too-easy fraud by taxpayers, the Code instead adopts a counterintuitive rule: gifts are ignored for income tax purposes. Emma need not include the $1,000 gift in income, and her parents cannot claim a tax deduction. The result is that Mom and Dad must make gifts out of after-tax income. For instance, if the parents are in a 40% bracket, then they need to earn $1,667 and pay taxes of $667 (40%) to have $1,000 left to buy Emma's gift.

To summarize: The Section 102 gift exclusion taxes true gifts at the wrong rate, the donor's rate, in order to prevent *income shifting* on fake or nonexistent gifts. The rule also tracks the way ordinary people think about gifts. Most people, strangely, don't think first of the IRS when birthdays and holidays roll around. The Section 102 exclusion for gifts ratifies that thinking—and avoids turning millions of Americans into unwitting tax evaders.

But the problem of gifts keeps on giving. The Section 102 exclusion, it turns out, opens up new avenues for tax evasion—including, ironically enough, *income shifting*. Crafty taxpayers quickly figured out a new way to use the Section 102 exclusion to extract money from the Treasury, a strategy illustrated nicely by *Commissioner v. Duberstein*.[5]

¶302 *DUBERSTEIN*

The transaction in *Duberstein* is a familiar one, albeit on a lavish scale. Two businessmen, Mose Duberstein and Morris Berman, each ran firms engaged in

[4] *See* Code Section 1(g).

[5] 363 U.S. 278 (1960).

buying and selling iron and other metals. Mose occasionally helped out Morris by providing him with the names of potential customers for products that Mr. B's firm sold (but Mr. D's did not).

One landmark day in 1951, when the two men had known each other seven years, Morris Berman called Mose Duberstein and related that, out of gratitude for these helpful tips, he wanted to give Mose a present. Mose protested:

> I told him he didn't owe me anything. And he said, well, he had a Cadillac car as a gift, and I should send to New York to receive it, which I finally did. But I told him he owed me nothing, and I didn't expect anything for the information, and I didn't intend to be compensated, but he insisted and I accepted this Cadillac car.[6]

Mose, we can surmise, enjoyed his new car and felt that his friend Morris was a generous sort. The Caddy was a princely gift, indeed, worth $4,250 in 1951, or the equivalent of $38,000 in 2013. Mose may well have thought no more about the matter — until he received a visit from an IRS agent.

The IRS, it turns out, expected Mose Duberstein to report the fair market value of the Cadillac as income on his tax return. From the IRS perspective, Morris Berman had paid Mose a referral fee, or compensation for the service of referring customers. Mose protested that the car had been a gift, excludable under Section 102. The two men had had no agreement for payment, and, indeed, Mose had told Morris that he owed him nothing for the referrals.

Duberstein illustrates how the taxation of gifts creates a line-drawing problem. When gifts are taxed one way and compensation another, taxpayers have an incentive to take the more favorable path. The Section 102 rule (exclusion) applies to some transfers of assets to others, while the Section 61 rule (inclusion) applies to other transfers (compensation). The IRS and the courts are left to classify transactions, even though, as in *Duberstein*, it can be all but impossible to do so. Realistically, Morris Berman probably had mixed motives. He may have enjoyed making a generous gift; he may have wanted to create a reputation for generosity; and he probably wanted to encourage Mose Duberstein to pass on customer tips in the future.

At first glance, *Duberstein* resembles the *valuation* problem we encountered in *Benaglia*,[7] with one party arguing that an item is business-related, while the other is arguing that it's personal. When we discussed the fringe benefit cases in Chapter 2, we saw that the tax law sometimes faces difficulties in deciding whether meals and lodging provided by an employer represent personal consumption or, instead, non-taxable business inputs.

But a closer look reveals that *Duberstein* isn't like *Benaglia* at all. There is simply no question that Duberstein's Cadillac represented personal consumption.

---

[6] Quoted in Duberstein v. Commissioner, 265 F.2d 28 para. 10 (1959).

[7] Benaglia v. Commissioner, 36 BTA 838 (1937).

(He didn't try arguing that he drove it only to see customers.) Duberstein is $4,250 richer than before the gift, and the Haig-Simons definition of income (recall $Y = C + \Delta S$) shouts, loud and clear: this man has income! But Section 102 muddies the waters by creating an exception to the Haig-Simons rule that income includes personal consumption. When personal consumption proceeds from a "gift," then the usual Haig-Simons outcome is reversed, and the recipient properly excludes the item from income.

Thus, it is Section 102, and not a *valuation* problem inherent in the concept of income, that gives rise to the problem posed by *Duberstein*. Past cases have held, and the *Duberstein* court reiterated, that the difference between a "gift" and "compensation" turns on taxpayer motive. In theory, Section 102 requires the IRS to peer inside Morris Berman's head (and heart) and determine whether the gift was motivated by "detached and disinterested generosity" or, instead, a compensatory motive.

By now you can sing the refrain: it is laughable to suppose that the IRS can detect motivation. If asked, most taxpayers will tell self-serving stories. And crafty taxpayers will arrange the setting to support their self-serving characterization. It's no surprise, then, that the two lower courts that decided *Duberstein* on its way to the Supreme Court reached conflicting conclusions on the same factual record. The Tax Court could find no evidence that Morris Berman intended to make a gift and inferred that the Cadillac represented remuneration for services. The Court of Appeals for the Sixth Circuit, by contrast, cited Mose Duberstein's testimony (quoted above) as "uncontradicted evidence" that the transaction was a gift.

The ironic result of all this is that Section 102, which is supposed to prevent *income shifting*, offers taxpayers ample opportunity to choose whether transactions are gifts or compensation. And when taxpayers can choose between compensation and gifts, they can also choose which taxpayer will be taxed—in a word, they can engage in *income shifting*.

To see why, consider a stylized rendition of the Berman-Duberstein transaction. Imagine that Berman wishes to pay Duberstein $100, and imagine (as in the *Duberstein* case) that the facts are sufficiently malleable that the parties can plausibly claim either compensation treatment or gift treatment, as they prefer. Table 3.1 illustrates the tax payoff. If the parties call the transaction compensation, the $100 is taxed at the recipient's rate, while if they call it a gift, it's taxed at the payor's rate.

Table 3.1 Taxing Compensation, Taxing Gifts

	Compensation	Gift
Payor	Deduct $100	No deduction
Recipient	Include $100	Exclude
Result	**$100 taxed at recipient's rate**	**$100 taxed at payor's rate**

Now, all this would be a big yawn if every taxpayer had the same tax rate. But the whole raison d'être of Section 102 is that taxpayers don't face the same tax rates: that's why *income shifting* is profitable. So in the (very common) case in which a payor and recipient have different tax rates, they can profitably collude to shift income. If the payor's tax rate is higher, then call the payment compensation. If the recipient's tax rate is higher, then call it a gift. Presto! Free tax dollars courtesy of Uncle Sam.

The paradox is that Section 102 aims to prevent *income shifting* within the family, but, because it reverses the usual income rules, it opens up a new category that invites unrelated taxpayers to collude to shift income. It's hard to know whether, on balance, Section 102 does more harm than good. The point, thus far, is simply that no good (tax) deed goes unpunished: Section 102 both forestalls tax planning and fosters it!

In fact, the legal record suggests that the real Berman and Duberstein did not collude in this way. The two of them—without any coordination at all—engaged in an even more profitable transaction. Morris Berman, it turns out, deducted the $4,250 cost of the Cadillac from his income, classifying it as a "finder's fee." That is, from his point of view, the Caddy was a business input, an expenditure made to advance his business interests, not a personal relationship. Putting the two sides together, the tax result was that *no one was taxed on the value of the Caddy*.

Put another way, the Berman-Duberstein transaction went well beyond *income shifting*. Instead of choosing whether to have the Caddy's value taxed at Mose's rate or Morris's rate, as in Table 3.1, the parties went one better—they argued (in effect) that it should not be taxed at all.

To see how the parties reached tax-planning nirvana (no one is taxed), we have to revisit Table 3.1 and add a column for this very special transaction, the "business gift," depicted in Table 3.2.

Table 3.2 The "Business Gift"

	Compensation	Gift	Business Gift
Payor	Deduct $100	No deduction	Deduct $100
Recipient	Include $100	Exclude	Exclude $100
Result	**$100 taxed at recipient's rate**	**$100 taxed at payor's rate**	**$100 is entirely untaxed**

Table 3.2 illustrates the "business gift" at stake in *Duberstein* and a host of cases like it. When taxpayers made or received a gift in a business setting, the recipient claimed an exclusion from income under Section 102, as Mose Duberstein did, while the payor claimed a deduction.

Now, you might reasonably think that these taxpayers were working a scam, taking inconsistent positions and daring the IRS to find them. But, in fact, the law *at that time* supported the taxpayers' claimed treatment of business gifts. Section 102, after all, says what it says: gifts are excludable. And, separately, Section 162 permits a deduction for ordinary and necessary business expenses. Nothing in the Code at that time prevented the Bermans of the world from taking a business deduction for gifts that legitimately served to further their business.

The business gift, then, arguably represented legal tax planning, with both taxpayers taking supportable positions under the law as it existed. (By contrast, colluding to mischaracterize compensation as a gift is illegal tax fraud.) Mose excluded his Cadillac, in all good faith as far as we can tell, as a gift, while Morris deducted the cost of the car, again in all good faith as far as the record shows, as a business expense.

We can now see why the IRS fought *Duberstein* all the way to the Supreme Court, which ultimately ruled against the taxpayer and for the agency. The Supreme Court upheld the Tax Court's determination that the transaction was not a gift. So the value of the Cadillac was, in the end, income to Mose Duberstein.

On the larger stage, though, *Duberstein* marked a defeat for the IRS in the war against the deductible-and-excludable business gift. The Court ratified the Tax Court's factual determination in the case of Duberstein but refused to adopt a presumption that gifts made in business settings usually are compensation. Instead, the majority opinion endorsed the motive test for gifts—"detached and disinterested generosity" is the oft-quoted phrase—leaving it to future factfinders to (somehow) untangle human motivations.

So the *Duberstein* decision left the door wide open for business gifts, deductible by the donor and excludable by the recipient. And the Supreme Court's opinion didn't do much except prevent future cases from reaching the courts of appeal. The opinion called for factfinders to apply their "experience with the mainsprings of human conduct to the totality of the facts of each case."

Realistically, though, there wasn't much the Supreme Court could do. The Court is, after all, an interpreter of the Code, and its interpretive power is limited. The real problem with business gifts lay in the structure of the statute: the income tax generally operates to implement something like the Haig-Simons measure of income. When Congress enacted Section 102, it apparently failed to realize how uneasily the gift exclusion would fit with the rest of the Code, including the deduction for business expenses. (Chapter 8 explains why business expenses should be deductible.)

Ultimately, it took two congressional enactments to pull up the business gift at its roots. First, Code Section 102(c) attacks the exclusion side, providing that employees may not exclude gifts made by an employer. This conclusive rule goes well beyond the weak presumption the IRS hoped for in *Duberstein*. The result is that no matter how detached and disinterested, how saintly an employer may be, gifts she makes to you are taxable as income. Second, Code Section 274(b) attacks the deduction side of the business gift, prohibiting a business deduction for gifts in excess of $25 per recipient per year.

Duberstein is still good law today. When no contrary statute applies, a "gift" consists of a transfer motivated by detached and disinterested generosity. But, thanks to Code Sections 102(c) and 274(b), the room for income-shifting mischief is much reduced. The primary significance of the case today is probably in the area of charitable contributions, where the *Duberstein* standard helps determine whether a purported gift to charity is really a gift or, instead, a payment for services.[8]

¶303 REAL-WORLD TRANSACTIONS: BONUSES, TIPS, AND BUSINESS GIFTS

Every year, it seems, Wall Street bonuses make headlines, whether, "Wall Street Bonuses Rise as Jobs Decline" or "Wall Street Bonuses Fall." But what is the tax perspective on bonuses? Must the lucky 1% include in income their $200,000 (and higher) annual windfalls?

It might be tempting to try to exclude bonuses as gifts. They come at year end during the holiday season and generate joy for the recipients. But, armed with *Duberstein*, you now know better. Bonuses are unquestionably *not* gifts. Employers do not pay them out of "detached and disinterested generosity" but rather out of cold calculation. Typically, bonuses are understood by both parties as part of the compensation package, intended to give employees an incentive to contribute to the firm's success. So, even when bonuses aren't guaranteed—that is, they may be zero if the firm doesn't meet financial targets—they are taxable as compensation when received.

The key question, as *Duberstein* reminds us, is not "Did the firm have an obligation to pay the bonus?" Instead, the key is motive: is the firm just being nice, with nothing at all to gain, or, instead, is the firm calculating that well-treated employees will work harder and stick around? Sorry to break it to you, but the answer in the business world is always, always cold calculation and not sheer niceness. Remember, too, that Code Section 102(c) mandates the result: employees may not claim exclusion treatment for even *true* gifts from their employers. From the tax perspective, gifts from employers are now something like vampires, zombies, and werewolves—fun to imagine, but nonexistent.

Tips are even more common than bonuses, and they may feel even more gift-like. Not only do diners face no obligation to tip, they often have little to gain from it. Unless you're a repeat customer at a restaurant, you don't gain anything in return for leaving money on the table as you are leaving. It might seem, then, that tips really are a real-world instance of "detached and disinterested" generosity.

Not so fast. Wait staff and Vegas dealers have tried the gift theory over the years, and they have uniformly lost to the IRS, which considers tips to be earned income. Diners and "21" players, the courts have held, aren't truly being generous in the way that the *Duberstein* standard imagines. Instead, diners are participating

---

8 *See, e.g.*, Winters v. Commissioner, 468 F.2d 778 (1972) (denying a charitable deduction for $2,000 paid by parents to their children's religious school).

in a tradition that tends to improve service from waiters who realize that a tip may be in the offing, and card players are attempting to improve their luck.

This is not to say that there is no element of generosity in bonuses and tips—often, there is. But to understand why the tax law so coldly disregards the warmer impulses of the human heart, we need only imagine what would happen if bonuses and tips *were* treated as gifts for tax purposes.

Employers and workers could readily collude to have compensation taxed to the lower-rate party, fine-tuning at will by paying a little more bonus to this worker, a little more "regular salary" to that one, even changing the mix year to year as tax positions change. Section 102(c) now forecloses that opportunity, but that's another way of saying that it reaches the same sensible result as the case law on tips.

Waiters and their customers would face a different set of incentives, because diners cannot deduct tips paid from their income. For them, treating the tips as gifts would be a win-win: the waiters would avoid tax entirely on their income, and diners could leave smaller tips, knowing they'd be tax-free.

Of course, gifts do occur in business. Entrepreneurs have built entire companies around corporate goodies like wine baskets, fruit arrangements, and cigar samplers. Most of these "gifts" probably should be taxed as compensation, thanks to *Duberstein* and Section 102(c). And those over $25 should be nondeductible under Section 274(b). Of course, what people actually report is another matter. Many people don't know enough tax law to realize that the Harry & David gift basket sent by the boss equals a $75 inclusion on their tax return. They may unwittingly violate the law. One of the costs of taking the tax course, however, is that *you* now know better! And the law probably operates, as intended, to forestall large-scale and deliberate *income shifting* and other kinds of tax planning.

In the end, perhaps the tax law is looking out for our better natures. By doing away with the tax advantages of the business gift, the IRS has nudged humanity (well, OK, that subset of humanity subject to and aware of U.S. tax law) toward small, token gifts and away from lavish but insincere presents. I think our mothers would approve: after all, it's the thought that counts.

CHAPTER 4

Marginal and Average Tax Rates

Introduction . . . . ¶400
Two Tax Rates . . . . ¶401
Real-World Transactions: The Value of Tax Breaks for Real Estate and Education . . . . ¶402
Distribution and the Average Tax Rate . . . . ¶403
Old Colony and Substance Over Form . . . . ¶404
Real-World Transactions: Signing Bonuses and the Gross Up for Taxes . . . . ¶405

¶400 INTRODUCTION

The simplest way to understand the income tax, or any tax for that matter, is as a rate times a base. Like this:

$$\text{Tax due} = \text{Tax rate} \times \text{Tax base}$$

The income tax uses income as its tax base. So if my tax rate is 40% and I have $1,000 of income, then my tax due is $400.

When non-lawyers discuss the income tax, they often talk about tax rates. When Uncle Richard complains about high taxes at the Thanksgiving table, or Aunt Sally recounts how her tax bill went down when she retired, they're mostly talking about tax rates.

Lawyers, by contrast, spend most of their time talking (and thinking) about the tax base. Tax rates, it turns out, are fairly simple for Congress to enact and for people to understand. (That's why we'll spend just this one short chapter on tax rates.) The tax base is far more complicated, and the income tax base is complex even by tax standards. Chapters 1, 2, and 3 have already introduced some of the complexities of defining income, and the rest of this book will tackle many more.

Still, before we proceed, there are a few fine points to note about tax rates, and we will spend this chapter pursuing them. And it turns out that a classic case on tax rates also introduces one of our six concepts, *substance over form.*

¶401 TWO TAX RATES

The term "tax rate" is ambiguous. Tax rates actually come in two different varieties—marginal and average—and it's important to know which one you're dealing with.

Marginal tax rates represent the tax rate payable on the next dollar of income, and they are the key tax rate for tax planning. Lawyers and bankers mostly think about the next deal down the line, and so they care about the marginal tax rate, which determines the tax cost or tax benefit of a new transaction. *Average tax rates reveal the tax rate payable on the taxpayer's income as a whole, and they measure the total tax burden on an individual, a family, or a class of taxpayers.* When someone complains that her tax bill is too high (or too low), she is talking about her average tax rate. And when government statisticians publish the tax burden on, say, the top 1% of income-earners, they too are measuring the average tax rate on that group.

Average tax rates are intuitive to most people, but the marginal tax rate takes a little more analysis. Begin this way: a flat-rate income tax would have just one marginal tax rate. For instance, a true flat tax of 20% would impose tax at the 20% rate on someone with $1,000 of income or $1 million of income. True, the person with $1,000 of income would pay only $200 in taxes, while the millionaire would pay $200,000. But the *average tax rate,* or percentage of income paid to the government, would be the same.

That result strikes some people as unfair, because the person with just $1,000 of income probably needs every dollar just to feed himself, while the millionaire can spare a greater percentage of her income to help fund the government. That fairness claim is controversial, with serious arguments on both sides.[1] But, for better or worse, the United States has a progressive tax system, in which marginal tax rates rise with income. The result is that taxpayers with higher incomes pay higher marginal and average rates of tax.

It's worth spending a little time to work through a few examples that illustrate rising marginal and average tax rates. Let's use this stylized tax system:

Table 4.1 Progressive Marginal Tax Rates

Income	Tax rate
$0-$50,000	10%
Over $50,000	10% on the first $50,000 and 40% on income over that amount

Table 4.1 reveals two key points about marginal tax rates. First, you can readily see that the marginal tax rates are progressive: the taxpayer pays 10% on the first $50,000 of income and 40% when the next dollar of income exceeds $50,000. Second, even someone who makes more than $50,000 still gets the benefit of the 10% rate (or "bracket") on the first $50,000 of her income.

These points may seem confusing. What does it mean to say that it is the tax rate on the "next" dollar of income? An example will help.

---

1 Some classics include Walter Blum and Harry Kalven, *The Uneasy Case for Progressive Taxation*, 19 U. Chi. L. Rev. 417 (1952) and J.A. Mirrlees, *An Exploration in the Theory of Optimum Income Taxation*, 38 Rev. Econ. Stud. 175 (1971).

EXAMPLE 1. Yvonne has $60,000 of income. Per the rate schedule in Table 4.1, she pays tax at 10% on the first $50,000, or $5,000 of tax. She pays tax at 40% on the remaining $10,000, or $4,000 in tax. In total, she owes $9,000 in tax.

So Yvonne pays a total of $9,000 to Uncle Sam. Her average tax rate, which measures her total tax burden, is $9,000/$60,000 or 15%. That may seem odd at first: why isn't her average tax rate 40%? The answer is that she, like all taxpayers in this kind of system, pays tax at the 10% rate on the first $50,000 of her income. Her marginal tax rate (40%) is her tax bracket or top tax rate. If she earned an additional $1,000, taking her to $61,000 of income, she would pay an additional (or "marginal") tax of 40% on that increment, or $400. But her overall tax burden *averages* across the 10% bracket and the 40% bracket. At her income level, the average tax rate is 15%.

Table 4.2 extends the example to show marginal and average tax rates for a range of taxpayers under the rate schedule shown in Table 4.1.

Table 4.2 Marginal and Average Tax Rates

Income	Total Tax Due	Marginal Tax Rate	Average Tax Rate
$15,000	$1,500	10%	10%
$40,000	$4,000	10%	10%
$60,000	$9,000	40%	15% ($9,000/$60,000)
$200,000	$65,000	40%	32.5%
$1 million	$385,000	40%	38.5%

Table 4.2 shows that marginal tax rates are incredibly easy to identify: they're the same as the taxpayer's tax bracket. The table also illustrates that average tax rates require a bit more work. The first two taxpayers offer a simple case: both their average *and* their marginal rates are 10%. That's because their incomes are taxed in only the 10% bracket.

The table also shows that, once taxpayers break into the 40% bracket, the average tax rate rises, as more and more income is taxed at the higher rate. The (comparatively) worse-off taxpayer earning $60,000 has a fairly modest 15% average tax rate, while the much better-off millionaire has a 38.5% average tax rate.

As a technical matter, we can apply the term "progressive" (or its opposite, "regressive") to either marginal or average tax rates. The tax rate structure examined in Table 4.2 has progressive marginal tax rates *and* progressive average tax rates as well: both rise as income increases.

The example in Table 4.1 mimics fairly closely the structure of the rates found in the actual income tax. If you take a look at Code Section 1, you'll find that it offers a number of filing statuses, which depend on family structure (marriage and the presence of dependents). It also includes a larger number of brackets. But the basic idea is the same: marginal rates are progressive, and even high-income taxpayers benefit from lower brackets.

The marginal tax rate is the key rate for tax planning, because tax planning is all about change. Should the client buy an asset (or sell one)? Should she agree to a new contract (or pay damages to back out of an old one)? These are all decisions made on the margin, which just means that we hold everything else constant and change just the one item.

For example, suppose that your client, Yvonne, earns $60,000 and that she faces the rate structure depicted in Table 4.1. She has $5,000 in savings and wants to think through the financial consequences of investing her money in a company that promises to repay the $5,000 plus an additional $1,000 in one year's time.

The $1,000 profit is income to her; we will see that profit and income are (mostly) the same thing, with a few refinements. Her marginal tax rate is 40%, and so you can tell her that she will keep $600 after taxes. Her after-tax return on the $5,000 investment, then, is 12% ($600 income after taxes, divided by $5,000 investment needed).

We use Yvonne's marginal tax rate of 40% instead of her average tax rate of 15% because the marginal rate accurately captures how her situation will change if she keeps everything the same but for the new investment. Without the investment, we know that she owes Uncle Sam $9,000 in taxes. With the investment, she earns a total (pre-tax) income of $61,000 and so owes a total of $9,400 in tax ($5,000 on the first $50,000). The marginal tax rate captures nicely the change in her situation—and avoids having to recalculate her entire tax liability!

The average rate, by contrast, does not offer a useful tool for tax planning at the margin. In fact, a new investment will actually change this client's average tax rate: paying $9,400 on $61,000 in income means an average tax rate of 15.4%, which makes sense because she's a bit richer.

We also use the marginal tax rate to evaluate tax deductions, which are amounts subtracted from income. Suppose Yvonne, starting with $60,000 in income, finds out that she is entitled to a tax deduction of $1,000. That means that her income will fall to $59,000. What is the tax impact? We could redo the entire tax calculation, but there's no need, since all that has changed is the $1,000 reduction in income. A $1,000 deduction will save her $400 in taxes at her 40% marginal tax rate.

¶402 REAL-WORLD TRANSACTIONS: THE VALUE OF TAX BREAKS FOR REAL ESTATE AND EDUCATION

Marginal tax rates are pretty much all you need to understand some fairly sophisticated tax planning. To illustrate, let's consider tax breaks for real estate investment and for college education.

Tax breaks come in two forms: tax deductions and tax credits. A tax deduction is an amount subtracted from income. Because deductions reduce income subject to tax, they reduce tax liability, and so they have economic value. Taxpayers generally like to show the government the smallest (legal) income, so that they pay the smallest (legal) tax. Deductions reduce income, and so they have value to individuals.

¶402.01 Real Estate

Real estate investments entitle their owners to an array of tax deductions. "Depreciation," for instance, refers to the tax rule that permits an investor to deduct the cost of a building over time. For example, suppose that your client pays $10 million for a downtown office building. Code Section 168 allows her to deduct that $10 million, not all at once, but over time. In the first year, suppose that the deduction is 1/40 of the cost of the building, or $250,000.

As your client decides whether or not to buy the building, she will look at economic factors, like the building's location and its physical condition. She will project future rents and make some predictions about whether the city is likely to flourish or decline in the coming years. She will also take into account the tax benefits (and detriments) of buying the building. In particular, the value of the tax deductions for depreciation will play a role in her calculations. The more valuable the tax deductions, the better the investment will look from a financial perspective. So how should you answer when your client asks: "So, how much is the depreciation worth?"

The answer is amazingly simple: the value of a tax deduction is the client's marginal tax rate times the deduction. Here, the deduction is $250,000. So if your client's marginal tax rate is 40%, then the value of the deduction each year is $100,000. That means she saves $100,000 in taxes she would otherwise pay thanks to the depreciation deduction.

Of course, depreciation is the gift that keeps on giving: it isn't just one year of deductions, but 40! Later on (in Chapter 10), we'll add some sophistication to our understanding of the value of a series of deductions over time. For now, though, you can see that the value of each year's deduction is determined by the marginal tax rate.

A second kind of tax break on real estate takes the form of a tax credit, which is a reduction in the amount of tax a taxpayer owes. Now, at first glance, that may sound just like a tax deduction, which ultimately reduces the taxpayer's tax bill. The difference, though, is critical: *A tax deduction reduces income, while a tax credit reduces the tax owed.*

For example, suppose that your client's taxable income is $1 million. His marginal tax rate, let's suppose, is 40%, and he pays $300,000 each year in taxes. (Remember that his *average tax rate*, here 30%, is lower than his *marginal tax rate*.) Now he is deciding whether to invest money in a low-income housing development. The sponsor of the project advises him that if he makes the investment, Code Section 42 will entitle him to a $100,000 tax credit. (The low-income housing tax credit offers tax breaks to investors to induce them to build affordable housing.)

How much is the tax credit worth? The key is that it reduces tax liability dollar-for-dollar, so that a $100,000 credit is worth ... $100,000. That is, the client's total tax bill will fall from $300,000 to $200,000.

A tax credit is very much like a credit on your bank account or your Visa bill: if you return a sweater to Macy's, and you receive a $100 credit on your Visa statement, that is worth the full $100 to you. A tax deduction, in contrast, is worth only a fraction of a dollar, because it reduces income subject to tax, not tax liability directly.

The link between marginal tax rate and value has stunning consequences for tax policy: *a tax deduction (but not a tax credit) has different value to different taxpayers, depending on their marginal tax rate.* Return to the real estate investor who can claim a $250,000 deduction for depreciation. An investor in the 40% bracket, as we have seen, will value the deduction at $100,000. An investor in the 10% bracket, by contrast, will value the same deduction at only $25,000. And, obviously enough, an investor with no taxable income will value the deduction at $0.

So when Congress uses tax *deductions* to encourage investments in real estate, then it is, *sub rosa*, offering more money to richer investors (in higher brackets) than to poorer ones. That might be a good idea, if Congress's goal is to encourage as much investment as possible, and if higher-income investors are highly responsive to tax incentives. Or it might be a bad idea, if we think tax giveaways shouldn't favor the rich. By contrast, a tax credit produces an even pattern of rewards across income classes, since its value isn't linked to marginal tax rates.

A slight complication is that a credit may not be worth its full amount if the taxpayer doesn't have sufficient tax liability to "soak up" the tax credit. So, for example, a client whose annual tax bill is only $75,000 couldn't fully use a $100,000 tax credit. The credit would be worth only $75,000 to her.

Congress can solve the problem of insufficient tax liability, when it chooses, by altering credit design. The best example is the earned income tax credit. The EITC is the largest federal cash transfer for working-age adults and their children. (It costs the federal government more than $60 billion per year,[2] compared to $20 billion for the federal share of Temporary Assistance for Needy Families, the transfer program sometimes abbreviated TANF.[3]) The EITC is a tax credit: if my EITC is $3,000, then I can offset my tax liability by that amount. But low-income people, the target group for the EITC, often have low (or even zero) federal income tax liability. Their low tax bills make a traditional tax credit a poor

---

2 See *Joint Committee on Taxation, Estimates of Federal Tax Expenditures for Fiscal Years 2012-2017*, JCS-1-13, available at https://www.jct.gov/publications.html?func=startdown&id=4503.

3 Budget of the U.S. Government, Historical Tables, Table 11.3, available at http://www.whitehouse.gov/omb/budget/historicals.

policy vehicle. To solve the problem, the Congress made the EITC refundable, so that if the credit exceeds tax liability, the U.S. Treasury will pay out the excess amount. So if my EITC is $3,000, but I otherwise owe only $500 in taxes, I would pay zero in taxes *and* receive a $2,500 check from the IRS.

¶402.02 Education

Congress has also provided tax deductions and tax credits to encourage people to go to (and stay in) college. There are an array of tax breaks for higher education,[4] but to illustrate the range of options, consider just two.

First, taxpayers who pay interest on student loans may be able to deduct their interest payments.[5] So, if Carl pays $1,000 in eligible student loan interest, he can deduct that amount. How much is the deduction worth? You know that one: the value is $1,000 times Carl's marginal tax rate.

Second, taxpayers may (depending on their income level) be able to claim a tax credit for college tuition. The Congress has provided two different tax credits, called the American Opportunity Credit and the Lifelong Learning Tax Credit.[6] Like any tax credit, these two provide a dollar-for-dollar offset to tax liability. So, if Dara is entitled to a $1,000 tax credit, it is worth $1,000 to her (provided that she otherwise would owe at least $1,000 in income taxes). The American Opportunity credit is partially refundable, while the Lifelong Learning credit is not.

¶403 DISTRIBUTION AND THE AVERAGE TAX RATE

Recall that *the average tax rate is used to measure tax burden and is defined as total tax liability divided by total taxable income.* Tax burden in this sense is intuitive: it measures the share of your income that goes to the federal government in taxes. So, if Henry earns $100,000 and pays $20,000 in income taxes, his average tax rate is 20%. That figure tells us nothing about his marginal tax rate, of course. But it does allow us to compare him to Isla, whose average tax rate is (say) 25%.

Individuals (and families) sometimes keep track of their average tax rate from year to year, just to measure their overall tax situation. Tax software like TurboTax, for example, makes the comparison easy by calculating average tax rate and tracking it year to year.

Policy wonks inside and outside government use average tax rates to track the tax burden on different classes of taxpayers. For instance, the Congressional Budget Office provides this historical perspective on average federal income tax rates for the top 1% of taxpayers (measured by their pre-tax incomes).

---

[4] For an overview, *see* Internal Revenue Service, *Tax Benefits for Education*, Publication 970, available at http://www.irs.gov/publications/p970/.

[5] For conditions that must be met, *see* Code Section 221.

[6] Code Section 25A.

Chart 4.1 Average Individual Federal Income Tax Rates on the Top 1% of Households, 1979-2009[7]

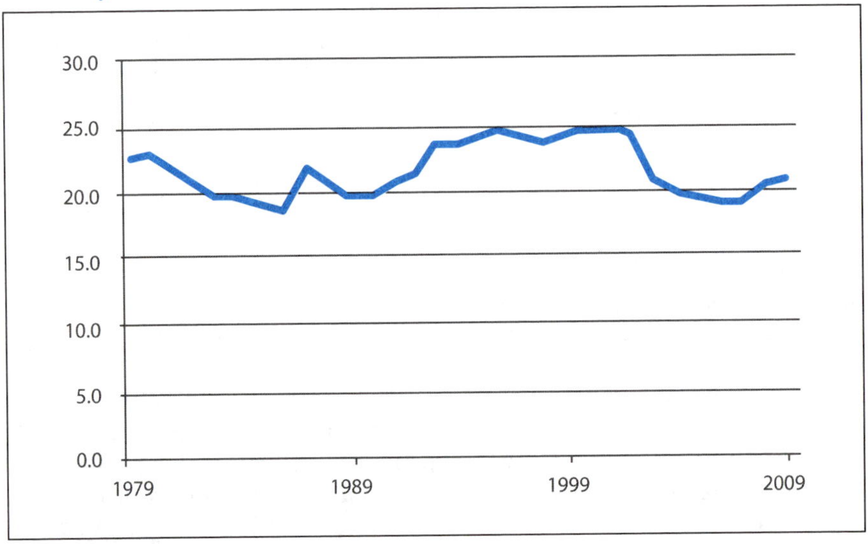

Whatever your political opinions about the top 1%, you now know that their average federal income tax rate has ranged from a low of 18.6% (in 1986) to a high of 24.7% (in 1996) and stands at 21% as of 2009. Depending on your views of government and the economy, that tax burden may strike you as laughably low or terribly high. But either way, comparing average tax rates over time is the accepted standard for measuring the distribution of tax burdens.

¶404 *OLD COLONY* AND SUBSTANCE OVER FORM

Every now and then, taxpayers figure out a creative new way to conduct a familiar transaction—and reduce their tax burden in the process. One famous example is a 1929 Supreme Court case, *Old Colony Trust.*[8]

The transaction at issue in *Old Colony* is straightforward. William Wood, the president of the American Woolen Company, earned a cash salary of about $1 million in 1918. A cool million would be a high salary today, but it was colossal at the time. Adjusting for inflation, Mr. Wood earned the equivalent of $15 million.[9] But Mr. Wood thought he deserved more, and the company

7 Source: Congressional Budget Office, The Distribution of Household Income and Federal Taxes, 2008-2009, available at http://www.cbo.gov/publication/43373 (Supplemental Table 1).

8 Old Colony Trust Co. v. Commissioner, 279 U.S. 716 (1929). The taxpayer was Old Colony Trust, acting as the executor of Mr. Wood's estate.

9 The Bureau of Labor Statistics provides a handy inflation calculator here: http://www.bls.gov/data/inflation_calculator.htm.

(er, that would be the company he co-owned with his father-in-law)[10] agreed. To sweeten Mr. Wood's compensation package, the company agreed to pay Mr. Wood's federal income taxes for him. Mr. Wood's taxes, paid by the company, were about $700,000. The result is that Mr. Wood kept the whole $1 million cash salary, free and clear.

Mr. Wood's arrangement is unusual. Typically, an employee receives a salary and pays her own taxes. If Gabby earns $100,000 at her job, she also expects to pay federal income taxes out of her paycheck. In fact, she doesn't usually have any choice in the matter: her employer withholds the taxes, reducing her paycheck, and sends the tax due directly to the IRS. But it isn't immediately obvious that there's a tax problem if a company follows the *Old Colony* route and pays an employee's taxes on top of her regular salary.

The tax issue posed in *Old Colony* is whether Mr. Wood's income for 1918 should include the $700,000 in taxes paid by the company on Mr. Wood's behalf. Mr. Wood's position (of course) was "no." He received $1 million, and the company paid the taxes due of $700,000. End of story. The IRS, in contrast, took the position that Mr. Wood's taxable income was $1.7 million (not the $1 million he reported), so that he owed additional taxes.

The IRS won the case, and it raked in a big monetary reward. The top marginal tax rate in 1918 was a bit more than 70%,[11] so that an additional income inclusion of $700,000 meant about $490,000 in additional income taxes. Today, that $490,000 would amount to nearly $7 million, adjusted for inflation since 1918.

But the irony of *Old Colony* is that the IRS should have sought—and won—a far bigger tax payment. To see why, we need to ask what Mr. Wood and the American Woolen Company were really doing when they arranged for the company to pay his taxes. In tax, we call this move *substance over form*, and it's one of the six key concepts that recurs throughout the income tax. *When we ask about the substance of a transaction, we are asking about the economics of a deal: what was motivating the parties to do what they did?*

When the American Woolen Company paid Mr. Wood's taxes, what happened in form is that one party paid the taxes of another. Paying taxes isn't normally a taxable event. When Gabby earns $100,000 and pays, say, $20,000 to the IRS, the tax payment itself isn't a taxable event. She's just paying what she owed. American Woolen and Mr. Wood did the very same thing *in form*.

But *in substance*, what was really going on is that American Woolen was paying Mr. Wood extra salary. By paying Mr. Wood's taxes for him, the company was putting extra dollars in his pocket. To see how, let's use some stylized tax numbers. Assume that the marginal and average tax rate for Mr. Wood was 70%.

---

[10] *See William Wood and the American Woolen Company*, Bread and Roses Centennial Exhibit website, http://exhibit.breadandrosescentennial.org/node/70.

[11] CCH, A Historical Look at Top Marginal Tax Rates, at http://www.cch.com/wbot2013/029IncomeTaxRates.asp (top marginal tax rate in 1918 was 73%).

(This is unrealistic: marginal tax rates at the time were steeply progressive. But the assumption makes the math easy.) Now, imagine two CEOs each earning cash salary of $1 million in 1918. William Wood gets to keep his entire salary free and clear, because his company pays his taxes for him. His counterpart—let's call him Terence—has to pay his own taxes of $700,000.

Now, it's clear enough that William is way better off than Terence: William has $1 million to spend as he likes, while Terence, who pays his own taxes, has only $300,000 left to spend. So the IRS was correct to infer that William Wood's real salary was higher than $1 million.

But the IRS made a costly mistake when it treated William Wood as having total income of only $1.7 million. Extend the example to suppose that Terence, the CEO who pays his own taxes, receives a raise to $1.7 million. The IRS position in *Old Colony* implies that William is in the same position as Terence. But Terence is actually still worse off. At a 70% rate, Terence will pay $1.19 million in taxes on his $1.7 million salary. That leaves him with only $510,000 to spend. Poor guy! (Let's pause to contemplate his plight.) There's no way he'll keep up with William Wood and his $1 million.

So to figure out who *would* be comparable, we should ask the question this way: at what level of salary would a CEO keep $1 million after paying his own taxes? The answer, it turns out, is a whopping $3.33 million in 1918 dollars (equivalent to a heart-stopping $52 million in today's terms, placing William Wood comfortably among the highest paid CEOs in the country today[12]):

Pre-tax income	$3.33 million
Tax at 70%	$2.33 million
After-tax income	$1 million

In substance, then, William was paid $3.33 million in 1918 dollars, and he should have paid the IRS $2.33 million. Viewed from this perspective, *Old Colony* looks less like an IRS victory and more like a defeat.

Why didn't the IRS pursue the full amount due? The Supreme Court's opinion contains a hint:

> It is next argued against the payment of this tax that, if these payments by the employer constitute income to the employee, the employee will be called upon to pay the tax imposed upon this additional income, and that the payment of the additional tax will create further income which will in turn be subject to tax, with the result that there would be a tax upon a tax. This, it is urged, is the result of the government's theory,

[12] *America's Highest Paid Chief Executives*, Forbes, available at http://www.forbes.com/lists/2012/12/ceo-compensation-12_rank.html. In fact, Mr. Wood might outpace many of the CEOs on that list, since his salary was paid all in cash, while many top CEOs are compensated in stock with various restrictions.

> when carried to its logical conclusion, and results in an absurdity which Congress could not have contemplated.[13]
>
> In the first place, no attempt has been made by the Treasury to collect further taxes upon the theory that the payment of the additional taxes creates further income, and the question of a tax upon a tax was not before the circuit court of appeals, and has not been certified to this Court. We can settle questions of that sort when an attempt to impose a tax upon a tax is undertaken, but not now.

The Supreme Court seems uneasy about the prospect of a "tax upon a tax," and so the IRS didn't press the point, content to wait for another day. But, in fact, the dreaded tax upon a tax produces just the right answer. Just as the taxpayer pointed out, the logic of *Old Colony* holds all the way down: if the payment of $700,000 in tax by the company should be taxed to William Wood, then so should the additional payment of $490,000, and every payment on down the line (assuming that the firm will keep paying the taxes so that Wood, as promised, receives $1 million after tax). In fact, had *Old Colony* been correctly decided, William would have owed 70% tax upon a tax as follows:

Table 4.3 Old Colony Trust

Income	Tax
$1,000,000	$700,000
$700,000	$490,000
$490,000	$343,000
$343,000	$240,100
$240,100	$168,070
...	...
TOTAL INCOME $3.33 MILLION	TOTAL TAX $2.33 MILLION

Eventually, the IRS got the calculation right. Today, the IRS will collect the full tax upon a tax should you be lucky enough to be in William's position and have your employer pay your taxes for you.

¶405 REAL-WORLD TRANSACTIONS: SIGNING BONUSES AND THE GROSS UP FOR TAXES

Old Colony (or, rather the correct result in *Old Colony*, as just described) has vigorous life today in a variety of corporate transactions that require one party to pay the federal income taxes of another party.

[13] Old Colony Trust Co. v. Commissioner, 279 U.S. 716, 730-31 (1929).

A common example is the signing bonus. Many corporate executives (and some lawyers) receive a signing bonus when they agree to work for a firm. The signing bonus is, obviously enough, income to the recipient: it represents compensation for changing employers. Some employers, though, sweeten the pot by offering a tax "gross up," which compensates the employee for taxes due on the bonus.

"Gross up" is a seriously ugly term, but it's just another name for the "tax upon a tax" process that showed us William Wood's true income in *Old Colony*. For instance, suppose that Lily receives a $500,000 signing bonus from her new employer, and she's savvy enough to ask for a tax gross up. What that means is that her employer agrees to pay all federal taxes due, so that she takes home $500,000 free and clear.

The "gross up" refers to the concept you now know: it isn't sufficient for the employer to pay taxes on just $500,000. Instead, the employer has to pay a higher amount equal to the taxes due on a pre-tax salary of $X that would yield an after-tax salary of $500,000. The formula is as follows, where *t* is Lily's marginal tax rate:

$$\$X = \frac{\$500{,}000}{(1 - t)}$$

For instance, suppose that Lily's marginal tax rate is 40%. The employer would have to report a total bonus of $833,333 to the IRS, which would result in taxes of $333,333 at the 40% marginal tax rate. The employer would send $333,000 to the IRS and cut a check for $500,000 to Lily.

The key task from a lawyer's perspective is to draft the gross up correctly. If you represent Lily in this example, which of the following contract clauses will produce the desired result—and which could leave Lily with a tax bill?

> **OPTION 1.** Employer agrees to pay Employee a signing bonus of $500,000 and to pay any and all federal, state, and local income taxes due on that amount.

> **OPTION 2.** Employer agrees to pay Employee a signing bonus in an amount equal to the amount that will permit Employee to retain $500,000 after the payment of all federal, state, and local income taxes due on the transaction.

It's Option 2, of course. Option 1 is, at the very least, ambiguous: it suggests that Employer could comply by simply paying Lily's tax on the first $500,000, without paying the tax upon the tax upon the tax. Option 2 could be drafted in other ways; you might include the gross-up formula, for example. And in the real world, you'd want to think about payroll taxes and any other relevant taxes. You'd also want to add a provision so that the employer is on the hook for any future tax adjustments if it somehow underpays Lily's tax. But this simple beginning illustrates the financial importance of the gross-up idea.

CHAPTER 5

Gains and Losses

Introduction . . . ¶500
The Concept of Basis . . . ¶501
Real-World Transactions: Corporate Acquisitions . . . ¶502
When is Basis Recovered? *Hort v. Commissioner* . . . ¶503
Allocating Basis and *Inaja Land Co. v. Commissioner* . . . ¶504
Basis Rules for Gifts and Bequests . . . ¶505
Real-World Transactions: Estate Planning and the Income Tax . . . ¶506
Basis and Pre-Nuptial Agreements: *Farid-Es-Sultaneh v. Commissioner* . . . ¶507

¶500 INTRODUCTION

Gains and losses are among the most intuitive concepts in the income tax. To see why, begin with a simple transaction. Suppose your roommate buys a used bicycle at a yard sale for $100. She spends the afternoon cleaning it up, touching up the paint and inflating the tires. Afterward, the old bike looks so much better that she resells it to a classmate for $150. How much did your roommate make for her afternoon's work? Fifty dollars, obviously.

But pause for a moment to reflect on that answer. Suppose you overheard your roommate telling another friend that she'd made $150 on the deal. You're probably too polite to correct her, but you'd know that she was exaggerating. She put in $100 to buy the bike to begin with, so her gain in the end was only $50—the excess of what she got out over what she put in.

The income tax treats gains as income. The tax law deploys some fancier terminology, which we'll get to shortly. But the notion of gain as making more than you put into something carries right over from common sense into the tax law.

Before we get to terminology and a few complexities (you knew they were coming), pause to consider why gains are includable as income for tax purposes. In Chapter 2, we first encountered the Haig-Simons definition of income, and it serves as a useful touchstone here. Recall that Haig and Simons agreed that income includes any increase in resources available for personal consumption or for savings.

The key concept is that the income tax seeks to tax *net income*, which includes only the increase or gain in resources, and not the total amount of resources on hand. Returning to the roommate example, after she resells the bike she has $150 in her pocket, and she's free to go out and spend it all. It's her money, after all!

But her gain, her profit, her *net income* is only the $50 increment she added to her wealth by fixing up the bike. Intuitively, the bike deal ultimately made your roommate better off by $50, and that's her net income.

The distinction between gains and total resources captures the difference between income and wealth. The aim of the income tax is to impose tax on those who get richer in a year. A wealth tax, by contrast, aims to tax total resources, whether or not the person is better off compared to last year. In our bicycle example, the roommate has $50 of income but $150 of wealth.

Later in this chapter, we'll see that the hardest issues—and this is generally true throughout the tax law—have to do with the timing of gain and loss. Problems of *valuation* force the law to take shortcuts and adopt inaccurate rules of thumb. And those shortcuts, in turn, open up big opportunities for taxpayers to cut their taxes via *income shifting* and *tax deferral.* We will turn to those matters shortly, but first, begin with the, er, most basic concept: basis.

¶501 THE CONCEPT OF BASIS

The Code rules governing gain and loss are quite intuitive once you understand a couple of terms. To capture the increase in resources, the income tax adopts a simple formula in Code Section 1001:

Gain = Amount Realized - Basis

"Basis" is a tax accounting term that measures what the taxpayer has invested in an asset. In our example, your roommate paid $100 to buy the bike, so that's her basis. (Basis includes the cost of an item, an intuition codified in Code Section 1012.) You can think of basis as the baseline for measuring profit. If your roommate can sell the bike for more than $100, she's made money, but if she sells for less than that, she's lost money.

The "amount realized" is pretty much what it sounds like: the total money realized on the deal. When your roommate resells the bike for $150, she *realizes* $150. But, intuitively, the amount realized is not her gain: we have to subtract out her investment, or her basis. Thus:

Gain ($50) = Amount Realized ($150) - Basis ($100)

The same concepts apply to business and investment transactions. Suppose that you purchase 100 shares of Microsoft stock for $5,000, or about $50 per share. Next week, the price of Microsoft has risen to $52 per share. You sell your 100 shares for $5,200. Your gain is $200: the difference between the amount realized ($5,200) and your basis ($5,000).

The notion of basis also provides a baseline for determining losses. Suppose that the block of Microsoft stock you bought for $5,000 declines in value to $4,200. In that case, you're actually worse off than before: you've lost $800 of the money you invested! The tax law treats this as a loss, and it reduces your net income. Intuitively, then, a loss occurs when your amount realized is less than your basis:

Loss ($800) = Basis ($5,000) - Amount Realized ($4,200)

In this example, you still have quite a bit of wealth left ($4,200). But you're worse off than you were before you put money into the stock market—worse off by $800. The Haig-Simons notion of income is broad enough to recognize that sometimes people lose money—they have *negative income*. Equivalently, a loss is subtracted from your other income in arriving at net income.

You might feel a little suspicious of losses at first. It may seem unfair or even fishy to permit taxpayers to subtract (or deduct) losses from their net income. You might even worry that the Tax Code is creating an incentive for investors to lose money so that they can deduct their losses on their tax returns!

But the concept of *net income* explains why the income tax should permit taxpayers to deduct losses. Imagine two taxpayers, Jed and Amy, holding equivalent jobs, each paying $100,000 per year. Now imagine that Jed trades stocks during the year and loses $8,000, while Amy just keeps her spare cash in a checking account. At the end of the year, Amy is better off by the full $100,000 she earned at her job. But Jed is better off by only $92,000. You can think of Jed's stock-market losses as offsetting part of what he earned: he lost roughly a month's income in the stock market.

We don't need to worry that the income tax is subsidizing stock trading by permitting loss deductions. Jed is worse off than Amy in real life, not just in the tax world, and his loss is correctly measured as $8,000. So Jed should report only $92,000, while Amy reports $100,000. It might be a different story if, as a society, we thought that people shouldn't trade stocks, but today it's very much a mainstream investment decision. (It might also be a different story if we thought that Jed hadn't really lost the money—that he somehow cooked the books or exaggerated his economic loss. We'll get to cases like that later on when we come to tax shelters, which often fabricate losses.)

Going forward, will taxpayers eagerly lose real money in order to take a tax deduction on the loss? No way. A real dollar of loss costs you, well, $1. You have $1 less to spend on your morning coffee or a candy bar. The tax deduction for that dollar will save you only a fraction of a dollar, measured by your marginal tax rate. If you're in the highest federal tax bracket, that's about 40%. So a dollar of deductible loss will save you only 40 cents in taxes.

Going out on a limb here, I'd say that 40 cents is less than a dollar. So the tax lesson is simple enough: never, ever sign onto a deal in which you lose real dollars in order to get a tax deduction for the loss. The public policy implication is the same; taxpayers should be able to deduct real losses, and we don't need to worry that they're making money at Uncle Sam's expense by doing so.

Armed with the concepts of basis and amount realized, you can readily figure out how much gain (or loss) someone incurs. These very same concepts govern the taxation of even complicated business deals.

¶502 REAL-WORLD TRANSACTIONS: CORPORATE ACQUISITIONS

Perhaps surprisingly, the same basic rules apply to big corporate acquisitions involving billions of dollars and millions of shareholders. Corporate acquisitions can take complicated forms, which we won't deal with in this course (you'll need to take Corporate Tax for those!). Still, when one corporation acquires another for cash, the seller will recognize gain or loss according to the rules of Code Section 1001.

A little background will clarify the business deal. Legally, as you may know, a corporation is a business entity owned by its stockholders. Many big businesses, like Target, Bank of America, and Microsoft, are corporations. Every corporation issues stock to its stockholders (or, equivalently, "shareholders'). Stockholders purchase their stock by contributing money to the corporation. In return for their investment, they receive an undivided ownership interest in the corporation's income and assets. Shareholders also have the right to vote for the corporation's board of directors. The stock market provides the venue for shareholders to sell their stock to others.

Corporations come in all sizes. A small business might have just one shareholder. A family business might have a handful of shareholders, all family members—Mom, Dad, and the adult children. A large, public corporation, by contrast, may have millions of shareholders. Consider Family Dollar Stores, Inc.—perhaps you've seen their stores or shopped in one. Founded in 1959, Family Dollar today has 58,000 employees and annual sales of $10 billion. The company has more than 100 million shares of common stock outstanding.[1]

In 2014, another dollar store proposed to pay $78.50 per share in cash for all the stock of Family Dollar.[2] From a business perspective, the acquirer's motive is easy to understand. Once the buyer owned all the stock of Family Dollar, the buyer could install its own board and management. The acquirer would then control the assets and operations of Family Dollar and could merge the businesses in ways that made business sense. Although the war of the dollar stores didn't end there, pause to consider how a stock purchase would be taxed.

---

1 For a description of the company, *see* Forbes Magazine, *Family Dollar Stores*, at http://www.forbes.com/companies/family-dollar-stores/; for data on stockholders, *see* the financial statements provided by the company at http://investor.familydollar.com/files/doc_financials/2014/Family%20Dollar%20Q3%202014%2010Q.pdf.

2 For details on the bid by Dollar General to acquire Family Dollar, *see* the news release at http://investor.shareholder.com/dollar/releasedetail.cfm?ReleaseID=866625.

Corporate stock is, of course, an asset, just as a bicycle is. When a taxpayer sells an asset, she recognizes gain or loss according to the (now) familiar formulas of Section 1001:

Gain = Amount Realized - Basis
and
Loss = Basis - Amount Realized

So every shareholder of Family Dollar would recognize gain or loss measured by the $78.50 selling price, or amount realized, and his or her basis. Suppose that one shareholder, Sarah, had bought her stock for $60 per share. When Sarah sold her stock to the acquirer, she would report gain of $18.50 per share on her tax return.

All the other millions of shareholders would do the same, calculating gain or loss based on their own stock basis. The corporate acquirer, in turn, would have a basis of $78.50 per share in the Family Dollar stock, because that's the purchase price it paid.

The same basic rules apply to another common corporate transaction, the partial acquisition. Many corporations own multiple businesses. Consider Procter & Gamble Co., which every year racks up $83 billion in sales of everything from Pantene shampoo to Bounty paper towels.[3] It would not be unusual for an acquirer to bid to buy, say, the Pantene shampoo business without also wanting to buy the rest of the company.

The deal would be taxed under the usual rules of Section 1001, with one additional wrinkle. P&G would recognize gain or loss based on the difference between its basis in the assets of Pantene and the amount realized on the sale. Thus, if a buyer paid $100 million for Pantene, and if P&G's basis were $70 million, P&G would report a total gain of $30 million.

The one new wrinkle is that gains and losses on different assets may be taxed differently. The tax law imposes special tax rates on some gains and disfavors some losses. The Pantene business probably comprises a number of different kinds of assets: plant and equipment, brand names, and goodwill. (Goodwill is the value of a going business over and above the value of its identifiable assets.) Accordingly, P&G would have to allocate the $100 million amount realized among the various assets of Pantene so that it could report gain and loss separately for each asset. This allocation can require some careful accounting, especially for a large business with hundreds or thousands of separate assets. But conceptually, it's a straightforward application of Section 1001.[4]

---

[3] For sales data, *see* the Procter & Gamble website at http://www.pginvestor.com/CorporateProfile.aspx?iid=4004124; for a list of brands, *see* the company website at http://www.pginvestor.com/GenPage.aspx?IID=4004124&GKP=1073748355.

[4] The allocation rules are specified in Code Section 1060 and the corresponding regulations. It might seem that allocation imposes needless complexity, since total gain or loss will be measured by total basis compared to total amount realized. But it turns out that special rates and limitations apply to gains and losses on different kinds of assets, making allocation necessary for accurate taxation.

¶503 WHEN IS BASIS RECOVERED? *HORT V. COMMISSIONER*

To this point, we've focused on determining the amount of a taxpayer's basis, which is usually straightforward. A harder problem for the tax law is to determine when a taxpayer should recover basis. The most famous case, *Hort v. Commissioner*,[5] concerns just this problem. In the end, the Supreme Court gets the right answer—but for the wrong reason.

To frame the problem in *Hort*, start with a simple example. Suppose you buy a downtown office building for $10 million. Then you rent out the offices to a tenant for $2 million per year. You hold the office building for three years and then sell it for $7 million.

From a tax perspective, it's clear enough that your basis in the building is its $10 million purchase price. (This result is intuitive, but formally, you'd cite Code Section 1012.) It's also obvious that the $2 million in annual rents is income to you. And when you sell the building in the third year, your amount realized will be $7 million. But how should you net your basis against the rents to arrive at *net income*?

Table 5.1 illustrates two plausible, but polar-opposite rules that the tax system might adopt. The first rule would permit the taxpayer to recover basis when the building is purchased (in year 1). That rule produces a big loss in year 1, but the loss is more than offset by net gains later on. The second rule would instruct the taxpayer to recover basis when the building is sold (in year 3). That rule produces more income in the first two years but a small loss in year 3.

Table 5.1 The Timing of Basis Recovery

		Recover Basis in Year 1		Recover Basis in Year 3	
Year	Gross income	Basis Recovery	Net Income	Basis Recovery	Net Income
1	$2 million in rents	$10 million	($8 million)	0	$2 million
2	$2 million in rents	0	$2 million	0	$2 million
3	$2 million in rents plus $7 million in amount realized	0	$9 million	$10 million	($1 million)
TOTALS			$3 million		$3 million

The first key point is that the taxpayer's total *net income* from owning the building is the same in either case: $3 million. That has to be the right answer, intuitively, since the taxpayer put in $10 million and ultimately received back $13 million ($6 million in rent over three years and the sales price of $7 million).

The second key point is that the timing of taxation is very different under the two rules. When the law permits the taxpayer to subtract her entire basis in

[5] 313 U.S. 28 (1941).

year 1, the taxpayer reports a net loss and then higher income later. When the law defers basis recovery, the taxpayer has higher income in the early years and a loss at the end.

This, then, is how basis rules can create—or avoid—*tax deferral*. Chapter 1, if you recall, established that taxpayers generally prefer to pay their taxes (just like their Visa bills) later rather than sooner. In this example, the taxpayer will report the same total income (and pay the same total tax) no matter what. *But the typical taxpayer will prefer early basis recovery because that rule defers her income* compared to a rule that postpones basis recovery.

Here's another way to see the same point. From the taxpayer's perspective, basis is a good thing—a tax "goodie," so to speak. Basis is a tax goodie because it reduces net income for tax purposes. And lower net income means a smaller tax bill. So, ask yourself the simple question: does the taxpayer want a goodie now or later? Now, of course! So, as a general planning rule, taxpayers have an incentive to claim basis at the earliest legal opportunity.

The tax law, it turns out, actually adopts a variety of rules for basis recovery, depending on the kind of asset involved. Stocks and bonds typically are taxed according to the rule of basis recovery when sold.

Real estate is a little—but only a little—more complicated. Taxpayers who own rental real estate (like the office building in our example) are permitted to recover basis gradually over time, based on the projected useful life of the building. For example, suppose the office building in our example were projected to be usable for 20 years. The taxpayer would divide the $10 million basis by 20 and would deduct $500,000 in basis every year.

The rule that permits gradual basis recovery is called depreciation. (Later, in Chapter 10, we'll revisit depreciation and add some detail, but the key point for now is that depreciation is a form of basis recovery.)

The result, in our example, is shown below in Table 5.2. The annual depreciation deduction offsets the rental income, reducing net income to a steady $1.5 million per year. In year 3, the taxpayer can not only take a final depreciation deduction but can also net her remaining basis of $8.5 million against the sales proceeds of $7 million.

Pause for a moment to consider why the remaining basis is only $8.5 million instead of $10 million. The reason is that the taxpayer's total investment in the transaction is $10 million. If the law permits her to deduct a portion of that basis every year ($500,000 in our example), then the depreciation deductions must reduce basis dollar-for-dollar. To see why, imagine that basis remained $10 million. In that case, the taxpayer would be double-counting, because she would receive tax goodies totaling $11.5 million ($500,000 per year for 3 years plus $10 million in year 3) instead of just $10 million.

Table 5.2 Gradual Basis Recovery

Year	Gross Income	Basis Recovery	Net Income
1	$2 million in rents	$500,000 depreciation	$1.5 million
2	$2 million in rents	$500,000 depreciation	$1.5 million
3	$2 million in rents plus $7 million in amount realized	$500,000 depreciation plus $8.5 remaining basis upon sale	$0
TOTALS			$3 million

We're ready now to see what went right—and wrong—in the famous *Hort* case. The facts present a fairly common business transaction. Walter Hort inherited an office building in Manhattan. Unhappily for him (and for the rest of America), the Great Depression hit shortly thereafter, and the value of Walter's building plummeted. As business contracted during the Depression, tenants demanded lower rents or, in some cases, sought to get out of their leases.

The transaction in *Hort* involved a tenant who made a payment in exchange for the cancellation of the tenant's obligations under a lease. Irving had a lease in Walter Hort's building but no longer wanted to rent the office space. To persuade Walter to tear up the lease, Irving made a one-time cash payment of $140,000 (just as you might have to pay your landlord if you want to move out of your apartment before the lease term is up).

Was this a good deal for Walter? He didn't think so. In fact, he reported to the IRS that he lost money on the deal—$20,000 in fact. After all, he had just lost a prime tenant, and new tenants were likely to demand lower rents. This was the Depression, after all. Walter most likely sighed, pocketed the cash, and hung out a "For Rent" sign.

But then the IRS took an interest in the case and slapped Hort with a gigantic tax bill. The IRS's view was that he had made a $140,000 profit on the lease-cancellation deal. Updated for inflation, these are sizable sums. The IRS claimed that Walter had a whopping $2.5 million of income, while he claimed a loss (in today's dollars) of almost $400,000.

Who was right? The solution, it turns out, lies in the concept of basis. Both Walter and the IRS were making claims about the timing of basis recovery. Let's begin by laying out what their claims were. We can then see which side had the more compelling case.

Recall that Walter claimed a loss of $20,000 even though he received $140,000 in cash. Recall, too, that a loss has a specific meaning in tax:

Loss = Basis - Amount Realized

The amount realized on the deal is pretty clearly the cash that Irving paid Walter Hort, or $140,000. So if Walter calculated a loss of $20,000, he was implicitly claiming that he should be entitled to claim basis that exceeded his amount realized by $20,000. In other words, Walter's position was:

Loss ($20,000) = Basis ($160,000) - Amount Realized ($140,000)

What was the legal authority for Walter's basis claim? He had inherited the building from his father in 1928, before the Depression, when real estate values were high. The basis of inherited property (according to Code Section 1014) is fair market value, so Walter's total basis was likely very high—millions or tens of millions of dollars. He certainly felt, understandably enough, that he was worse off when Irving exited the scene. His tax position reflected that common-sense view: the $160,000 claimed basis represented the lost rentals he would incur from re-renting the space (at a lower rate) to a new tenant. The net $20,000 loss reflected the excess of his lost rentals over the compensation Irving paid.

From one perspective, Walter's claimed loss is quite modest. Given the scale of the Great Depression, he had probably lost substantially more than $20,000 by the early 1930s, when Irving Trust backed out of its lease. But, absent a sale of the building for cash, the tax law faced a *valuation* problem. There was no reliable way to crystallize the total amount he had lost. We can understand Walter's legal position in light of the *valuation* problem: he wanted to use Irving's payment of $140,000 as an occasion for claiming a portion of his overall loss.

By contrast, the IRS position seemingly defied common sense. The IRS treated Walter as if he had gained something when Irving paid to get out of the lease—as if he had profited to the tune of the entire $140,000 payment. In Haig-Simons terms, Walter surely has the better argument. The Depression tanked his property values, and Irving's exit compounded his loss. If our income tax were run entirely on Haig-Simons principles, Walter's perspective seems compelling.

But the income tax doesn't operate according to the principles of Haig-Simons. Instead, it operates according to rules. The key virtue of the IRS position in *Hort* was that the agency was seeking to enforce legal consistency against a taxpayer's attempt to accelerate basis recovery.

To see the inconsistency in the taxpayer's position, recall the idea of depreciation developed in our initial example. The law permits owners of office buildings to recover their basis gradually over the expected life of the building. Thus, if Walter Hort had (say) a $10 million basis in his building, the law would permit him to deduct some basis every year. He wanted to deduct even more than that: he attempted to deduct *extra* basis to offset the Irving payment.

But the law doesn't permit taxpayers to choose the timing of basis deductions. (If it did, virtually all taxpayers would deduct their basis as soon as possible!) Taxpayers must, instead, stick by the rules. And the applicable rules permitted only depreciation deductions to the owner of an office building.

The irony, then, is that the victorious IRS position in *Hort* was economically indefensible but legally sound. Walter, like nearly everyone in the Depression, was hurting economically. He was legitimately worse off than he had been, and probably by quite a bit more than the $20,000 he claimed on his tax return.

But the basis rules do not track economic reality; instead, they simply bind all similarly-situated taxpayers to report income in the same way.

The Court's opinion in *Hort* contains none of this reasoning. Instead, the Court proceeds by analogy, reasoning that the $140,000 payment from Irving was a substitute for rents and so, like rents, should be taxed in full. The doctrine of substitution has endured, and the tax law still uses it to test the taxability of lease-cancellation payments.

But the logic of substitution is, ultimately, unsatisfying. Office buildings are valuable, in the end, because they generate rents to the owner. If you own an office building, you can either rent out the space or sell it to someone who will. In the latter case, the sales price of the building will be—in an economic sense—a substitute for the rents you will forgo. But the law imposes starkly different basis rules on holding and selling. An owner (like Walter Hort) recovers basis only via depreciation. A seller, by contrast, can offset the entire basis of the building against the sales price he receives.

The real question in *Hort*, then, isn't whether Irving's payment was a substitute for rents. Of course it was! The real question is whether Walter Hort was a building owner or a building seller. And while it is interesting to consider whether the Court could have framed him as a (partial) seller of the building, in the end the Court opted for common-sense consistency and deemed him the owner. Given the Court's holding, there was only one route for Walter to claim the loss on his building: sell it.

¶504 ALLOCATING BASIS AND *INAJA LAND CO. V. COMMISSIONER*

When taxpayers buy and sell bundles of assets, *valuation* can pose headaches for the tax system. Suppose that Kara buys a five-acre tract of land for $5 million. She's paid $1 million per acre, obviously enough. So if she waits a year and then sells off one acre for $1.25 million, then she's made a profit of a quarter of a million dollars, or $250,000.

Kara's case is intuitive, because the proportions are easy. Another way to reach the same result is to say that she sold one-fifth of her land for $1.25 million, so she recovers one-fifth of her basis, or $1 million. That proportional method produces gain (under the usual Code Section 1001 formula) of $250,000.

But even a simple case like Kara's can quickly grow complicated if the five acres of land are very different. Some of the land, like the one acre Kara sold, is ideal for building—flat, well-drained, with easy access to a road. But other portions of the land might be quite poor building sites. If that's the case, then we can't assume (as we implicitly did in the simple case) that each acre is equally valuable. The result is a *valuation* problem: we can't be at all certain whether Kara has made any profit, because we can't know (without more information) what proportion of the value of the land she sold. Put in tax terms, all we know is her amount realized of $1.25 million. We can't be certain about her basis in the acre she sold. If the value of each of the original five acres is quite variable, it might be that she paid, in effect, far more than $1 million for the best acreage, and far less than $1 million for the worst.

This kind of *valuation* puzzle is common in the real world. Consider the famous case of *Inaja Land Co. v. Commissioner*.[6] Simplifying a bit, twenty-five friends got together in 1928 and pooled their money to buy land for a private fishing club. They formed a corporation, Inaja Land Co., and paid about $60,000 for 1,200 acres of land on the Owens River in California. Some of the members built cabins on the land, and the club restricted the use of the property to guests.

In the mid-1930s, however, the fishing club members got a nasty surprise. The state of California built a large tunnel and dumped debris into the Owens River. The crystal-clear river became a muddy stream of trash, and the fishing was ruined. The club members got together and sued the state, contending that the dumping had impaired the value of their land. After some legal wrangling, in 1939, the California government paid the Inaja Land Co. about $50,000. But as part of the settlement, Inaja Land agreed to grant the state a permanent easement to dump into the Owens River. Put another way, the fishing club had sold, for a cool $50K, its right to clean water.

The *valuation* issue in Inaja Land is clear enough. The cash isn't hard to value, of course: $50,000 is, well, $50,000. But what isn't clear is what portion of the value of the land had been sold. We know that Inaja Land paid a total of $60,000 for its land. But what portion of that $60,000 investment did the company sell when it gave up its right to clean water?

We can speculate, of course. Inaja Land was, after all, primarily a fishing club. So the polluted water might have rendered the land nearly valueless from the perspective of the would-be fishermen. If we really thought the land was otherwise worthless, then we might grant Inaja Land a loss of $10,000, calculated as basis ($60,000) less amount realized ($50,000). The taxpayers would certainly like that solution, which grants a big upfront loss, giving them the value of *tax deferral*.

But the case isn't really that clear. The land might have been valuable to other people as, say, farmland or home sites. Even though the fishing was ruined, there might be farmers or builders still willing to pay quite a bit for it. In that case, the water easement might represent only a fraction of the value of the land, say, 10%. On that logic, only 10% of the basis of the land (or $6,000) should be recovered, and Inaja Land should report a gain of $44,000, calculated as amount realized ($50,000) over basis ($6,000).

So what's the right answer—a loss of $10K or a gain of $44K? That's an awfully large swing in tax liability, and the truth is that we can't solve the puzzle based on logic alone. Without an accurate *valuation* of the property and the easement, we simply cannot tell what portion of the basis should be allocable to the sale of the clean water rights.

---

[6] 9 T.C. 727 (1947).

Faced with this puzzle, the Tax Court threw up its metaphorical hands. The court concluded:

> Apportionment with reasonable accuracy of the amount received not being possible, and this amount being less than petitioner's cost basis for the property, *it cannot be determined that petitioner has, in fact, realized gain in any amount.*[7]

Reluctantly, the court applied the "wait and see" rule of *Burnet v. Logan*[8] and held that the entire $50,000 should be treated as a return of basis. The result may have soothed some of the pain of the would-be fishermen, since they pocketed the $50,000, tax-free for the moment. Going forward, the land basis was lower by $50,000 (*i.e.,* the land basis was now $10,000 instead of the original $60,000). But the lower basis wouldn't have any tax "bite" until they sold the land, potentially much later on. In the meantime, the taxpayer could reap the economic value of *tax deferral.*

Courts generally dislike the "open transaction" doctrine of *Burnet v. Logan,* precisely because it presents taxpayers with such massive *tax deferral.* More and more, Congress and the IRS have created *valuation* conventions that allocate an aggregate basis among separate properties so that taxpayers must report some proportion of their gain or loss. For example, the installment sale rules of Code Section 453 require taxpayers who sell property for a stream of payments to allocate their basis among the payments in order to calculate gain or loss on a current basis. Code Section 72 imposes a similar basis allocation rule for annuities. And the regulations under Code Section 1012 provide rules for determining the basis of securities acquired at different times and for different prices.[9]

¶505 BASIS RULES FOR GIFTS AND BEQUESTS

The basis rules for gifts and bequests (found in Code Sections 1014 and 1015) may seem dry at first. But, in fact, they contain one of the most stupendous giveaways of tax dollars in the Code. The rules authorize taxpayers to shift income and defer tax, and it's all perfectly legal. In fact, wealthy decedents and their heirs can go further: the Code grants them tax forgiveness. Tax nirvana!

If you read Chapter 3, you should be feeling a strong sense of disorientation right about now. In that chapter, we saw that the whole purpose of the tax rules on gifts is to prevent *income shifting*! Recall that Code Section 102 deliberately taxes the donor rather than the donee, because the drafters of the Code suspected—quite correctly!—that gifts typically are made by high-bracket parents

---

7 9 T.C. 736.

8 283 U.S. 404 (1931).

9 Regulations Section 1.1012-1.

to lower-bracket children. Section 102 protects the fisc by preventing parents and kids from shifting income to lower brackets.

It is especially ironic, then, that the basis rules on gifts undo much of the effect of Section 102. The two basic rules (found in Code Sections 1001 and 1015) are that donors realize no gain on the transfer of property by gift and that the donor's basis transfers over ("carries over") to the donee. The easiest way to understand the rules is by example:

EXAMPLE 1. Suppose that Adam owns 100 acres of undeveloped land. He bought the land years ago for $100,000 and hasn't done anything with it. Over time, the land has appreciated in value to $150,000. Adam's son, Brent, has decided to become an organic farmer, and his dad has agreed to give him the land to farm.

When Adam transfers the land to Brent, we know that Brent can exclude the value of the gift from his income, thanks to Section 102. The basis rules of Section 1015 provide that Brent takes a carryover basis of $100,000 in the land. And implicit in Section 1001 is that a gift is not a *realization* event: a gift is not a sale or exchange from Adam's perspective, and so, Adam also has no income upon the transfer.

At first glance, these rules seem fairly intuitive. Most people don't think of a gift as a transaction that triggers an income tax. From an administrative perspective, it would be difficult to detect every birthday present and holiday gift anyway. Not to mention the considerable *valuation* problems in valuing illiquid gifts like the farmland in the Adam-Brent example. So it may seem just fine to treat Brent, in effect, as if he's stepped into Adam's shoes. After all, if Brent sells the land any time soon, he will recognize the built-in gain of $50,000.

But if you take a closer look, you'll recognize that the basis rules permit Adam and Brent to shift a considerable amount of income (here, $50,000) from high-bracket dad to low-bracket son. This kind of *income shifting* permits taxpayers to reduce their taxes at will (and it is precisely the tax gambit that Section 102 aims to prevent).

The result, then, is a deep discontinuity in the law. If Adam gives Brent $150,000 in cash, the entire amount is taxed at Adam's rate (because gifts are not deductible—see Chapter 3). But if Adam can, instead, give Brent property with a low basis (relative to fair market value), then the pair can readily shift income and have it taxed at Brent's rate.

The carryover basis rules also permit Adam and Brent to defer tax until the property leaves the family, and maybe forever. As long as Brent doesn't have to sell, he can avoid paying tax on the gain. Of course, any taxpayer can defer gain by not selling, but the carryover basis rules permit transfers without taxation. Another nice gift, so to speak, from Congress to property owners!

The rules on inherited property are even more favorable. Heirs take property with a basis equal to fair market value. Returning to the Adam-Brent example, suppose that Adam dies and leave the land to Brent in his will. Consulting Code Section 1014, Brent learns that he will take a "stepped-up basis" in the land equal to $150,000. The result is that no one will ever pay tax on the $50,000 of gain that accrued while Adam owned the property. Basically, it's 100% tax forgiveness, which is even better than *income shifting* and *tax deferral*!

Once again, though, only the propertied class can take advantage of the give-away. If Adam leaves Brent $150,000 in cash, there is no gain to be eliminated by a step-up. The whole amount will have been taxed to Adam at Adam's rate.

If Congress means to teach a lesson with all this, it's clear enough: buy property, and don't hold cash!

You might think that this conclusion is too hasty. After all, the basis rules do impose a tax disadvantage on people who make gifts (or bequests) of *depreciated* property. For example, suppose that Adam bought a second parcel of land, years ago, for $25,000. The land is now worth only $10,000. If Adam gives this land to Brent, Section 1015 will reduce Brent's basis to $10,000.[10] The result is that Adam's loss is erased completely! Section 1014 has the same effect: Brent acquires a fair-market-value basis, which is the stepped-*down* basis of $10,000 in this case.

At first glance, the tax disadvantage in giving depreciated property seems quite large. Donors (and decedents) who give away loss property are saying goodbye to a valuable tax loss, one that their donees (and heirs) cannot claim.

But savvy taxpayers can easily avoid this apparent tax disadvantage by simply selling the property! A well-advised Adam will never give Brent the depreciated land. Instead, he will sell the land, claim the $15,000 tax loss, and give Brent the $10,000 instead. Adam is better off (because he can use the tax loss on his tax return to offset other income), and Brent is no worse off (he can use his $10,000 to buy other land).

¶506 REAL-WORLD TRANSACTIONS: ESTATE PLANNING AND THE INCOME TAX

Tax considerations play a major role in estate planning, which is the task of determining how (and when) to pass on wealth to the next generation. Tax planners must navigate two separate tax regimes: the estate and gift tax and the income tax.

The estate and gift tax is separate from (and imposed in addition to) the income tax. The tax applies to the total amount of wealth transferred by any individual by gift or at death. But because the federal tax applies only to lifetime transfers totaling more than $5.43 million (in 2015), only the very wealthy need pay attention to it.[11] You'd need a whole course in estate and gift taxation

---

[10] To be precise, Code Section 1015 reduces Brent's basis to $10,000 only if Brent ultimately sells at a loss. *See* Code Section 1015(a). If the land eventually rises in value beyond $25,000, Brent will be able to claim the higher carryover basis.

[11] The relevant Code provisions are at Section 2001 *et seq*. The exemption amount is adjusted annually for inflation. *See* Rev. Proc. 2014-61, 2014-47 IRB 860, available at www.irs.gov/irb/2014-47_IRB/.

to understand the ins and outs of estate planning. Still, the basic direction is clear enough: because the estate and gift tax is imposed on the value of assets transferred, tax planners aim—within the boundaries of the law—to minimize the value of assets for tax purposes. But implementing those tax plans can involve complex trusts, charitable gifts and complicated business restructuring.

By contrast, income tax considerations can—and often do—drive estate tax planning even for the middle class, and tax strategies are fairly straightforward. Three rules of thumb shape most income tax planning in this area:

First, taxpayers should hold onto appreciated assets until death to ensure that heirs can take advantage of the Code Section 1014 step-up in basis. Section 1014 is pretty much the best tax deal around: it forgives 100% of the gain accrued during the decedent's lifetime. Heirs walk away with a basis equal to fair market value, so that they can sell immediately (if they choose) and pay zero income tax. In effect, the government has added tax forgiveness to the bequest.

Second, if a taxpayer needs or wants to make a lifetime gift, she should usually avoid giving cash and should instead give appreciated assets (on the plausible assumption that the donee is in a lower marginal tax bracket). The gift of appreciated property doesn't trigger any immediate income tax to the donor or donee. And Section 1015, recall, grants a carryover basis to the donee, so that any eventual gain realized when the property is sold will be taxed at the donee's (presumptively lower) rate.

Third, a taxpayer should avoid giving or bequeathing depreciated assets. Instead, he should sell them and give or bequeath the cash. Depreciated assets (which have a basis in excess of fair market value) incorporate a potential tax loss, but that loss is only worth something in the hands of the donor. Section 1014 (and, in most cases, Section 1015) prevent the transfer of the loss to the heir (or donee). Transferring depreciated property basically means destroying a tax goodie. And a tax goodie is a terrible thing to waste! So a taxpayer is far better off if she sells the property, claims the tax loss herself, and gives away the cash.

EXAMPLE 2. Marian bought General Electric stock for $10,000 years ago. It is now worth $8,000. If Marian dies and leaves the stock to her son, he will take a fair market value basis of $8,000. The tax loss will disappear. Instead, Marian should sell the stock, claim the $2,000 tax loss on her return now, and leave the $8,000 cash to her son.

While these three rules serve most taxpayers fairly well, two caveats are important. The first caveat is that taxpayers should deviate from these rules of thumb if tax savings are outweighed by other considerations. For example, suppose that Peter, at age 75, holds undeveloped land that has appreciated over time. A developer has offered Peter an excellent price for the land, and Peter believes that he can make far greater profits if he sells the land and reinvests the money in the stock market. In this case, a tax planner should make sure Peter understands the tax costs of giving up the Section 1014 step-up. But if Peter thinks that the potential economic gains outweigh the tax detriment, he should go ahead and sell.

A second caveat won't make sense until you know more about capital gains (the subject of Chapter 13), but I include it here for completeness. Some investment gains are subject to a special, low tax rate, and some investment losses are limited. These rules do not change the basic direction of death-time income tax planning. But they complicate the picture by reducing the tax cost of selling (some) appreciated assets and by reducing the tax benefit of selling (some) depreciated assets.

¶507 BASIS AND PRE-NUPTIAL AGREEMENTS: *FARID-ES-SULTANEH V. COMMISSIONER*

In a fascinating older case that is still good law today, the tax law forced the federal courts to decide whether financial motives or love explain transfers of property in pre-nuptial agreements.[12] This was an awkward position for the judges, who are not selected for their expertise on matters of the heart. But the tax rules on basis required the courts to opt one way or the other, and, in the end, the Second Circuit found that pre-nups reflect an exchange and not a gift.

Doris Mercer, the daughter of a Pittsburgh police captain, was destined to be a princess. But along the way, she married Sebastian S. Kresge, the founder of K-Mart, when he was 57 and she was 32.[13] The only hitch in their romance was that Kresge was, er, already married. Apparently worried that the glamorous Doris might get tired of waiting for him, Sebastian transferred to her some valuable stock in the family corporation "for her benefit and protection in the event that the said Kresge should die prior to the contemplated marriage."

Sebastian's divorce went through, and he and Doris proceeded to marry in 1924. But before the wedding, the two signed a pre-nup terming the stock a "gift" and "an ante-nuptial settlement" for Doris in exchange for her release of her legal rights to Kresge's property.

The two divorced in 1928, in part because Sebastian's penny-pinching ways annoyed Doris. (He owned real estate worth $400 million but wore his clothes and shoes till they fell apart and quit golf because it cost too much to replace lost golf balls.) Doris took her Kresge stock and went her own way. Later, she married a Persian prince and took the name Doris Farid-Es-Sultaneh.

Doris sold some of her Kresge stock in 1938, and when the IRS called her to account for her gain on the transaction, the main issue was the determination of her basis. The IRS claimed that Sebastian had transferred the stock to Doris as a gift and, accordingly, Doris had a low carryover basis (under Section 1015). Doris (or her lawyers, anyway) took a very different view of the facts: they

---

[12] Farid-Es-Sultaneh v. Commissioner, 160 F.2d 812 (2d Cir. 1947).

[13] Details of Mercer's life can be found at http://glenalpin.org/the-princess-period.html.

characterized the pre-nup as an exchange. Doris had given up her legal rights to Kresge's property in exchange for stock and so, they said, she should claim a higher fair market value—or cost—basis in the stock (under Section 1012).

The financial stakes for Doris Farid-Es-Sultaneh were high. She sold the stock for $230,000, which established her amount realized. Her gain, of course, would be determined by the gap between basis and amount realized. The higher her basis, the smaller her gain. In court, Doris took the position that her basis was $10 per share, or a total of about $120,000—equal to the fair market value of the stock in 1924. Under the IRS theory, by contrast, her basis in her stock would have been just 15 cents a share, or roughly $1,800—that is, Sebastian's carryover basis.

The tax rules thus backed the Second Circuit into an uncomfortable corner. For tax purposes, the Sebastian-Doris prenup had to be classified as either an exchange or a "detached and disinterested" gift. (Remember the *Duberstein* standard from Chapter 3.) Confronted with this binary, the court ruled that—for tax purposes, anyway—pre-nups should be understood as cold, commercial transactions, value-for-value exchanges that produce for the recipient a cost basis under Section 1012.

Certainly, Doris must have been pleased at the outcome. And many people find her a more sympathetic character than the miserly Sebastian. Still, the holding in *Farid-Es-Sultaneh* should give you pause. Think, for instance, about what the holding implies for Sebastian. If the pre-nup was an exchange for Doris, it must also have been an exchange for Sebastian. And if that's true, then Sebastian should have reported taxable gain equal to the difference between the $120,000 fair market value of the Kresge stock in 1924 and his $1,800 basis.

The prospect of gain for Sebastian may not seem too worrisome. Taxing Sebastian ensured that Uncle Sam had a chance to tax the gain that would justify Doris's basis step-up. And Sebastian certainly had the money to pay the IRS!

But step back and consider the position that *Farid-Es-Sultaneh* creates for the IRS. The holding of the case is that an "exchange" that is invisible to the tax system and involves no cash can trigger taxation of the transferor. This is a potential recipe for tax evasion, because in pre-nups and divorce cases, there is often a long lag between the transfer of property and the sale of the property. In *Farid-Es-Sultaneh*, 14 years had passed. In many divorces, similarly, spouses will divide property that is sold only much later. The time lag can make it difficult—or impossible—for the IRS to impose tax on the initial transfer. By the time the property is sold, the statute of limitations (typically, 3 years in tax, sometimes 7) will often have run out.

Understood this way, the holding in *Farid-Es-Sultaneh* creates a potential "whipsaw." ("Whipsaw" is a favorite term among tax lawyers. It means a situation in which the taxpayer wins and the IRS loses either way—sort of heads-I-win-and-tails-you-lose.) The IRS would typically not be aware of a pre-nup or divorce settlement; these are private matters, typically, and governed by state law, not federal law. But then when one of the spouses sells property much later, she is entitled to a stepped-up basis (as was Doris), and it is too late for the IRS to proceed against the other spouse for the earlier gain! Putting all this together, the parties get a tax-free step-up in basis.

Today, divorces (but not pre-nups) are governed by Code Section 1041, which prevents this kind of whipsaw by adopting the position the court rejected in *Farid-Es-Sultaneh*. Section 1041 provides that the transferee of property in a divorce takes a carryover basis. This rule denies a step-up in basis and ensures that the tax system ultimately captures any gain on the property.

But there's a catch. Section 1041 retires one problem but spawns several more. The carryover basis rule, it turns out, offers new opportunities for clever taxpayers to cut their taxes, while creating nasty traps for unwary (or poorly-advised) divorcing couples. Chapter 12 dishes the dirt on tax planning for divorce.

CHAPTER 6

The Realization Requirement

Introduction . . . . ¶600
Valuation, Realization and Tax Deferral . . . . ¶601
Realization and Windfalls . . . . ¶602
Defining Realization: *Eisner v. Macomber* . . . . ¶603
What is a "Sale or Other Disposition"?
Cottage Savings Association v. Commissioner . . . . ¶604
Real-World Transactions: Year-End Stock Trading . . . . ¶605
Real-World Transactions: Real Estate Swaps . . . . ¶606

¶600 INTRODUCTION

In this chapter, we forge links among three of our six concepts: *realization*, *valuation*, and *tax deferral*. Policy makers concerned about problems of *valuation*, we will see, created the *realization* requirement. But the *realization* doctrine also opens the way for taxpayers to achieve tax reduction through *tax deferral*.

At this stage, you may still be a little shaky on the concepts and their relationships. Understandably so—since we haven't worked much with *realization* or *tax deferral* yet! Generally speaking, *realization* is the rule that requires taxpayers to include gains in income (or deduct losses from income) only when they sell their property. Most people find the realization requirement intuitively appealing.

But by the end of this chapter, and for the rest of this book, you'll see that this shiny surface masks one of the biggest villains in the tax law. The *realization* doctrine feels easy and natural, but it has a hidden dark side: it offers *tax deferral* to the well-off, warps investment patterns, and sets hidden traps for the unwary. Chapter 14 illustrates how many tax shelters incorporate *realization* games, and when those games pay off, the taxpayer wins big.

¶601 VALUATION, REALIZATION AND TAX DEFERRAL

But for now, let's start with the basics. The *realization* requirement governs the timing of gain or loss, but it does not affect the total amount of gain or loss. Imagine that a taxpayer, Tara, buys land for $1,000. Next year, it's worth $3,000, but she chooses to hold on rather than sell. And in 10 years, Tara sells it for $7,000.

Thanks to Chapter 5, we know that Tara's basis in the land is $1,000 (under Code Section 1012, if you must know). Now, in principle, there are two different ways of measuring her gain on the transaction.

Year-by-year or "mark to market." One approach to measuring gain would look at the change in the value of Tara's land each year. By the end of the first year (Year 1), Tara has gained $2,000, in the sense that *if* she sold the land, she'd sell it for $3,000. By the end of 10 years, she has gained an *additional* $4,000, for a total of $6,000 of gain. This economic method is sometimes called "mark-to-market," because the amount of gain is measured by the changes in market price, whether or not the taxpayer sells her property.

Mark-to-market seems odd to many people when they first consider it. After all, Tara only has a paper gain at the end of Year 1. She doesn't have $2,000 in extra cash. And the price of the property might change again. Only when she sells the property, finally, can we fix her total gain on the deal. But this intuition overlooks an important fact: Tara's property is worth $2,000 more than she paid for it, so in an *economic* sense, she has gain. Think about it this way. Suppose Tara goes into a bank at the end of Year 1, seeking a loan. The bank will want to assess her credit and will be interested in the current value of her land ($3,000) as it calculates her net worth. Why? Because the bank will want to know what would happen if Tara sold her assets to pay off the loan, and current value is the best measure.

Realization. A different approach waits until sale to measure gain. The *realization* approach disregards the market gain and postpones reporting the entire $6,000 gain to Year 10, when the property is sold, as Table 6.1 illustrates.

Table 6.1 Realization and the Timing of Gain

Year	Value	Gain (Mark To Market Method)	Gain (Realization Method)
0	$1,000		0
1	$3,000	$2,000	0
10	$7,000	$4,000	$6,000
TOTAL		$6,000	$6,000

The table reveals that the realization requirement does not affect the amount of gain reported. It affects only the timing. But the key point is that timing matters because *tax deferral is valuable to the taxpayer.*

Think about all this from Tara's perspective. She would rather use the realization method, because it lets her put off paying taxes until Year 10. The postponement is valuable to her, because instead of having to pony up cash to pay the IRS as early as Year 1, she can hold onto the money and use it in other ways. With 9 years of *tax deferral,* Tara has plenty of time to invest the tax money that would otherwise be claimed by Uncle Sam. From Tara's point of view, *realization* is way better than mark-to-market, because Tara—and not the IRS—captures the time value of money.

The Haig-Simons definition of income, which we've used as a touchstone, implies mark-to-market accounting. After all, Messrs. Haig and Simons were interested in economic income—the accretion to net worth—not sales and other realization events. But what Haig and Simons didn't include in their calculation was the real-world problem of *valuation*. It's easy enough to assume the value of property in a classroom hypo. But it's far more difficult in the real world to know what property is worth until it is sold. *Realization* responds to the *valuation* problem by not attempting to value property until a market transaction—a sale—establishes the value with certainty. When a willing buyer meets a willing seller, the IRS can be pretty sure that the sale price is a fair measure of value.

Realization has other virtues too. It avoids the huge administrative headache of having taxpayers running around every year getting appraisals of their property. Can you imagine if you had to value, every single year, all the stuff you own, from your car to your bike to your clothing and jewelry? The costs to taxpayers would be high, and we can imagine that opportunistic taxpayers would be tempted to cheat, while honest ones would be nervous. Realization also avoids what economists call the liquidity problem: the fact that taxpayers may not have the cash to pay the tax until they sell the property. In the example in Table 6.1, for instance, a mark-to-market system would saddle Tara with a hefty tax bill in Year 1. But unless Tara has a big cash reserve, she may not have the cash on hand to pay the tax. She would either have to borrow against the property or sell it to pay the tax, and both of these are potentially costly options.

Sales are the prototypical realization event, and they're extremely handy from the IRS's point of view. The taxpayer has parted with the property in a way that fixes its value and puts cash in the taxpayer's hand. But there are other kinds of events that have some of these characteristics. Gifts, for instance, are another way of disposing of property (but aren't *realization* events, as we saw in Chapter 5). Property swaps are another kind of disposition. If Tara swaps farmland for an in-town condo, for instance, she no longer has the farmland but also doesn't have cash.

To see how the law has dealt with the challenges of *realization*, let's begin with the case of the mysterious cash in the piano. Seriously.

¶602 REALIZATION AND WINDFALLS

In *Cesarini v. United States*,[1] a federal district judge sitting in Ohio faced an unusual set of facts. In 1957, Ermenegildo and Mary Cesarini bought a used piano at an auction for $15. Their daughter practiced on the piano, but apparently no one cleaned the piano for, well, seven years. In 1964, they finally gave the old

[1] 296 F. Supp. 3d (N.D. Ohio 1969).

piano a bit of cleaning, and they found $4,500 in old currency stuffed into the piano case. (Updated for inflation, that's about $35,000 in today's dollars. A nice payoff to housework, but I wonder if they were a little uneasy about whose cash it was and whether they'd come knocking some day.)

The Cesarinis proceeded to do a very scrupulous, but—let's be honest—unusual thing: they reported the income to the IRS. Ermenegildo and Mary then brought suit to reclaim the taxes they paid, arguing that the cash in the piano didn't fit the Tax Code's definition of "income."

(Handy bit of obscure tax knowledge: This litigation posture is called a "refund suit," because the taxpayer is, in effect, suing the U.S. Treasury to get back the money they paid. You can always tell whether a tax case is a refund suit, because if it is, the parties will be the taxpayer and the United States. If the other party is the Commissioner of Internal Revenue, then the procedural posture is that the taxpayer has not paid up, and the Commissioner wants his (or her) money.)

The district judge made short work of the lawsuit, and the 6th Circuit affirmed in a quick opinion. The court emphasized, rightly enough, the broad language of Section 61, which requires the taxpayer to include all income "from whatever source derived." And the court found a key piece of law that both parties had apparently overlooked: er, a regulation on point.[2] The regulation provided then (and still provides today) that "treasure trove" is income in the year the taxpayers take "undisputed possession" of it.

The regulation pretty much sank the Cesarinis' case. Cash in a piano isn't exactly like a pirate's chest full of gold doubloons, but it's not a stretch to include it in the "treasure trove" category.

Cesarini is usually cited for the holding that windfalls are income, and that's sound enough. But the case also raises interesting questions about *realization*. The Cesarinis found cash, which is easy to value. But what about items that may be hard to value? The law requires taxpayers to report the value of windfalls as income, but if taxpayers haven't sold the item, its value may be quite unclear.

Turner v. Commissioner[3] provides a good illustration of the *valuation* problem. In 1948, Reginald Turner answered the phone to find that a radio host had picked his number at random. If Reginald could identify the song being played, the host gushed, he'd win a valuable prize! Well, Reginald knew his stuff, and he won two steamship tickets to Buenos Aires. The prize was especially welcome to the Turners, since Reginald's wife, Marie, had been born in South America.

All was peachy until the IRS got wind of the Turners' good fortune. The tax man told Reginald and Marie to pay up. The value of their steamship tickets was taxable income. The Tax Court agreed, although it cut the Turners a break on *valuation*. The IRS tried to tax the couple on the full retail price of the tickets,

---

[2] Regulation Section 1.61-14(a).

[3] 13 T.C.M. 462 (1954).

a whopping $2,220 in 1948 (a heart-stopping $22,000 in today's dollars). The court cut down the includable income to $1,400, noting that the tickets were not transferable or saleable. The Turners, unlike the Cesarinis, didn't have cash to spend as they chose. Still, the Turners may have felt a financial pinch, since their total income for the entire year (excluding the tickets) was just $4,500.

We can understand the tax rules on windfalls as part of the *realization* doctrine. Finding money is clearly a *realization* event, per *Cesarini*. Receiving steamship tickets for participating in a radio quiz is also a taxable event, per *Turner.* Code Section 74 requires taxpayers to include prizes in income; keep that in mind if you're ever on the short list for a Nobel. But we shall soon see that the law is not entirely consistent. Many other forms of economic gain are not treated as *realization* events, and the problem of *valuation* is one major reason why.

¶603 DEFINING REALIZATION: *EISNER V. MACOMBER*

The connection between *valuation* and *realization* is the central theme in the leading case of *Eisner v. Macomber.*[4] The case concerns a stock dividend, which is an odd transaction, but easily understood.

Recall that corporate stock represents an undivided interest in the earnings and assets of a corporation. (We discussed corporate stock in Chapter 5.) Corporations sometimes declare and pay cash dividends on their stock. A dividend is simply a cash payout that represents a share of corporate earnings. So, if you own ten shares of Microsoft, and Microsoft declares a dividend of 50 cents per share, you will receive a check for $5. Cash dividends are taxable as income to the shareholder. So you would have to include the $5 on your income tax return for the year.

The transaction at issue in *Macomber*, though, was a "stock dividend" rather than a cash dividend. Myrtle Macomber, the taxpayer, owned stock in the Standard Oil Corporation, the massive oil enterprise originally founded by John D. Rockefeller. Standard Oil decided not to pay out cash. Instead, it simply issued new shares of stock. So people who already owned Standard Oil stock (like Myrtle) got a few more shares.

The IRS claimed that the fair market value of the stock dividend should be taxable income for Myrtle. And the IRS seemed to be on firm ground here. Congress had passed a special Code Section that said, in so many words, that stock dividends were taxable!

But Myrtle (or, really, her lawyer) was determined to avoid taxation, and so she kicked things up a notch: she claimed that the taxation of stock dividends was unconstitutional, a violation of the Sixteenth Amendment. In other words, she challenged the Code itself by arguing that Congress had exceeded

---

4 252 U.S. 189 (1920).

its constitutional authority. The Sixteenth Amendment was necessary because a prior Court had struck down an income tax under the Direct Tax Clause (which requires apportionment among the states according to population). Long story short, the Sixteen Amendment authorizes Congress to impose an "income tax," and so the question boiled down to whether the taxation of stock dividends was consistent with the whole notion of income taxation.

Justice Holmes had very little patience with what he saw as a tangle of tortured constitutional reasoning. He wrote that "most people not lawyers" would assume that the Sixteenth Amendment had put to rest complicated questions about the Direct Tax Clause. But Holmes was a dissenter in this case, and the majority sided with Myrtle Macomber, holding that, in fact, stock dividends are not income and, therefore, are not permissibly taxed by Congress under the Sixteenth Amendment.

Justice Pitney's opinion emphatically rejects the Haig-Simons, mark-to-market notion of economic income. Income is not, he writes, "a gain *accruing to* capital [or] a *growth* or *increment* of value *in* the investment" (italics in the original). Instead, he writes, income occurs only upon the "realization of profits of the stockholder." And a stock dividend, the majority concludes, is not such a realization. The "essential and controlling fact," Pitney asserts, is that the "stockholder has received nothing out of the company's asset for his separate use and benefit."

Eisner v. Macomber, then, opted firmly for *realization* over mark-to-market. That choice still resonates today because, as we shall shortly see, the realization requirement—as sensible as it may first seem—gives taxpayers enormous power to choose the timing of taxation. It isn't an exaggeration to say that the *realization* requirement costs the Treasury billions of dollars a year and provides the legal foundation for most income tax planning.

Ironically, Myrtle's particular asset—Standard Oil stock—was quite easily valued and very liquid. (Standard Oil was, at that time, one of the country's largest companies.) But the majority was probably thinking ahead to the many assets that are less-readily valued and may be quite illiquid. Even very modest assets, like a home, can be difficult to value, because real estate is unique in location and attributes. Even a cookie-cutter condo is different from its neighbors (higher floor, corner unit, different kitchen layout, and so on). And real estate is highly illiquid: it can take months to sell, and initial valuations can be quite uncertain.

The *realization* requirement remains firmly embedded in the Code, even though *Eisner v. Macomber* has limited precedential value in constitutional law today.[5] Code Section 1001 requires a sale or other disposition for the measurement of gain, and we shall see that many features of the Code are built around the notion of *realization*.

---

[5] *See, e.g.*, Michael Graetz and Deborah Schenk, Federal Income Taxation 151 (7th edition, 2013) (noting that although "the Court has not overruled *Macomber*, it has confined the decision to its facts").

¶604 WHAT IS A "SALE OR OTHER DISPOSITION"? *COTTAGE SAVINGS ASSOCIATION V. COMMISSIONER*

Macomber established that a stock dividend is not a *realization* event, but it left open the question whether other events—short of a sale for cash—might satisfy the *realization* requirement and require taxpayers to report gain or loss. Taxpayers' incentives are clear enough: they will usually want to postpone *realization* in order to postpone the taxation of gains and achieve *tax deferral*.

But the incentive is reversed when a taxpayer has an unrealized loss. Recall that a loss is a "tax goodie" because it reduces the taxpayer's tax bill. A $1,000 loss, for instance, can offset $1,000 of taxable income. For a taxpayer in the 40% bracket, a $1,000 loss saves $400 in tax. The typical taxpayer will want to claim that $400 goodie now rather than later, and the *realization* requirement permits her to do so—by selling now.

So, when a taxpayer has property that has declined in value, she will want to claim that loss as early as possible, because a loss, like any tax goodie, is something that is generally more valuable now than later. In more formal terms, the time value of money rewards a taxpayer who claims a loss sooner. A tax loss reduces income taxes, which leaves more cash in the taxpayer's pocket. In most circumstances, the taxpayer should claim that cash now (not later) so that she can make use of the money.

Taxpayers can usually sell their property to claim a loss, and we will see shortly that tax considerations can indeed drive people to sell their assets. But sometimes, a taxpayer faces non-tax constraints that prevent her from selling. This kind of situation is a recipe for tax frustration: the taxpayer wants the loss (the tax goodie) now, but if she cannot sell, she cannot realize the loss for tax purposes.

Well, where there's a will (or an enormous tax loss), there's a way. In *Cottage Savings Association v. Commissioner*,[6] a savings and loan association ("S&L"), held a large portfolio of home mortgage loans that had declined in value by more than $2 million. Cottage Savings engineered a swap of its loans for the loans held by another S&L and claimed that the swap triggered the *realization* of its $2.5 million loss. The IRS, for its part, was unimpressed. The Commissioner challenged the transaction on the ground that the swap of loans did not constitute a "sale or other disposition of property" within the meaning of Code Section 1001.

To understand the transaction, the key point is that, to an S&L, just as to a bank, a loan is an asset. (It's a liability to the borrower.) Cottage Savings, like a lot of other S&Ls, found that many of its loans had declined in value, due to rising interest rates in the 1970s. The S&Ls had made long-term, low-interest mortgage loans to many borrowers, and the value of these loans declined because market rates rose. (To see why the loans declined in value, think about it this

6 499 U.S. 554 (1991).

way: suppose you could invest $100 and get 5% interest or invest $100 and get 20% interest. You'd clearly pick the 20% investment. So anyone holding $100 loans bearing 5% interest will find that they are worth a lot less than $100 when market interest rates rise to 20%.)

The economic plight of the S&Ls threatened to roil the entire U.S. banking system. If the S&Ls sold their loans on the open market, they would have realized losses so gigantic that many of them would have been deemed insolvent by regulators and would have been forced to close. Regulators faced a puzzle: they wanted to improve the cash position of the S&Ls, but, at the same time, they needed to avoid a "fire sale" of assets that would force the S&Ls to close.

The answer to the puzzle, curiously enough, lay in the Tax Code. As we have seen, tax losses are valuable to taxpayers because they reduce taxable income. Cottage Savings and other S&Ls were sitting on a major tax asset. If they could realize their tax losses, they could claim tax savings that would reduce their tax liability and improve their cash position.[7] Regulators hoped that the extra cash would help the S&Ls weather the crisis, at least for a time.

For the bank regulators, the problem was one of *realization*. The S&Ls needed to trigger *realization* for tax purposes (to claim their tax losses). At the same time, the S&Ls needed to avoid *realization* for regulatory purposes (because recording their losses officially would force the regulators to classify them as insolvent and shut them down). Engineering around this problem, the bank regulators came up with the famous (or infamous, depending on your perspective) Memorandum R-49.

Memorandum R-49 threaded the needle by ruling that S&Ls could swap mortgage loans among themselves without triggering *realization* for regulatory purposes. In effect, the ruling said that the swap would be treated as a nonevent for regulatory accounting. But the swap would, the regulators believed, count as a *realization* event for federal income tax purposes. Tax nirvana, then, was to claim valuable tax losses without accounting for the losses on the S&Ls' own books.

The transaction in *Cottage Savings* involved a swap of mortgage pools between Cottage Savings and another S&L. A mortgage pool is just a collection of mortgages. The pools were carefully constructed so that the economic values would be the same: that is, Cottage Savings (and the other S&L) could be sure that they were receiving an overall pool of loans that would perform just the same as the pool they gave up.

Consistent with the tax planning intended by Memorandum R-49, Cottage Savings reported a loss on the exchange, calculated (pursuant to Code Section

[7] Here's how tax losses translate directly into cash. Tax losses first reduce the current year's taxes. When the taxpayer owes less in taxes, she can keep more of her income. If tax losses exceed the year's income (as in the case of a business that is losing money), the taxpayer can carry back the losses to past years and claim an immediate tax refund of past years' taxes. *See* Code Section 172, which currently permits a two-year carryback of net operating losses.

1001) as the difference between the basis in the loans (roughly $7 million) and the fair market value of the loans (roughly $4.5 million). The IRS, for its part, took a dim view of Memorandum R-49, and it hauled Cottage Savings into court. Viewed in this light, the case was really a battle between two federal agencies: the S&L regulators and the IRS.

The key issue facing the Supreme Court in *Cottage Savings*, then, was the scope of the *realization* requirement. The Court upheld the Treasury regulation that interprets Code Section 1001 as requiring "the exchange of property for other property differing materially either in kind or in extent." But the Court ruled that the swap of mortgage pools met the material difference standard, because the mortgages given up and the mortgages received in the swap embodied "legally distinct entitlements." Because the mortgages represented obligations of different individual borrowers and were secured by different properties, they were materially different from a legal perspective, even though they were economically fungible.

From a tax planning perspective, the decision in *Cottage Savings* is a gift to well-advised taxpayers. Sophisticated investors now have one more tool to use when they want to realize a valuable tax loss: they can swap similar properties, and as long as they meet the formalistic "legally distinct entitlements" criterion, the exchange will be a *realization* event.

But *Cottage Savings* has a hidden sting for unwary taxpayers, who can trigger a *realization* event without meaning to do so. For example, suppose that you buy a bond from Company X for $1,000. (A bond is a debt instrument. When you buy a bond, you lend money to the bond issuer, typically a business or government entity. The bond issuer pays you interest and will repay the principal at maturity.) The bond pays 10% interest and has a 10-year term. Several years later, the bond is worth $1,200. At that point, the management of Company X (the bond issuer) comes to you with a proposal: they have an exciting new business opportunity, and they'd like to extend the maturity of your bond by six years. Company X, in other words, will keep paying you 10% but just for six years more. The deal sounds good to you, so you send back your consent form.

What you may not realize is that the change in maturity date (from the original 10 years to the new 16 years) constitutes a realization event under *Cottage Savings*. Even though the bond holder (you) and the bond issuer (Company X) remain unchanged, the bond itself is different. Sixteen years is longer than ten, and so the two bonds are materially different—"legally distinct," in the Court's terms. The result is that the tax law treats you as if you sold your old bond for the new bond. Your consent to the debt modification, in other words, constitutes a *realization* event, even though you did not literally sell your bond.[8]

---

[8] Regulation Section 1.1001-3 contains rules governing when debt modifications meet the material difference standard.

¶605 REAL-WORLD TRANSACTIONS: YEAR-END STOCK TRADING

The *realization* requirement is a huge gift from Uncle Sam to the taxpayer. The ability to hold or to sell may seem like a very ordinary power, one that every property owner has. But *realization* turns the ability to choose when and whether to sell property into a kind of tax super-power, because it permits the taxpayer to select the optimal timing for gain and loss on each asset she holds. In other words, *realization* fosters *tax deferral* and makes tax planning cheap and easy.

The *realization* rules are especially rewarding for wealthy investors who own a diversified portfolio of investments. Like many tax goodies, *tax deferral* is most valuable to high-income taxpayers, just because they face the highest marginal tax rates. This makes sense if you think about it: someone whose income is so low that they face a 0% federal income tax rate can't save any tax at all from tax planning. By contrast, someone in the 40% bracket may be able to save big bucks.

Now, diversification is a legitimate investment strategy and not (intrinsically) a tax dodge. Financial planners recommend that investors diversify their holdings so that, well, their eggs aren't all in the same basket. To take a simple example: someone who invests their entire wealth in Microsoft stock will find it hard to sleep at night if the new Windows operating system is a lemon or if Apple introduces a new must-have device. But if the investor instead spreads her money out, buying not only Microsoft but also Apple and a bunch of other stocks, she will reduce her risk that any one company will go bust in a big way.

But even though diversification isn't a tax-motivated strategy, it definitely has a tax-planning payoff. The simplest strategy can be captured in a five-word mantra:

Hold gains and sell losses

(This slogan is so useful that you may want to have it embroidered on a throw pillow. Go ahead; I'll wait.)

What the slogan means is that, all else equal, taxpayers should hold off on selling appreciated assets but should sell depreciated assets at the first chance. Holding onto gains gives the taxpayer the benefits of *tax deferral*. And if the taxpayer can hold onto his appreciated assets until death, his heirs will benefit from the Code Section 1014 step-up—which turns tax deferral into tax forgiveness.

On the loss side, a depreciated asset offers a tax goodie—a deductible loss—that most taxpayers would prefer to claim sooner rather than later. As Chapter 5 showed, a well-advised taxpayer should never give away depreciated property or leave it to heirs, since Sections 1015 and 1014 will deny the tax loss to donees and heirs. Far better, instead, to sell the property, take the tax loss, and give away (or leave) appreciated property.

Any taxpayer can adopt this mantra and will benefit. But diversification multiples the opportunities for tax savings, because diversified portfolios tend to produce a welter of gains and losses that can be "cherry-picked" by the clever taxpayer.

EXAMPLE 1. Derek has a portfolio of 50 stocks. Based on today's stock market values, his total gains are $25,000, and his total losses are $20,000. Financially speaking, Derek has made a profit of $5,000. As a matter of tax planning, though, Derek should sell some (or all) of his losing stocks while holding all of his gaining stocks. He will then report a $20,000 loss on his tax return—and zero gains. The tax losses will offset his salary or other income. Tax-wise, Derek will appear to be worse off by $20,000, when, in fact, he's better off by $5,000. And all perfectly legal.

Of course, Derek will eventually owe income tax on the $25,000 in gains. But *tax deferral* is the game here. And if he wants to reduce his taxes still further, he might give the appreciated stocks to a family member who is in a lower tax bracket: recall that Section 1015's carryover basis rules will (in effect) transfer the gain to the donee. Of course, if Derek holds the stock until he dies, Section 1015 will eliminate the gain entirely.

A few caveats are important. Did you catch the waffle words "all else equal" several paragraphs ago? The "all else" here contains two important assumptions that usually hold, but not always. One important assumption is that tax rates aren't about to change. If tax rates are about to go way up, for instance, some taxpayers might find it worthwhile to sell appreciated assets, paying lower rates now rather than higher rates later.

A second critical assumption is that holding investments (or selling them) will not materially change the taxpayer's real economic returns. This assumption will often hold when a taxpayer has a diversified portfolio and a large number of very liquid investments. But taxpayers should always weigh the nontax gain (or loss) in holding or selling an asset against the tax payoff.

EXAMPLE 2. Suppose Elspeth, who is in the 40% tax bracket, holds stock in Company Z with a basis of $10,000. Company Z so far has performed poorly, and Elspeth's stock has depreciated quite a bit, falling in value to $4,000. The tax loss would be $6,000 if she sold the stock (basis of $10,000 minus amount realized of $4,000). That's a very tempting tax goodie, worth $2,400 ($6,000 loss times the 40% marginal tax rate), and the usual advice would be to sell. But suppose Elspeth believes strongly that Company Z is about to announce a breakout innovation, and the stock will surge back to $20,000. In that case, the $2,400 value of the tax loss is swamped by the $14,000 predicted gain on the stock. (Even after paying taxes at 40%, the taxpayer will have $8,400 left.) The best advice in that case would be to hold and wait.

A very clever taxpayer might try to claim her tax loss and keep the stock too. The strategy would be to sell the stock in Company Z and buy it right back, one second later, for $4,000. That plan would seem to offer the best of both worlds: a tax loss on the sale and a continued investment in the stock for a low price. But if this smells too good to be true, it is. The tax law terms the sale-and-immediate-repurchase a "wash sale" and disallows the loss. The idea is that a sale isn't really a sale if the taxpayer continues to hold the asset. Section 1091 of the Code requires a taxpayer who sells a stock at a loss to refrain from buying that stock for 30 days afterward. If the taxpayer repurchases the stock within the 30-day period, the Code disallows the loss. (Chapter 11 revisits wash sales in more detail.)

A third and final caveat concerns the mysterious subject of capital gains. We won't learn the details until Chapter 13, but in a real-world setting it is important to take notice of capital gains and losses. Capital gains, we will see, may be eligible for a special, low tax rate, which lowers the tax cost of selling. Capital losses, though, may not be deductible in full in some cases, reducing their tax value. For most taxpayers, most of the time, our tax-planning mantra (hold gains and sell losses) still holds. But capital gains and losses can affect the balance between tax and non-tax considerations in any given case.

¶606 REAL-WORLD TRANSACTIONS: REAL ESTATE SWAPS

To this point, we've treated *tax deferral* as an unintended consequence of the *realization* requirement, and that's fair enough. But some Code provisions explicitly approve *tax deferral*. Code Section 1031, for example, permits real estate investors to engage in "like-kind exchanges" of property without triggering a *realization* event.

A like-kind exchange is simply a swap of one property for another. The Code requires the taxpayer to carry over her historic basis from the old property to the new. The result is that any gain is deferred until the taxpayer sells the new property (for cash).

> **EXAMPLE 3.** Cameron bought a New York office building for $50 million five years ago. The office building is now worth $60 million, and Cameron is tempted to sell, because he'd like to move to Seattle and reinvest his cash in real estate there. But Cameron's lawyer has a clever plan: swap the New York building for a building in Seattle. If—and it's not too hard—the lawyers follow the rules of Section 1031, Cameron will be able to reinvest without triggering tax on his $10 million gain! (Of course, Cameron's basis in the Seattle building will be just $50 million, but the carryover basis is just the mechanical rule that defers the gain.)

Section 1031 is pretty close to tax heaven. Cameron can reinvest without triggering a *realization* event, and he can defer taxes as long as he keeps swapping rather than selling for cash.

Of course, not all property owners are interested in swapping. In Cameron's case, the owner of the Seattle building may not be willing to participate: perhaps that person has a tax loss and prefers a cash sale. But don't spend any sleepless nights worrying about the Camerons of the world. Section 1031 permits taxpayers to engage in a three-way exchange. The way that works is that Cameron finds a buyer for his New York building. The buyer then goes out and buys (or arranges to buy) the Seattle building. When the dust clears, the Seattle seller has received cash, and Cameron has made a qualifying like-kind exchange. Yeah, that works.

A naïve person (not you!) might suppose that Section 1031 occasionally works in the IRS's favor. After all, if Cameron had a $10 million loss on his building, then the loss would be deferred too. Cameron would, in that case, be holding off on taking advantage of the tax goodie that the loss represents.

But this is a naïve view, because any taxpayer with a built-in loss simply wouldn't engage in a like-kind exchange. Cameron's lawyer advised him to take the Section 1031 route so that he could defer tax on the gain. If Cameron had had a built-in loss, he would certainly have sold for cash—and then bought the Seattle building for cash.

Now, if Section 1031 applied to all assets, it would pretty much do away with the *realization* requirement—and nudge the U.S. economy back to a barter system. But Section 1031 contains two restrictions that limit the scope of the like-kind exchange rules. First, not all property is eligible. Section 1031(b) excludes stocks, bonds, and other assets. So you can't engage in a like-kind exchange of your Apple stock for Microsoft stock.

Second, even eligible property can be exchanged only for other property of "like kind." So a delivery van, say, cannot be exchanged for a commercial refrigerator. Livestock of different sexes, Section 1031(e) helpfully informs us, are not property of like kind. But the regulations give wide leeway for exchanges of real estate, helpfully noting that taxpayers are permitted to swap improved property for unimproved property, and city properties for rural ones.[9] We can only infer that the real estate lobby was more influential than the farm lobby on this one.

9 Regulation Section 1.1031-1(c).

CHAPTER 7

Borrowed Funds

Introduction . . . ¶700
Valuation and the Exclusion of Borrowed Funds . . . ¶701
Cancellation of Indebtedness: *U.S. v. Kirby Lumber Co.* . . . ¶702
Zarin v. Commissioner and Code Section 108(e)(5) . . . ¶703
Commissioner v. Tufts and Nonrecourse Debt . . . ¶704
Real-World Transactions: Tax Planning for Bankruptcy and Insolvency . . . ¶705
Borrowing and the Time Value of Money . . . ¶706

¶700 INTRODUCTION

Borrowing and lending are among the most frequent transactions that people and businesses undertake. Ordinary people borrow to buy a house or to buy a car. Businesses borrow to construct buildings and fund purchases of inventory. On the flip side, individuals act as lenders when they deposit money in a bank account and earn interest. And a whole range of businesses act as lenders, including banks, obviously enough, but also car dealers, credit card companies, and furniture-rental stores.

Most loans are straightforward. The borrower receives cash, say, $1,000 from a bank. The $1,000 is the principal amount of the loan. The loan carries an interest rate, expressed as a percentage of principal per time period (for instance, five percent per year). The borrower makes periodic payments of interest and, in the end, must repay the $1,000 principal amount.

But it turns out that problems of *valuation* surface surprisingly often in borrowing and lending transactions, posing difficulties for both taxpayers and the IRS.

¶701 VALUATION AND THE EXCLUSION OF BORROWED FUNDS

Suppose that Bill borrows $10,000 from the bank. You might initially suppose that he has a corresponding $10,000 in income. After all, he now has $10,000 to spend on anything he likes. You might even feel a little envious if Bill uses the money for something fun, like a dream vacation to Japan or New Zealand.

But in Haig-Simons terms, Bill isn't $10,000 better off, because he has an obligation to repay the $10,000 (with interest) to the bank. All the loan has accomplished is to reshuffle Bill's portfolio of assets and liabilities. He has $10,000 more cash than before, but he also has $10,000 more debt than before. If he does spend the money on a fabulous vacation, he'd better have a plan for how to earn enough to pay back the loan.

In a simple case like this one, *valuation* isn't a problem. Bill borrowed $10,000 and will repay $10,000. There's no uncertainty involved as to the amount of the loan. But take a harder case: suppose that Beth is shopping for a new delivery van for her computer-repair business. She answers a Craigslist ad posted by Laura, who has a 2012 Toyota Scion for sale. Laura wants $20,000 for the Scion, which is a little high compared to Blue Book value. (The Blue Book is a reference tool that lists prices for used cars.) But Laura is willing to let Beth pay over time ($500 a month for 40 months) instead of paying the whole price up front.

When Beth signs on the dotted line, the contract may be titled "purchase agreement," but what's really going on is that Beth has stepped into the position of borrower, while Laura (Ha! You guessed it!) is in the position of the lender. It is as if two transactions—a car purchase and a loan—took place at the same time. In essence, Beth paid $x in cash for the Scion, borrowing $x from Laura. The terms of the loan are that Beth will pay $500 per month for 40 months. In other words, Beth is wearing two hats: as buyer and borrower. Laura, on the other side of the deal, is wearing two hats too: as seller and lender.

The *valuation* problem in the deal is that the tax law can't readily observe the purchase price of $x. You might think, at first glance, that the purchase price is $20,000. After all, that's what the contract says: 40 payments of $500 equals a total of $20,000. But the real purchase price is less than that, because the $20,000 will be paid over more than three years. No bank would lend you money for three years interest-free, and so we assume that Laura wouldn't either. So, in effect, the $500 payments consist of principal plus interest (just as payments on any car loan do).

The task for the tax law is to separate out the purchase price (the principal amount of the loan) and the interest rate. But doing this is tricky, because it's hard to know exactly what Laura's particular van was worth. The Blue Book value might be $17,000 for a van of similar make and model. Still, that value could be considerably off base if Laura has taken especially good (or poor) care of her particular van, or if she added upgrades like leather seats or a really great CD player.

The tax law sometimes takes a second route to *valuation* in cases like these. Instead of trying to value the asset involved (here, the van), the tax law estimates the interest rate that should be paid on the loan. If we knew the interest rate that a car dealer would have charged Beth to buy a used van, then we could calculate the interest on the loan from Laura. And if we can calculate the interest rate, then we can also determine the principal amount.

For example, suppose that market interest rates are about 5% per year. In that case, the transaction is equivalent to a loan of $18,500 (or so). (That number represents the "present value" of a loan with 40 payments of $500, assuming the interest rate is 5%. Paragraph 706 of this chapter goes into more detail on present value.) If, however, market interest rates are higher, say 10%, then the transaction amounts to a loan of just $17,000 (or so). The clear takeaway is that the interest rate matters—a lot.

We can generalize the *valuation* problem illustrated by the car purchase. When a transaction involves seller financing, the parties each play two roles. The seller is also a lender, and the buyer is also a borrower. The result is that the tax law may have difficulty ascertaining the value of the components of the transaction to each party. And the value of the two parts—sale and loan—may have a big impact on the parties' tax liability. The sales price determines the buyer's basis, and the interest rate determines the buyer's interest deduction, if allowable. On the other side of the deal, the sales price determines the amount realized by the seller (and, thereby, her gain or loss). The interest rate determines the seller/lender's interest income.

The tax stakes are high enough that taxpayers may try to misstate values to their advantage. For instance, a buyer/borrower might want to overstate the interest rate in order to take larger interest deductions (albeit at the cost of a lower basis for depreciation). A seller/lender will find that a higher interest rate and lower sales price lower her gain on the sale but increase her interest income.

In some cases, the parties will face competing tax incentives, and they will not, in the end, distort the value of their transaction. But in other cases, depending on the parties' relative tax rates, they might find it profitable to collude in misstating values. (Deliberately misstating values is, you should know, tax fraud, and you should not do it. Ever! But tax policymakers should anticipate the kinds of games taxpayers may be tempted to play.) We will see, in Chapter 14, that wily taxpayers have used seller financing in just this way to enable *valuation* misstatements that reduce the parties' taxes—at the Treasury's expense.

¶702 CANCELLATION OF INDEBTEDNESS: *U.S. V. KIRBY LUMBER CO.*

The plot thickens when we take notice of one more real-world fact: sometimes, people don't repay their loans. In the Great Recession, many people found themselves unable to meet their mortgage payments. And in any economy, some individuals—and businesses—just don't have the cash to pay off their debts when they come due.

A borrower's failure to pay his debt is, in legal jargon, a default. Lenders can respond to a default by pursuing their legal remedies (which might include confiscating other assets, if there are any). Lenders may also respond to a default (or a likely default) by simply cancelling the debt in whole or in part. A borrower who cannot pay 100% of her debt may still be able to pay off, say, 50% of it.

The cancellation of debt is a welcome relief to the borrower, of course. But it turns out that debt cancellation poses a problem for the income tax. Recall that when an individual borrows money, she doesn't include it in her income, because she faces an offsetting liability. A $1,000 loan makes the taxpayer richer by $1,000 in cash but poorer by the obligation to repay $1,000. On net, the transaction is a wash.

But when a debt is cancelled, the obligation to repay no longer offsets the initial cash infusion. If the taxpayer can settle her $1,000 loan by repaying only $800, for instance, the transaction *as a whole* has made her better off by $200. The Tax Code recognizes that gain by including cancellation of indebtedness income under Section 61(a)(12).

The idea that cancellation of indebtedness is income dates back to an old case from the early thirties. In *U.S. v. Kirby Lumber Co.*,[1] a company issued bonds. (Bonds are simply debt instruments: the bond issuer is the borrower, and the bond buyers are the lenders. Bonds are typically issued in relatively small denominations to a large number of buyers.) Kirby Lumber issued the bonds at par value, meaning that each $1,000 bond (say) was purchased for the full $1,000 face value. Later, Kirby Lumber was able to retire the bonds by repurchasing them from the holders for less than par value. Justice Holmes made short work of the problem, endorsing Treasury Regulations providing that the company had income equal to the difference between the borrowed amount (par value) and the repurchase price (a smaller amount).

The logic of cancellation of indebtedness is sound enough. After all, if two people borrow $1,000, and one repays in full, while the other repays only $800, then the second person is better off (by $200). But the *realization* requirement distorts the timing of the gain, sometimes rather badly. Companies in financial trouble typically see their creditworthiness decline over time. The tax law, by contrast, includes cancellation of indebtedness income only when it is realized by a formal debt retirement.

The result is that companies can—and often do—face enormous hits of taxable income at the worst possible time. If you think about it, a company in enough financial hot water to merit a debt cancellation is probably teetering on the edge of bankruptcy. Cash is probably scarce. And yet the IRS, thanks to the *realization* requirement, picks just this occasion to join the line of creditors clamoring for the debtor's assets.

EXAMPLE 1. Jerry had terrible business timing. He borrowed $2 million from a bank to build a state-of-the-art car wash in 2008. Jerry hoped to make big bucks, but the Great Recession had other ideas. For many people, little luxuries like a $20 car wash were the first budget item to be cut when times got hard. Jerry's $2 million debt came due in 2010, and he simply didn't have the cash to pay. Teetering on the brink of bankruptcy, Jerry persuaded the bank to let him off the hook for $500,000. Jerry heaved a sigh of relief—until his accountant told him that he owed taxes on a whopping $1.5 million of taxable income.

---

1 284 U.S. 1 (1931).

The Congress isn't completely clueless about cases like Jerry's. Paragraph 705 of this chapter discusses some Code rules that cut a break for insolvent and bankrupt debtors.

¶703 *ZARIN V. COMMISSIONER* AND CODE SECTION 108(e)(5)

Cancellation of indebtedness income is often easy to measure, as in our example of Jerry's $2 million loan settled for $500,000. But in some cases, the value of the cancelled debt can be disputed, and the tax law has a difficult time adjudicating the competing claims.

One of the best illustrations of the *valuation* problems posed by borrowing comes to us from Atlantic City, New Jersey.[2] David Zarin, a wealthy construction contractor, was also a compulsive gambler and a valued customer of a casino called Resorts International.[3] David lost $2.5 million at the Resorts gaming tables in 1978 and 1979, and he paid those gambling debts in full.

But by 1980, David (according to the court's findings) had begun gambling compulsively, sitting at the gaming tables for up to 16 hours a day. In 1980, he lost another $3.5 million. He told Resorts he intended to pay this debt too, but his check bounced. David's lawyers eventually proved that Resorts had not followed New Jersey regulations applicable to casinos involved in lending money. Faced with a debt that might have been found legally unenforceable, Resorts agreed to settle with Zarin in 1981 for just $500,000.

David Zarin surely felt great about the settlement. Until, that is, the IRS spoiled the party yet again. The IRS contended that David owed taxes on $3 million of cancellation of indebtedness income. Just as in *Kirby Lumber*, the IRS argued, David had borrowed a large amount ($3.5 million) and had managed to settle the debt for a smaller amount (the $500,000 settlement). The difference of $3 million, the IRS concluded, was taxable income. David, of course, took the position that he didn't owe the IRS anything, and the legal battle was joined.

The *valuation* problem in *Zarin* is clear enough once you realize that Resorts' loans to David Zarin involved seller financing. Resorts played a dual role, as both the seller (of gambling services) and the lender (of the money needed to gamble). Resorts certainly recorded the amount of the debt as $3.5 million. But David didn't use the loan to buy anything demonstrably worth that much. Instead, what he got was the ability to sit at the table and bet on rolls of the dice. And it isn't at all clear that the value of that opportunity was anything like $3.5 million.

---

[2] Zarin v. Commissioner, 916 F.2d 110 (3d Cir. 1990), *rev'g*, 92 T.C. 1084 (1989).

[3] *See* Richard Haitch, *Follow-Up on the News; High Rolling*, N.Y. Times, March 21, 1982, available at http://www.nytimes.com/1982/03/21/nyregion/follow-up-on-the-news-high-rolling.html (reporting that Zarin had settled his debt with Resorts and was working to raise awareness of compulsive gambling).

Now, you might object—as the IRS did—that plenty of customers walk into Resorts and pay cash for the privilege of gambling. Those customers surely believe that, say, $100 of tokens for the slot machines are worth their face value of $100. We know that because they plunk down cold, hard cash.

But David Zarin's situation is different, both in scale and in context. Pretty much no one in real life walks into a casino and plunks down $3.5 million in cash. Gamblers at that level are, arguably, playing a very different game. They may anticipate that the house will let them settle for something less in order to keep them coming back. The $100 slot machine gambler has no bargaining power with the casino, but the $3.5 million gambler surely does.

Compounding the *valuation* problem was David's gambling addiction. By the time he was sitting at the tables for 16 hours a day, betting the maximum on each throw of the dice, he probably was unaware of the amount of his debt, and the casino surely knew (or reasonably should have known) that. And yet, the casino kept letting him take on more and more debt.

Given the situation, it is difficult to put a value on the gambling opportunities that Resorts provided to David. On the one hand, he surely didn't feel as if he received $3.5 million in value. On the other hand, he did sign his name to documents attesting to that amount.

What is striking about *Zarin* is what a hard case it proved for the legal system. The *valuation* problem is clear enough in concept, but what proved much harder was finding a legal theory that would excuse David Zarin from owing tax on cancellation of indebtedness income. The Tax Court majority opinion, written by Judge Mary Ann Cohen, examined—and rejected—numerous legal arguments offered on Zarin's behalf. Several dissents offered additional theories.

One of the more promising legal theories offered by Zarin's counsel involved Code Section 108(e)(5), which is intended to resolve valuation uncertainties in cases of seller financing. Very generally, Section 108(e)(5) provides that in cases of seller financing, if the seller and buyer later agree to reduce the amount of the debt, the transaction will be treated as a purchase price reduction. That is, the parties will both be treated as if they simply reduced the agreed-upon price of the purchased item.

EXAMPLE 2. Suppose that John sold an apartment building to Karen in exchange for Karen's $2 million promissory note (which bore interest at a market rate). Within a year, Karen discovered that the property was contaminated with asbestos. Karen's tenants protested, and she incurred $600,000 in asbestos-abatement costs. In the contract of sale, John warranted the building to be free of asbestos. John now agrees to reduce the amount of Karen's debt by $600,000 to avoid a lawsuit. It may appear that Karen has $600,000 of cancellation of indebtedness income when John reduces her debt from $2 million to $1.4 million. But under Section 108(e)(5), the debt reduction is treated as a purchase price adjustment. John and Karen will be treated, for tax purposes, as if the initial sales price had been $1.4 million all along.

But Section 108(e)(5), by its terms, applies only to purchases and sales of "property." The difficulty for the judges in *Zarin* was that gambling chips didn't seem to be property in any standard sense. They represented, instead, something like a ticket to gamble.

Ultimately, the Third Circuit relied on a different set of theories to reverse the Tax Court and award Zarin what must have been a very welcome legal victory. The Third Circuit took note of the irregularities in Resorts' lending procedures and concluded that there was no debt for which the taxpayer was liable under New Jersey law. WIthout debt, there could be no cancellation of indebtedness income, the court reasoned. Instead, the Third Circuit concluded, the *Zarin* transaction involved a disputed liability, the settlement of which does not create income.

There is just one problem with the Third Circuit's theory, but it's a big one: the disputed debt theory simply doesn't apply to the facts of *Zarin*. The idea of a contested debt comes into play when there is genuine uncertainty about the amount of money that someone has borrowed. For instance, suppose you're in line at the deli, and your friend Jayne says, "Hey, I forgot my purse. Can you lend me enough to pay for my sandwich, and I'll pay you back?" You hand over a $20 bill. Later, when you ask Jayne to repay you, she hands you just $10, insisting that you gave her only a ten. That's a disputed debt, and if in the end you both agree to accept $15 as repayment in full, then there is no cancellation of indebtedness income. The theory is that, in the absence of good evidence establishing the amount of the initial loan, the final bargain establishes the amount of the liability.

By contrast, in *Zarin*, the record showed clearly, and David Zarin didn't dispute, that he had borrowed $3.5 million from Resorts and had received the full amount in gambling chips. There was no contest as to the amount of the liability that David owed to Resorts. The dispute went to the enforceability of the debt. And, as the Tax Court pointed out, the illegality or unenforceability of a debt has never provided the taxpayer with a way to sidestep *Kirby Lumber*. Even illegal debts, when cancelled, produce income under Code Section 61(a)(12). Take that, loan shark clients!

Now, *Zarin* may seem like a way-out case. But the problem of *valuation* posed by seller financing poses a serious problem for the tax law. Indeed, the *valuation* uncertainty inherent in seller financing paved the way for a decade (or more) of tax shelters, which Chapter 14 discusses. Those tax shelters combined seller financing with nonrecourse debt, so that buyers could document inflated prices for low-value property—and claim inflated, but highly-valuable depreciation deductions.

¶704 *COMMISSIONER V. TUFTS* AND NONRECOURSE DEBT

Valuation uncertainty can also afflict borrowing transactions at a later stage—when the value of the property and the amount of the debt diverge. The Supreme

Court faced just this kind of problem in *Commissioner v. Tufts*,[4] which is illustrated (in simplified form) in the following example.

Suppose that Tim buys an apartment building for $3 million. Tim finances the entire purchase with a $3 million bank loan. The bank loan, like many commonly used in real estate, is nonrecourse. Nonrecourse debt means that the bank has a security interest in the building but, in the event Tim fails to pay, the bank's sole remedy is to foreclose on and take possession of the building. The bank cannot, consistent with the terms of the nonrecourse loan, attempt to seize any of Tim's other assets to pay off the unpaid debt. (Nice deal! But you would expect the banks to charge a higher interest rate to offset their potential losses on deadbeat nonrecourse loans.)

After a few years, Tim has taken depreciation deductions of $500,000, so his adjusted basis (under Code Section 1016) is $2.5 million. But in the meantime, the real estate market has turned sour, and the apartment building is worth only $2.4 million. Tim hasn't paid any principal on the debt, which remains at $3 million. In circumstances like these, Tim will be tempted simply to walk away from the deal. Because the debt is nonrecourse, the bank will foreclose on the building, and the debt will be extinguished in full. Tim can simply move onto the next deal.

In business parlance, Tim's debt here is "underwater," because the face amount of the debt ($3 million) exceeds the value of the property securing it ($2.4 million). Underwater nonrecourse debt poses a *valuation* puzzle for the tax law, because the parties have agreed that the borrower can satisfy his debt with property worth less than the original amount he received in borrowed funds.

The terms of the nonrecourse debt contract make it difficult to calculate Tim's gain on the transfer of the property to the bank. We know that Tim's basis is equal to $2.5 million (that is, the original $3 million purchase price less $500,000 in depreciation deductions). We also know that a foreclosure is a "disposition" within the meaning of Code Section 1001. But what is his amount realized?

Think about the *valuation* puzzle this way. The tax law normally presumes that parties operating at arm's length engage in value-for-value exchanges. For instance, if two companies exchange parcels of real estate, we assume that the fair market value (and, thus, the amount realized by each party) is the same. Why? Because there is no reason that unrelated parties would give up more (or less) than they received.

But in Tim's case, there are two different values in the transaction: the value of the building and the value of the remaining debt. So there are two ways to think about Tim's amount realized. One possibility is that he realizes $2.4 million—the fair market value of the building—when he transfers the building to the bank in foreclosure. After all, that value is what the bank is receiving. The other possibility is that he realizes the face amount of the $3 million debt, which is the amount that the bank will treat as settled by the transfer.

---

[4] 461 U.S. 300 (1983).

The results of the two calculations differ dramatically. On the first view, Tim has lost $100,000. On the second view, he has gained $500,000!

(1)	Loss	=	Basis - Amount Realized
	$100,000	=	$2.5m - $2.4m
(2)	Gain	=	Amount Realized - Basis
	$500,000	=	$3m - $2.5m

Tim would obviously prefer calculation (1), and indeed, the taxpayers in the *Tufts* case reported a loss, relying on a similar calculation. But which value is correct? Put another way, should the tax system view Tim as having made a profit or lost money on the deal?

The most elegant—and conceptually sound—way to solve the *valuation* problem is to recognize that Tim and the bank have engaged in two simultaneous but distinct transactions: a loan and a sale of property.[5] On the loan side, Tim has made money, because the bank must (according to the terms of the nonrecourse debt) accept property worth only $2.4 million in payment of a $3 million debt. Thus, on the debt side, Tim has gained $600,000 in cancellation of indebtedness income.

On the property side, though, Tim has fared badly. He bought property for $3 million and depreciated it to $2.5 million but now faces a market price of only $2.4 million. He has lost $100,000 on that portion of the transaction.

Putting the two transactions together, Tim has gained $500,000 on net. (Looking ahead to Chapter 13, you should keep in mind that the gain and loss may have different character. The cancellation of indebtedness income is ordinary income, while the loss may be a capital loss, depending on the use of the property in a specific case.)

The tax law, unfortunately, adopts a less elegant approach. The bifurcated treatment (discussed above) applies only to foreclosures of property encumbered with recourse debt.[6] Instead, the tax law (following the decision in *Tufts*) adopts calculation (2) above for all other cases, including sales of property (whether debt is recourse or nonrecourse), *and* foreclosures involving property encumbered by nonrecourse debt.

The tax rule, then, is that Tim realizes the amount of his outstanding debt. If the debt exceeds his basis, the result is a taxable gain. The net result of this calculation (gain of $500,000) is correct. But the unitary calculation adopted by the *Tufts* court ignores the substance of what is happening. The result is that taxpayers can often convert what should be ordinary income from cancellation of indebtedness into tax-favored capital gains. (Capital gains are discussed in Chapter 13, *infra*.)

---

5 The bifurcation analysis in the text reflects the approach considered (but ultimately rejected) in Justice O'Connor's concurrence in *Tufts*.

6 *See* Regulation Section 1.1001-2(c), examples 7 and 8.

The takeaway is that *Tufts* appears on the surface to be a tough, pro-IRS decision, saddling the taxpayer with a large (capital) gain. Still, compared to the conceptually right result (an even larger hit of ordinary income), the *Tufts* Court let the taxpayer off easy. Investors in real estate are among the continuing beneficiaries of the Supreme Court's tax gift.

¶705 REAL-WORLD TRANSACTIONS: TAX PLANNING FOR BANKRUPTCY AND INSOLVENCY

Cancellation of indebtedness poses a policy problem for the income tax. Debt cancellation gives rise to taxable income under Code Section 61(a)(12), but it doesn't generate any cash that the taxpayer can use to pay the tax. Adding insult to injury, debt cancellation is most common when taxpayers are already in financial trouble. It isn't hard to see why lenders are more likely to grant debt relief to a borrower with shaky finances than to one who has plenty of money.

To mitigate the harshness of the cancellation of indebtedness doctrine, Code Sections 108(a) and (b) provide relief to taxpayers in financial trouble. Section 108(a) provides that, in certain cases, taxpayers need not report cancellation of indebtedness income at all. Among those who can claim this relief are the insolvent—those whose liabilities exceed the fair market value of their assets.[7] Debt relief ordered by a court in a Chapter 11 bankruptcy case also qualifies for the Section 108(a) exclusion.[8]

But the exclusion carries a price tag. Section 108(b) provides that taxpayers who exclude cancellation of indebtedness income must, in exchange, reduce certain tax attributes by an equivalent amount. The logic is that, in return for tax forgiveness now, the taxpayer must surrender some tax goodies that would otherwise shelter her income later on.

EXAMPLE 3. Bigco issued $4 million in bonds five years ago. Today, Bigco has filed for bankruptcy under Chapter 11, and the court has ordered Bigco's bondholders to accept 10 cents on the dollar in full payment of the bonds. Accordingly, Bigco retires its bonds for $400,000.

Under Section 108(a), Bigco excludes the $3.6 million in cancellation of indebtedness income that the transaction would otherwise generate. But, under Section 108(b)(2)(E), Bigco must surrender $3.6 million in tax goodies. Accordingly, suppose that Bigco reduces its basis in its factory from $10 million to $6.4 million. When Bigco later sells its factory for (say) $10 million, it will incur a larger gain—larger by exactly the $3.6 million of excluded cancellation of indebtedness income!

---

7 Code Section 108(d)(3).

8 Code Section 108(d)(2).

In effect, then, Section 108 offers temporary relief to the hard-pressed taxpayer. The IRS backs away, letting the taxpayer conserve its cash for other purposes and—hopefully—get back on a financially sound footing. But when the business turns around, the taxpayer will owe higher taxes, since the IRS has reclaimed some tax goodies, like basis, that would otherwise shield the taxpayer.

For obvious reasons, tax lawyers pay special attention to Section 108 when they represent a client in financial trouble. Section 108 looms especially large in recessions, when many clients may be insolvent on a fair market value basis. The key to planning in these circumstances is to ensure that debt cancellation, whenever possible, falls within the Section 108(a) exclusion—and that clients can defer paying the Section 108(b) price for as long as possible.

¶706 BORROWING AND THE TIME VALUE OF MONEY

The tax treatment of loans, as we have seen, rests on the idea that borrowing doesn't make taxpayers better off. The borrower has more cash (or a new car or business asset), but he also has an equal and offsetting liability to repay the loan. But some readers may be skeptical. Why *isn't* a borrower better off (in Haig-Simons terms) due to the time value of money? After all, she receives cash now and repays her loan later!

If this question isn't bothering you, go ahead and skip this section. But just in case you have some nagging doubts, here's the explanation.

The basic answer is that when a loan carries a market rate of interest, the present value of the payments to be made by the borrower will equal the principal amount borrowed. Thus, a borrower does not gain, even though she borrows $100 now and repays $100 later—say, in 10 years.

To see the point intuitively, think about it this way. It must be the case that borrowers aren't better off (in time-value-of-money terms) by borrowing. If they were, lenders would be doing something wrong! In a competitive market, lenders should not lose money on every loan (which would be true if borrowers systematically repaid less than they borrowed).

The following examples illustrate that lenders (and borrowers) have Haig-Simons income (or deductions) when interest accrues but do not have Haig-Simons income (or deductions) upon the issuance of a loan or the repayment of borrowed funds. Throughout the examples, assume that all taxpayers face a 40% marginal tax rate.

Begin with Borrower. She borrows $100 from Lender for 10 years at 10% interest, payable annually. At the moment she receives the loan, Borrower has an obligation with a present value (and basis) of $100. (That is, the interest payments plus the principal payment in year 10 have a present value of $100.) Thus, the loan itself generates no gain nor loss.

At the end of the first year of the loan, Borrower pays $10 of interest. At that moment, she has a liability that costs her $110: (a) a $10 cash interest payment and (b) a contract with payments with a present value of $100 (once again, the *remaining nine* interest payments plus the year-10 principal payment have a PV of $100). Hence, she should be able to deduct $10 of interest.

The same will be true of each interest payment. So the right result (given my assumptions) is that the borrower deducts $10 at the end of each year.

The treatment of the lender is parallel to the treatment of the borrower. The PV of the lender's asset grows from $100 to $110 when each annual interest payment is made and thereafter falls back to $100. The lender must thus include the $10 increment in income. When the borrower repays $100 to extinguish the obligation in year 10, there is thus no gain or loss to the lender.

To be sure, this analysis ignores possible changes in market interest rates, which can affect the fair market value of a loan. But on an ex ante basis—at the time the loan is made—the analysis should hold.

Just in case you're wondering: the value of the interest deduction to the borrower (like the interest inclusion to the lender) does not fundamentally change the analysis. The key is that the introduction of an income tax reduces the appropriate discount rate to the after-tax rate. So the borrower now has an after-tax obligation of $6 per year, which is properly valued at her 6% after-tax discount rate (10% pretax becomes 6% after-tax at a 40% MTR). Thus, the examples above still hold: the borrower deducts $10 of interest per period and, at the end of the period, owes a liability with a present value of $100.

CHAPTER 8

Business Deductions in General

Introduction . . . ¶800
Net Income, Deductions, and Exclusions . . . ¶801
Welch v. Helvering . . . ¶802
Exacto Spring Corporation v. Commissioner . . . ¶803
Real-World Transactions: Disguised Dividends and Disguised Gifts . . . ¶804

¶800 INTRODUCTION

We have seen that the income tax strives mightily, and with some success, to tax *net income*. The alternative is to tax gross income, a system that many people would consider unfair and inefficient.

To see why, consider a real-world example. The film "Avatar" is, by some estimates, the highest-grossing movie of all time, bringing in more than $2.5 billion (yes, *billion*) worldwide for the movie studio Twentieth Century Fox.[1] But "Avatar" cost about $500 million to make.[2] On these numbers, the Fox movie studio will care very much whether the federal government taxes its gross income ($2.5 billion) or its net income ($2 billion, after subtracting the cost of making the movie). At a 35% corporate tax rate, Fox would pay $175 million more in taxes to the feds on "Avatar" alone if it were not permitted to deduct the cost of making the film.

A gross income tax would overtax businesses that incur substantial costs. The result would be what many policy makers would consider an unfair and inefficient tax penalty. For instance, grocery stores operate at a low profit margin, meaning that their costs are high relative to their receipts. In one recent year, the grocery chain Safeway earned gross income of $2.1 billion. Nice! Until you see that the operating expenses for the business were more than $1.9 billion, leaving a profit of less than $200 million.[3] Safeway would be badly overtaxed if it were unable to deduct its costs of doing business.

---

1 The website Box Office Mojo collects statistics on the all-time box office records. *See* http://boxofficemojo.com/alltime/.

2 Michael Cipely, *A Movie's Budget Pops from the Screen*, N.Y. Times, Nov. 8, 2009, available at http://www.nytimes.com/2009/11/09/business/media/09avatar.html?_r=2&src=twr&pagewanted=all&.

3 Safeway Inc. (SWY) data available at http://finance.yahoo.com/q/is?s=swy.

So any income tax must take seriously the task of measuring *net income*. But the task is tricky, because *valuation* problems can make it difficult to determine the costs of doing business. The remainder of this chapter will introduce the kinds of *valuation* issues that can complicate net income determinations. The next two chapters take a closer look at *valuation* as it affects mixed business-personal expenditures and the timing of net income measurement.

¶801 NET INCOME, DEDUCTIONS, AND EXCLUSIONS

The concept of *net income* underlies many rules in the tax law. In Chapter 5, we saw that the goal of taxing net income explains the rules on basis, gain, and loss. Basis measures the taxpayer's investment in an asset, and gain and loss measure her profit after subtracting (netting out) her investment.

We can generalize now to say that the ideal of taxing *net income* requires that the tax system subtract ("net out") the costs of earning income. We call these subtractions from income "deductions." And deductions, it follows, are the key to transforming gross income into *net income*.

The concept of *net income* is closely linked to the Haig-Simons ideal. If we seek to tax people on their accretion to economic power, we should tax them on the net amount they have left to consume or to save after paying their business expenses. In the Safeway grocery example above, for instance, we saw that we must subtract Safeway's operating costs from its gross income in order to arrive at net income. The result, we saw, is that Safeway's net income is less than $200 million, despite total revenues (or gross income) of $2.1 billion. Put another way, how much will Safeway's shareholders be able to spend as they choose? They can only spend the *net income* ($200 million) and not the entire gross income of $2.1 billion.

The general principle, then, is that the tax law should permit taxpayers to deduct the costs of earning income. We will see important exceptions and will encounter line-drawing problems. Still, a useful starting point is Code Section 162(a), which provides an expansive general rule: "There shall be allowed as a deduction all the ordinary and necessary expenses paid or incurred during the taxable year in carrying on any trade or business."

Deductions may feel familiar, and there's a good reason. In concept, a deduction is no different from an exclusion. Both reduce income subject to taxation, as the following example illustrates.

> **EXAMPLE 1.** Samantha and Raphael work as law-firm associates in different firms. Samantha's firm pays her a salary of $95,000 and also pays for her business travel, which costs about $5,000 per year. Raphael's firm pays him $100,000, but he must pay for his own business travel (which also runs about $5,000 per year).

If you think about it for a moment, you'll see that Samantha and Rafael are in the same position financially: each one has a net salary (after paying business expenses of $95,000). In Haig-Simons terms, each has $95,000 in economic power: that is the sum they can spend on consumption or savings.

The tax law, though, treats some business costs as exclusions and others as deductions. Generally speaking, when an employer provides valuable items that are business-related, the employee excludes their value. These are the fringe benefits we studied in Chapter 2. Think of meals and lodging for the convenience of the employer. By contrast, when a business owner pays the costs of running his business, that's a deduction. Employees also can deduct business expenses, although with some limitations.[4]

Returning to our example, Rafael reports $100,000 in gross income and deducts his business travel costs under Code Section 162(a) to arrive at *net income* of $95,000. Samantha excludes the $5,000 her employer pays for her business expenses under Section 132(d) and reports—no surprise—*net income* of $95,000.[5]

¶802 *WELCH V. HELVERING*

It's all well and good to posit that the costs of earning income should be deducted. But, in the real world, expenditures often have both business value and personal value. In those cases, the tax law has trouble teasing apart the deductible business expense from the nondeductible personal expenses. The result is that the tax law may mismeasure *net income* and either over- or undertax the taxpayer.

The famous case of *Welch v. Helvering*[6] illustrates the issue. Thomas Welch was co-owner of a grain brokerage firm that went bankrupt in 1922. Thomas decided to try to stick it out in the grain business and took a job with Kellogg (the cereal company). To try to regain his standing in the local farming community, Welch undertook to repay the debts of the bankrupt company himself. He had no legal obligation to pay these debts. But you can imagine that the local grain farmers would be none too happy to see him darkening their doors again—unless he took strong steps to address the bad feeling generated by his family company's bankruptcy.[7]

As it happens, Thomas prospered in his new venture, and he shared his good fortune with his neighbors. In 1928, for instance, he earned $26,000 in commissions from Kellogg and made debt repayments of $11,000—more than 40% of his salary. (If these seem like small amounts, just update them for inflation to 2014: it's as if a modern-day Welch earned $360,000 and paid $153,000 out of his own pocket to debtors of his former company.)

---

[4] *See* Code Section 67, which imposes a floor on employee business deductions equal to 2% of adjusted gross income.

[5] Samantha's business travel is a working condition fringe because it would be deductible under Section 162 if Samantha (like Thomas) paid for it herself. *See* Code Section 132(d).

[6] 290 U.S. 111 (1933).

[7] Some of the details are provided in Joel S. Newman, *The Story of Welch v. Helvering: The Use (and Misuse) of the "Ordinary and Necessary" Test for the Deductibility of Business Expenses*, in Tax Stories (Paul L. Caron ed., 2003).

All was well—until the IRS took an interest. Thomas had deducted the debt repayments from his income, taking the view that they were ordinary and necessary for his new job and, therefore, deductible under Code Section 162. The IRS disallowed the deductions and presented Thomas with a whopping tax bill.

The case went all the way to the Supreme Court, which seemed dazed and confused by the unusual facts. Justice Cardozo's opinion deems Thomas Welch's actions "extraordinary" and adds, none too helpfully:

> We try to classify this act as ordinary or the opposite, and the norms of conduct fail us.... The standard set up by the statute is not a rule of law; it is rather a way of life. Life in all its fullness must supply the answer to the riddle.

Seriously? One strongly suspects that lower court judges were more befuddled than enlighted by Cardozo's instruction.

Still, even though the Court's opinion is opaque, there are two reasons why *Welch* is a hard case—and both have to do with puzzles, not of life in all its fullness, but of *valuation*.

The first *valuation* problem is one we've encountered before—the mixed business and personal expenditure. When Thomas repaid the debts incurred by his family firm, he was repairing not only his business reputation but his personal reputation. At least for smallish communities, the two are closely linked, and Thomas's actions showed that he was a good person, not just a canny grain merchant.

The Court's opinion hints at the point, when it worries that ruling in favor of Thomas would permit deductions for a man whose family name is "clouded" by thefts committed by an ancestor or a man who "enriches his culture" by gaining an education. In those cases, and arguably in *Welch* itself, there is no way to measure—to value—the business component of the expenditure and to distinguish it from the personal component.

A second *valuation* problem concerns the timing of Thomas's deductions. Suppose that we made the generous assumption that his motivation for repaying the debts was primarily to enhance his business reputation. Even so, the repayments very likely created a long-term benefit to Thomas. You can imagine the positive buzz in the community: "Can you believe what Tommy Welch is doing? He's paying us all out of his own pocket!" This positive reputation is likely to endure over time, making it inappropriate to permit him to deduct the entire cost upfront.

An analogy helps clarify the point. If Thomas bought a $30,000 truck to drive around to his business appointments, he couldn't deduct the entire cost in the first year. Why not? Because the truck would last for more than one year. In other words, Welch would be using up the business value of the truck over a number of years—not just one. Accordingly, the tax law would permit him a total deduction of $30,000, but spread over several years.

The *valuation* puzzle arises because the law cannot measure how long a positive reputation endures. Conventional assets (*e.g.*, trucks) don't pose much of a *valuation* problem. There may be a little variability depending on driving patterns, climate, and so on, but it isn't impossible to make a reasonable estimate of a truck's useful life. Call it five years. By contrast, there is no standardized way of improving one's reputation, and no measurable useful life.

Welch, then, was a hard case times two. The *valuation* problems were insoluble, not only because he mixed business and personal life, but because reputation is so evanescent. And so the Court denied him any deduction at all.

But don't be misled by *Welch* into thinking that the IRS devotes serious scrutiny to Code Section 162 business expenses. In most garden-variety business settings, the IRS respects the taxpayer's bona fide determination. So, if the management of Safeway grocery stores decides that, say, it's good business to offer fresh flowers in every store, the IRS will not question the deduction of the costs of offering flowers.

¶803 *EXACTO SPRING CORPORATION V. COMMISSIONER*

The tax law confronts a potential *valuation* problem whenever an expenditure represents both a deductible business expenditure and a nondeductible item. An important real-world problem concerns corporate dividends, which are—you guessed it—nondeductible.

To understand the problem, you need a little (but only a very little) background on the corporate tax. The United States has a "double tax" on corporate income: the system aims to impose one tax on the corporation itself and a second tax on the shareholder who receives a corporate dividend.

The system relies on three tax rules to ensure collection of the double tax. One rule is that corporations are taxable entities. Every year, every corporation must calculate its (net) income and pay tax, generally at a rate of 35%. The second rule is that dividends are income, reportable on shareholders' tax returns when received. The third rule is that corporations may not deduct dividends.

The nondeductibility of dividends is critical to the design of the double tax: if corporations could deduct dividends, the Treasury would collect, in the end, only one tax instead of two. To see why, consider a simple example.

> **EXAMPLE 2.** Corporation X earns $100 and immediately declares a dividend of $100. Under current law, the corporation must include in income the $100 it earns, and shareholders must include in income the $100 they receive. By contrast, if dividends were deductible, the deduction would reduce the corporation's net income to zero. In that event, the Treasury would collect just one tax (from the shareholder) instead of two (one from the corporation and one from the shareholder).

But clever taxpayers can blur the line between dividends, which are not deductible, and compensation to workers, which is. In *Exacto Spring Corporation v.*

Commissioner,[8] the Seventh Circuit confronted an allegation that a closely-held corporation had done just that. The central character in the drama was William Heitz, the chief executive and majority shareholder of the corporation.

William earned a salary of more than $1 million per year, and the corporation justified his salary by noting his extensive qualifications, his unique knowledge, and his valuable role as founder and all-around workhorse for the corporation's interests.

But the IRS suspected that a portion of the $1 million in "salary" paid to William Heitz as CEO actually represented a dividend to William as a shareholder. The government's challenge relied on Code Section 162(a)(1), which permits businesses to deduct "reasonable" compensation. The IRS took the position that Heitz's salary was so high that it was unreasonable, noting, among other facts, that Exacto Spring had paid very limited dividends even though the company's business had prospered overall.

We can understand the IRS as making a *substance over form* argument here. In form, Exacto Spring was paying a deductible business expense—salary. In substance, the IRS claimed, the $1 million paid comprised $400,000 in compensation for services and $600,000 in dividends.

The IRS position implied a hefty tax bill for the Exacto Spring Corporation but not for Heitz himself. Under the law at the time, William would have had to pay tax on the $1 million at his marginal tax rate whether it was called "compensation" or "dividend." The corporation, by contrast, stood to lose a $600,000 deduction if the IRS succeeded in recharacterizing that amount as a dividend.

The *valuation* problem in *Exacto Spring* arises because the corporate tax aims to impose a double tax on income earned as a shareholder but not on income earned as an employee. The problem is that William Heitz wore two hats—one as CEO, and one as majority shareholder. Heitz's dual role made it difficult, but essential, for the IRS to differentiate the value he generated as a worker from the value he generated as an owner of capital.

In the Seventh Circuit's decision in *Exacto Spring*, Judge Posner targeted the multi-factor test traditionally used in unreasonable compensation cases. In a sharp and amusing opinion, Posner criticized the test as unreliable in concept and misapplied in practice. The multi-factor approach, he writes, "does not provide adequate guidance to a rational decision."

Judge Posner instead endorsed the "independent investor" test, which he described as providing an indirect market test. Under the independent investor test, a judge (or the IRS) asks what rate of return a shareholder would expect, *ex ante*, to receive on an investment in the particular corporation, taking into account the riskiness of the venture and so on. If the investor ultimately receives at least that return, then the tax law treats any compensation paid as reasonable. The logic is that executive compensation is economically reasonable if shareholders as a group have received an adequate return on their capital. Under this test,

[8] 196 F.3d 833 (7th Cir. 1999).

compensation would be excessive only if compensation is so high that investors have been denied their expected return.

Judge Posner's criticism of the conventional seven-factor test has considerable merit. Judges have very limited ability to determine whether a given executive is overpaid, and the multi-factor test requires them to do just that.

The catch is that the independent investor test doesn't avoid the *valuation* problem—it just shifts it to a new arena. The problem, keep in mind, is to come up with a method of measuring the relative value of labor and capital contributed by an individual to a corporation. (William Heitz, for instance, contributed his labor as CEO and his capital as a shareholder.) The conventional test attacks the problem by attempting to value the labor component: that's why the seven factors focus on the executive's training and on the services he provides to the firm. The logic is that if we can value the labor portion, then the remainder of the payment can be attributed to capital. The independent investor test flips the inquiry: it attempts to value the return on capital and then assumes that the rest can be attributed to labor.

The catch is that setting a value on the return to capital is not, in principle, any easier than determining reasonable compensation. The facts in *Exacto Spring* are atypical here, because the IRS's own expert found that investors expected a 13% return. Given that finding, the way was open for Judge Posner to apply the independent investor test and resolve the case. Bam!

But once the independent investor test is adopted, the IRS and taxpayers will face the considerable task of determining what rate of return investors in a specific corporation would have demanded, years ago, in order to make their investment. The expected rate of return is not an item stated in corporate documents: corporate equity by its nature does not guarantee any particular return.

And expected rates of return vary from company to company based on the risk and return profile of the particular business and industry. So the independent investor test, in practice, may ultimately prove as messy and variable as the despised seven-factor test. The unavoidable problem is that the law demands *valuation* in the context of closely-held businesses, where valuing either labor or capital is likely to be difficult.

¶804 REAL-WORLD TRANSACTIONS: DISGUISED DIVIDENDS AND DISGUISED GIFTS

Individuals in closely-held businesses, especially family businesses, often have multiple roles. The CEO may also own most of the stock, and her parents, spouse, and children may also be involved. These overlapping relationships can tempt the players to manipulate payments in tax-advantageous ways, requiring the IRS to deploy the substance over form doctrine.

Disguised dividends are one well-known tax game that draws IRS scrutiny when the business is incorporated.

EXAMPLE 3. Amanda, Bruce, and Christy are siblings. Each owns 33.33% of the stock in their family corporation, which has performed quite well financially. If the business pays each one a salary of $200,000 but pays no dividends (or pays only occasional dividends), the IRS may suspect a disguised dividend. The suspicion is that by hiding a (nondeductible) dividend in an inflated (deductible) salary, the siblings are trying to reduce the corporation's tax bill. The savings can be considerable. If the disguised dividend is (say) $50,000 per sibling per year, the IRS is losing up to 35% of that amount in foregone tax revenue. (Keep in mind that the top corporate tax bracket is 35%.)

But, just as in *Exacto Spring*, the IRS will seek to assemble facts to deploy the *substance over form* doctrine. The approach the IRS takes will vary depending on the relevant circuit's legal test. Some circuits still focus on whether salaries are excessive. Others have adopted the independent investor test embraced by Judge Posner in *Exacto Spring*.[9] But under either type of theory, these cases are fact-intensive and expensive to litigate, because they require the parties to litigate *valuation*—either the value of the workers' services or the value of the stock investment.

Family businesses—whether incorporated or not—are sometimes tempted to try a second tax gimmick, one that also draws IRS scrutiny when detected. The idea is to put a family member on the company payroll in order to convert (nondeductible) gifts into (deductible) compensation.

EXAMPLE 4. Evelyn runs a small but profitable (unincorporated) business with her wife, Marianne. Marianne's elderly father, Paul, is in poor health and has fallen on hard financial times, and the couple would like to pay him $2,000 per month to help pay his living costs. Evelyn and Marianne are in the 40% federal tax bracket, while Paul has no other income. It occurs to Evelyn that instead of giving Paul a gift, which would be nondeductible, they ought to "hire" him at a salary of $2,000 per month. Evelyn comes to you to ask whether her idea will fly.

The answer you should give is no, unless Paul will really be doing $2,000 worth of work for the company. The *substance over form* doctrine insists that the arrangement should be taxed for what it really is. And if what is really happening is that Evelyn and Marianne are supporting Paul, then they cannot paper the arrangement as salary.

Which brings us to a word on tax fraud. New students of taxation sometimes get the mistaken impression that tax planning can involve stretching or hiding the truth. But that's tax fraud, not tax planning. Tax planners work within the law and advise their clients on how to avoid pitfalls hidden in the rules. Lying about the facts of a business or family situation is unethical and illegal, and it can mean jail time and hefty civil penalties.

---

[9] The Second Circuit follows a variant of the independent investor approach. Dexsil Corp. v. Commissioner, 147 F.3d 96 (2d Cir.1998). For recent cases in other circuits reaffirming the use of the traditional test, *see* Eberl's Claim Service, Inc. v. Commissioner, 249 F.3d 994 (10th Cir. 2001); Haffner's Service Stations, Inc. v. Commissioner, 326 F.3d 1 (1st Cir. 2003); Metro Leasing and Development Corp. v. Commissioner, 376 F.3d 1015 (9th Cir. 2004); and Brewer Quality Homes, Inc. v. Commissioner, 122 Fed. Appx. 88 (5th Cir. 2004) (unpublished op.).

CHAPTER 9

Deductions for Business Meals, Commuting, Clothing and Child Care

Introduction . . . . ¶900
Business Meals and *Moss v. Commissioner* . . . . ¶901
Commissioner v. Flowers and the Problem of Commuting . . . . ¶902
Real-World Transactions: Tax Lobbying and the Restaurant Industry . . . . ¶903
Work Clothing and *Pevsner v. Commissioner* . . . . ¶904
Child Care and *Smith v. Commissioner* . . . . ¶905

¶900 INTRODUCTION

Chapter 2 introduced one of the core difficulties facing any income tax: the problem of distinguishing business and personal expenditures. We saw that many fringe benefits provide a mix of business and personal value. The result is a *valuation* puzzle for the income tax.

The same *valuation* problem recurs in the context of business deductions. When taxpayers spend money on items that produce both business value and personal satisfaction, the law finds itself in a ticklish position. To preserve the income tax base, the tax must not permit taxpayers to deduct personal consumption. (Recall that the Haig-Simons concept treats personal consumption as one of the two core items, along with an increase in savings, that define what income is!) And yet, in order to tax *net income*, the income tax must permit taxpayers to deduct the costs of doing business.

The *valuation* problem arises because items like food, shelter, clothing and entertainment are core examples of personal consumption. You may not deduct your breakfast, your rent, or your Broadway tickets. And yet, when taxpayers consume these items in a business context, they may credibly claim that the costs represent an expense of earning income. How is the tax law to tell the difference?

In most cases, we will see, the tax law brings little finesse to the *valuation* problem. Very rarely does the law inquire into a taxpayer's unique situation. Instead, more often than not, the law adopts an all-or-nothing approach, which endorses—or prohibits—deductions for whole categories of expenses. The predictable result is that the law too often mismeasures income (relative to the Haig-Simons ideal).

¶901 BUSINESS MEALS AND *MOSS V. COMMISSIONER*

Everyone has to eat, and perhaps nothing is more personal than what we eat. Some people cook, while others live on take-out. It isn't surprising, then, that the tax law generally treats food as non-deductible personal consumption. Whether you whip up a thrifty meal of bean stew or splurge on filet and lobster, either way, you must pay the cost in after-tax income.

But meals can have business value too. In *Moss v. Commissioner,* [1] for example, John Moss and the other partners at a law firm scheduled daily lunch meetings for all the firm's lawyers (partners and associates alike) at Cafe Angelo, a restaurant near the office. Most of the lawyers typically spent the day in court, and the lunch hour was the only time that most could regularly attend a meeting. The partners deducted the cost of the lunches, treating them as a business expense under Code Section 162.

Moss illustrates the *valuation* problem posed by business meals. On the one hand, any meal has personal value, because it nourishes our bodies. And any meal we eat at work substitutes for a meal we would otherwise eat at home—so a business meal saves us buying our own meal.

On the other hand, meals consumed while working (or while at work) also have business value. Indeed, the facts in *Moss* seemed to be quite favorable to the taxpayers: These were efficient business meetings, not leisurely meals with casual conversation. Also relevant is cost: Business necessity can force the taxpayer to buy more expensive meals than she would otherwise consume. John Moss and his partners spent nearly $8,000 in 1977 (or $30,000 in today's dollars) on Cafe Angelo lunches for the firm's seven lawyers. Many of the lawyers might have preferred an easy (and cheap) sandwich brought from home, but the restaurant meals facilitated the firm's business.

In principle, the income tax should bifurcate the cost of a business meal into its personal and business value. The problem, of course, is that the tax law cannot easily separate the personal component and the business component of a given meal. Suppose, for example, that the meals in *Moss* cost an average, in today's dollars, of $20 per person and included a sandwich, a small salad, a drink, and a dessert. It's pretty clear that $20 exceeds, by a large margin, the cost of a basic meal at home. (We've all eaten peanut butter and jelly for lunch!). And perhaps some of the lawyers didn't particularly like the food or thought it too rich or fattening. Still, the lawyers in *Moss* did enjoy a sit-down restaurant meal, with all the shopping, cooking, and clean-up done by someone else. That enjoyment is surely as personal as the enjoyment people feel when they go out to a restaurant on their own dime.

So it's not surprising that the *Moss* opinion wrestles with the *valuation* dilemma:

---

[1] 80 T.C. 1073 (1983).

> The expense in question is close to that evanescent line dividing personal and business expenses....The dual nature of the business lunch has long been a difficult problem for legislators and courts alike.[2]

In the end, the Tax Court denied John Moss's deduction, reasoning that, although the Cafe Angelo meetings were helpful to the business, the lawyers were not sufficiently different from the ordinary worker who eats lunch at her desk: "petitioner is much like employees in all fields who find it necessary to devote their lunch hour to work-related activities."[3]

The court's reasoning is logical enough, but only if you accept the premise that the ordinary worker should not be able to deduct a lunch eaten at her desk. But that assumption begs the question: *should meals eaten at work be deductible?* The analogy to the worker who lunches while working just kicks the metaphorical can down the road. On the one hand, she probably (certainly!) would prefer to eat a meal of her choice at home while channel-surfing. And her sandwich at work is likely more expensive than a home meal (or, if brought from home, will suffer in quality from sitting in a brown bag). On the other hand, the worker, like every human being, has to eat something.

Hearing *Moss* on appeal, Judge Richard Posner of the Seventh Circuit took the opportunity to quip that "the framework of statutes and regulations for deciding this case is simple, but not clear."[4] And he got it quite right when he wrote:

> "The problem is that many expenses are simultaneously business expenses in the sense that they conduce to the production of business income and personal expenses in the sense that they raise personal welfare."[5]

The drafters of the Tax Code, then, find themselves once again between a rock and a hard place. If the law denies taxpayers a deduction for business meals, it will overtax businesses in which meals have business value. But if the law permits a deduction for business meals, it will (to some degree) permit the deduction of personal consumption.

The *Moss* decision may strike you as ungenerous to the taxpayers, but don't shed too many hot tears over the fate of American business. The courts and Congress have left plenty of room for taxpayers to deduct their meals. Business meals with clients (rather than co-workers) can almost always be deducted, as can meals with potential employees. Meals eaten while traveling overnight on business are deductible too.

By the mid-1980s, many policy makers believed that the deductibility of business meals had become a subsidy for expensive meals for, well, fat cats. In

---

[2] 80 T.C. 1076, 1077.

[3] 80 T.C. 1080.

[4] Moss v. Commissioner, 758 F.2d 211, 212 (7th Cir. 1985).

[5] 758 F.2d 211, 212.

the 1986 Tax Reform Act, the Congress enacted Section 274(n), which limited deductions for business meals and entertainment to 80% of the amount paid. In 1993, the Congress cut back the deduction to 50%. The result is that a $100 business meal is only half deductible: the payor can deduct only $50.

The 50% rule has its appeal: it's a rough-cut way of apportioning business and personal value. And those of us in the sandwich-at-our-desk crowd can be pleased that the fat cats can only deduct half of their lavish meals at the Four Seasons. But, as with all bright-line solutions to any *valuation* problem, the 50% rule probably overtaxes some and undertaxes others:

EXAMPLE 1. This year, Karen, a new lawyer in town, paid $100 to attend the local business club's "rubber chicken" awards lunch. She's a vegetarian and can't eat most of the food, and she doesn't yet know anyone, so she isn't having lunch with her buddies. But the networking opportunities are good enough to warrant the expense. Karen clearly has only a business rationale for paying the $100, but she is limited to a deduction of $50.

EXAMPLE 2. Phillip is a partner and Charlotte is a job candidate at Big Law Firm. The two were law school classmates, and they share a group of friends. Phillip takes Charlotte out to a gourmet lunch on Big Law Firm's dime, and the two happily spend the hour catching up while consuming a $500 meal with wine. Philip deducts 50% of the cost of the lunch as a recruiting expense.

It isn't hard to spot that Karen is overtaxed, while Philip (and maybe Charlotte) are undertaxed. Karen received only business value for her $100 but can only deduct $50, while Phillip took a friend to a (partly) tax-deductible lunch.

¶902 *COMMISSIONER V. FLOWERS* AND THE PROBLEM OF COMMUTING

Nothing is drearier than a long commute. (If you haven't yet tried it, I don't recommend it.) Sitting in a car, bus, or train, just waiting to get to work and perhaps trying to do a little reading or writing along the way, is a sure recipe for exhaustion. Most people, if asked, would consider the costs of commuting to be a cost of working: no one I've ever met commutes for fun.

But the tax law takes the opposite view. Commuting is considered a personal expense and, therefore, nondeductible. The doctrine originates in a Supreme Court case from the 1940s called *Commissioner v. Flowers*.[6] A lawyer (Flowers) lived in Jackson, Mississippi and worked in Mobile, Alabama. He made 40 trips per year to Mobile, and he deducted his travel costs under the provision now

[6] 326 U.S. 465 (1946).

found in Code Section 162, which permits the deduction of expenses of traveling "while away from home in the pursuit of business."

The Supreme Court disallowed the deduction, reasoning that the cost of the commute reflected a personal decision to live and work in two different places. Flowers incurred his travel costs "solely as the result of the taxpayer's desire to maintain a home in Jackson while working in Mobile, a factor irrelevant" to business.[7]

The Court's reasoning is logical enough, but it still isn't quite satisfactory. It is true enough that Flowers' decision about where to live reflected personal preference. He had lived in Jackson his whole life; he voted there, attended church there, and had personal ties there. But it is equally true that the exigencies of his job forced him to leave that home and travel a good distance in order to work.

In fancier language, the court deploys a but-for theory of causation that can readily be reversed. But for his decision to live in Mississippi, Flowers would not have had to commute. At the same time, it's equally true that but for his job in Alabama, Flowers would not have had to commute.

The real problem in Flowers is, of course, one of *valuation*. Commuting costs reflect a nested set of personal and business decisions. We can imagine a pure business reason: perhaps Flowers could have worked in Jackson but would have earned a lower wage or had no chance of advancement. We can just as easily imagine a personal rationale: perhaps the schools were better in Jackson, or perhaps his spouse had a job or social ties there.

Policy makers, reasonably enough, have declined to inquire into the mix of personal and business factors motivating individual commuting decisions. Instead, following the pattern we've seen in other cases, the law simply denies any deduction for commuting expenses, no matter how sympathetic the facts.

Implicitly, then, the law presumes that taxpayers could—if they chose—live so close to work that they would have zero commuting costs. When taxpayers do incur commuting costs, it must be—the law presumes—because of a personal choice to live elsewhere. Sometimes, of course, the presumption is absurd. My favorite example is the nuclear test site case: In *Coombs v. Commissioner*,[8] Lee Coombs and more than a dozen workers at the U.S. government's Nevada nuclear test site claimed deductions for commuting and travel expenses. The nuclear test site, for obvious reasons, was located in a remote desert, and the closest "habitable area" was 65 miles away. So Lee and the others, reasonably enough, chose to live far away from their workplace. But the IRS stuck to its, er, guns, and the courts agreed, holding that the costs of commuting and overnight stays were not deductible.

The law applies even to two-career couples who work in different places. In *Hantzis v. Commissioner*,[9] Catharine Hantzis was a law student at Harvard who accepted a summer associate job in New York City. Catharine attempted to deduct the costs of her meals and lodging as travel expenses under Code Section 162(a)(2),

---

[7] 326 U.S. 465, 473.

[8] 608 F.2d 1269 (9th Cir. 1979).

[9] 638 F.2d 248 (1st Cir. 1981).

which permits a deduction for taxpayers "away from home." The court found that even though Catharine and her husband maintained a home in Boston, she was not entitled to a deduction for her New York expenses, because she had only a personal connection to Boston, and not a business connection. (Being a law student, it turns out, is not a business.) The court, in essence, assimilated Hantzis's case to the *Flowers* case, emphasizing the personal reasons for Catharine's extra costs and setting aside her business reasons for working in New York.

¶903 REAL-WORLD TRANSACTIONS: TAX LOBBYING AND THE RESTAURANT INDUSTRY

When you think about deductible business meals (which I'm sure you do frequently), you might reasonably suppose that the benefit of the deduction goes to business people, particularly the rich ones who can afford to eat at places like the Four Seasons. After all, a 100% deduction for business meals reduces the cost of a $100 meal to just $60 for someone in the 40% tax bracket. But an economist would point out that the "incidence" of the tax benefit can shift if restaurants can charge more due to the tax-favored nature of the expenditure.

"Incidence" is a cool and useful word in tax policy discussions: it signifies an analysis that identifies the taxpayer who really bears the economic burden of a tax or reaps the economic benefit of a deduction or credit. The neat insight is that tax burdens and benefits can travel around, or shift, as markets adjust to the presence of the tax burden or benefit. So a tax that is formally paid by Taxpayer A might work its way through the markets and end up burdening Taxpayer D.

> **EXAMPLE 3.** Suppose that, initially, the tax law does not permit the deduction of business meals. Even so, Kathleen, a lawyer in the 40% tax bracket, spends $100 per month to take her best client out to a nice meal at Cafe de France, where they catch up on the client's legal issues and bond a little bit as they get to know each other. (That personal touch is very, very important in any service business.) Now, suddenly, the Congress acts to permit full deductibility of business meals.
>
> It would seem that the new tax deduction would permit Kathleen to put $40 back in her pocket, since the tax deduction of $100 saves her that much. Sweet deal! But, as a little time passes, the savvy owners of Cafe de France realize that they can mark up their prices to, say, $120. Kathleen still feels better off than before the legal change, since her after-tax cost is just $72 (60% of $120). But Cafe de France is better off too, since its revenue has increased by $20.

You can imagine a chain reaction that involves even more people. Perhaps the cafe's wine merchant spots the new prosperity of the restaurant and hikes wine prices a little bit. Perhaps the wait staff bargains for a higher base wage. And so on. Market forces will determine which market participants can claim a bit of the "tax goodie" that Uncle Sam has thrown onto the bargaining table. But the key point is that Kathleen, who pays for the meal and takes the tax deduction on the return, may not reap the full economic benefit. Indeed, if the price of the Cafe de France meal eventually rises to $167, then Kathleen will be no better off than she was before: the deduction will save her $67, and her out-of-pocket cost will be $100.

This isn't just a classroom hypothetical. Economists have studied the incidence of tax benefits for restaurant meals, and they've concluded that the deductibility of business meals affects the restaurant industry's profitability.[10] The restaurant industry knows about incidence too: its lobbyists fought hard (if unsuccessfully) to oppose the 50% limitation on the deductibility of business meals, and it remains a legislative target for the industry's lobbyists today.[11]

¶904 WORK CLOTHING AND *PEVSNER V. COMMISSIONER*

Back in the 1970s, Sandra Pevsner worked at the Yves St. Laurent boutique in Dallas.[12] This boutique sold extremely expensive designer clothing, and the management required salespeople to wear St. Laurent clothing so that they could look like peers to their customers and could, if complimented, say that their clothes were St. Laurent.

But even though St. Laurent clothes were perfect for Dallas socialites, they didn't suit Sandra's lifestyle. She worked all day and went home, most nights, to be with her husband, Barry, who had suffered a heart attack. The Pevsners didn't go out much, and Sandra was careful not to wear her pricey St. Laurent clothes outside work, so that they would last longer.

In 1975, Sandra spent $1600 to buy and maintain her work clothes. In today's dollars, that's $7,000—a pretty hefty clothing bill for someone working as a store manager. She deducted the cost of the clothing on her tax return, reasoning that she bought and wore the clothes solely for work.

The Tax Court upheld Sandra's tax deduction, finding her a credible witness when she testified that she never wore the work clothing outside work. But the Fifth Circuit ruled against Sandra, holding that even though she did not wear the clothing outside work, she could have done so. The standard, the judges opined, should be an objective rather than a subjective one, looking to the nature of the clothes and not to Sandra's individual situation.

Pevsner is, of course, another case that straddles the business-personal fault line that runs through the Tax Code. Everyone has to wear clothes, and we typically think that clothing choices are highly personal: just ask my daughter whether she'd

---

10 *See* Stephen J. Hiemstra and Steven T. Kosiba, Recession and Tax Impacts On the U.S. Restaurant Industry, 17 J. Hospitality and Tourism 17 (Feb. 1994).

11 Michael Wines, *Congress is Feeling Pressure to Preserve Meal Deduction*, N.Y. Times, July 27, 1993, available at http://www.nytimes.com/1993/07/27/us/congress-is-feeling-pressure-to-preserve-meal-deduction.html. National Restaurant Association, Taxes, available at http://www.restaurant.org/advocacy/Taxes.

12 Pevsner v. Commissioner, 628 F.2d 467 (5th Cir. 1980).

ever be caught wearing one of my outfits! But clothes worn to work also serve a business purpose: our bosses, colleagues, and clients judge us by what we wear. And, unfortunately, in many businesses expensive clothes project success, reliability, and stability. Sure, the famous litigator David Boies can get away with wearing suits from Lands End and Sears,[13] but I don't suggest that a young associate imitate his sartorial choices. You're going to have to scrounge up the cash to go to Nordstrom.

What is curious about *Pevsner* is that Sandra's particular case didn't pose much of a *valuation* problem. For Sandra, the expensive Yves St. Laurent clothes were clearly a cost of working. She didn't wear designer clothes outside work, and she bought the clothes only because her job required them. In effect, St. Laurent was reducing her pay by the $1600 cost of the required clothes.

But the Court of Appeals' judges in *Pevsner* were skeptical—and probably rightly so—about the IRS's (and courts') capacity to take notice of individual circumstances. Sandra Pevsner was an especially credible witness with a documented simple lifestyle, but other managers might have more opportunity to wear their work clothes outside work. It would be difficult for the IRS to monitor whether workers wear their work clothes when they're off the job.

More generally, the judges may have—and should have—been worried about the *valuation* problem inherent in permitting a general deduction for work clothing. When a lawyer chooses a $3,000 suit instead of a $300 suit, he may be making a sound business decision. But it's also possible that he gains personal consumption value out of looking good in Armani. As always, the IRS has no magic way of peering inside people's heads to measure just how much business value and personal value they reap from their self-presentation.

Despite the merits of Sandra Pevsner's individual case, then, a favorable ruling would have created a double danger. A deduction for work clothing could invite people to, er, stretch the truth about whether they wore work clothing outside the workplace. And a clothing deduction would understate the Haig-Simons income of taxpayers whose work clothing choices brought them significant personal benefits.

Still, the decision in *Pevsner* itself is costly in just the opposite way: The tax law overtaxes people who, like Sandra, must buy relatively expensive clothing in order to work. After *Pevsner*, only a narrow class of taxpayers—those who wear uniforms unsuited to general wear—can deduct their work clothing. So lab coats are deductible, but starter suits for young lawyers are not.

¶905 CHILD CARE AND *SMITH V. COMMISSIONER*

In *Smith v. Commissioner*,[14] Henry and Lillie Smith sought to deduct the cost of hiring "nursemaids" to take care of their young children while both parents

---

13 Edward Lewine, *An Open Case*, N.Y. Times, March 26, 2006, available at http://www.nytimes.com/2006/03/26/magazine/326wwln_domains.html?_r=0.

14 40 B.T.A. 1038 (1939).

worked outside the home. The Board of Tax Appeals, the predecessor of the Tax Court, made short work of the taxpayers' claim. The Board rejected the argument that child care was a cost of working for Henry and Lillie, treating the expenses instead as entirely personal. Deploying the gender-role assumptions of the time, the court emphasized Lillie's duty to care for the couple's children:

> We are not prepared to say that the care of children, like similar aspects of family and household life, is other than a personal concern. The wife's services as custodian of the home and protector of its children are ordinarily rendered without monetary compensation.... Here the wife has chosen to employ others to discharge her domestic function and the services she performs are rendered outside the home.... But that does not deprive the same work performed by others of its personal character nor furnish a reason why its cost should be treated as an offset in the guise of a deductible item.[15]

By now, you can spot the *valuation* problem in a second. Child care involves a personal element, to be sure. Choices about how to care for children are among the most personal that we make. But child care also represents a marginal expense of working outside the home. The stay-at-home parent need not pay for child care.

Child care, like business meals and commuting, then, mixes personal and business elements. Having children is, today, a personal choice. But the conditions of work require parents to make more expensive and extensive arrangements for child care than they otherwise would. Just like business meals and business clothing, child care mixes the satisfaction of meeting basic personal needs with an additional expense related to business.

The holding in *Smith* takes what is, by now, the familiar all-or-nothing approach to the *valuation* problem. (In this case, the taxpayers walked away with nothing.) *Smith* is still good law. Code Section 162 does not permit a deduction for child care costs.[16] But members of Congress apparently saw more merit in the argument that child care is a cost of working. Code Section 21 provides a dependent care tax credit, which offers a partial reimbursement for a capped amount of child care expenses. But the credit provides only modest dollars, and it is nonrefundable, so that low-income families receive little benefit.[17] The cost of child care remains a serious issue for many families.[18]

---

15 40 B.T.A. 1038, 1039 (1939).

16 For a modern reaffirmation of *Smith*, *see* Settimo v. Commissioner, T.C. Memo. 2006-261 (2006).

17 Amy E. Dunbar, *Child Care Credit*, Tax Policy Center, available at http://tpcprod.urban.org/taxtopics/encyclopedia/Child-care-credit.cfm.

18 David Blau, *Rethinking U.S. Child Care Policy, Issues in Science and Technology*, Winter 2002, available at http://issues.org/18-2/blau/.

CHAPTER 10

Capitalization and Depreciation

Introduction . . . ¶1000
The Value of Tax Deferral . . . ¶1001
Capital Expenditures and *Indopco, Inc. v. Commissioner* . . . ¶1002
Depreciation and *Simon v. Commissioner* . . . ¶1003
Real World Transactions: Bonus Depreciation and the Great Recession . . . ¶1004

¶1000 INTRODUCTION

The task of measuring *net income* poses high stakes for the income tax. If the law gets it wrong, the system may over- or undertax some people, some investments, even some whole industries. The result is that the income tax will impose an unintended penalty on—or award an unintended subsidy to—those individuals, those investments, and those industries.

In the last generation, tax policy makers have realized that the timing of deductions matters as much as the total amount. If the tax law gets the timing wrong, it can award unintended *tax deferral* to the taxpayer, and *tax deferral*, as we know, amounts to a subsidy via the tax law. To see why, consider a simple example.

EXAMPLE 1. Tatyana invests in an asset that costs $600. The asset will produce gross income of $300 per year for three years and will then be worthless. Intuitively, Tatyana's basis of $600 should be recovered over the three-year useful life of the asset, as in Case A in Table 10.1 below. If, instead, the law permits her to deduct the $600 cost immediately, as in Case B, her income is inappropriately deferred or pushed back to later years. If, as a third possibility, the law denies her a deduction until the asset is disposed of (discarded) in year 3, as in Case C, Tatyana's income will be inappropriately accelerated.

Table 10.1 Measuring Net Income Over Time

Year	Item	Case A	Case B	Case C
1	Gross Income	$300	$300	$300
	Deduction	-$200	-$600	0
	Net Income	$100	-$300	$300

Year	Item	Case A	Case B	Case C
2	Gross Income	$300	$300	$300
	Deduction	-$200	0	0
	Net Income	$100	$300	$300
3	Gross Income	$300	$300	$300
	Deduction	-$200	0	-$600
	Net Income	$100	$300	-$300
	Total Net Income	$300	$300	$300

Table 10.1 illustrates one of the tax lawyer's favorite sayings: "Timing is everything." Tatyana's total net income over the three-year investment is the same in all three cases: $300. That makes total sense, since she invested $600 and ultimately earned a total of $900.

But the three legal regimes (represented by Cases A, B, and C) produce very different patterns of income and loss over time. In Case A, Tatyana has a level $100 of income in each year. In Case B, Tatyana reports a big loss in Year 1 and large amounts of income in Years 2 and 3. Case C is just the opposite; generating large amounts of income for Tatyana in the first two years followed by a big loss in Year 3.

Cases A, B, and C might be called level basis recovery, immediate deduction, and basis recovery upon sale. Pop quiz: which one does the taxpayer prefer?

Well, in the usual case, Tatyana prefers immediate deduction. Remember, taxpayers (usually) want deductions now and income later, and that's exactly what Case B does. Case C is the worst from a timing perspective, because it accelerates income and defers deductions.

It turns out that we can quantify the value of *tax deferral*. Let's see how.

¶1001 THE VALUE OF TAX DEFERRAL

Tax deferral isn't just a psychic benefit. Sure, it provides breathing room to the taxpayer, who can pay later, and perhaps that reduces some anxiety. But even laid-back types can benefit from *tax deferral*, which has objective financial value due to the simple fact that money in a bank account earns interest.

> **EXAMPLE 2.** Suppose that you earn extra income of $100 this year. Your marginal tax rate is 40%, and so you should owe the IRS $40 now. But a quirk in the tax law defers your tax for 10 years. That is, in 10 years you'll be required to pay the $40. (Importantly, it's the same $40 obligation, and not $40 with interest!)

In this example, the 10-year *tax deferral* has financial value measured by the interest you could earn by investing the $40 for ten years. In a sense, the IRS is letting you use the government's money for ten years—and is permitting you to keep any interest (or other investment return) you earn in the meantime. Put another way, the IRS has given you an interest-free loan of $40.

One way to think about the value of the interest-free loan is to calculate what you could earn over the 10 years. It turns out that if you put $40 into a 5% bank account for 10 years, you would have about $65 in the account. After paying the IRS its $40, you could pocket the $25 difference. Maybe $25 isn't too, too exciting these days, when even a fast-food meal runs $10. But just add some zeros, and all of a sudden we're talking about $25,000. Or $25 million!

Another way to think about the value of *tax deferral* is that you can put less than $40 in a bank account today, and the investment will grow to $40 by year 10. How much less? Well, at a 5% interest rate, you can deposit just $25 today, and that sum will grow to a touch more than $40 by year 10. So you can pocket $15 today, thanks to *tax deferral.*

In case you're wondering, the two ways of looking at *tax deferral* are equivalent. Financial types would say that the "present value" of $25 to be received in 10 years, at a 5% discount rate, is about $15. Put another way, $15 today is equivalent (in this financial sense) to $25 in a decade, if we're right that the prevailing interest rate is 5%.

So *tax deferral* is valuable even if your preferred investments are, say, stocks and bonds rather than bank accounts. As long as the taxpayer can expect to earn a positive return, *tax deferral* has financial value.

In a real-world setting, tax planners understand that the value of *tax deferral* may be outweighed by other factors. Most importantly, changing tax rates may reduce (or increase) the payoff to *tax deferral.* If a taxpayer now in (say) the 40% bracket will be in the 0% bracket in the future, then the imperative to defer is even stronger. But if a taxpayer faces rising tax rates over time, it might be prudent to pay taxes now rather than later. The best course will depend on the magnitude of the change in rates, the period of deferral, and the taxpayer's discount rate (*i.e.*, her investment opportunities).

> **EXAMPLE 3.** Return to the example above, in which you earn $100. Suppose that you can (at your option) pay $40 of taxes now or can defer the tax 10 years. We have already seen that if your tax rate remains constant, you should defer the tax, because at a 5% discount rate, the deferred tax costs her only $25 in today's dollars. But if her tax rate in 10 years will be 50%, so that she will owe tax of $50, should she still defer?

To answer that question, a tax planner should run the numbers to determine the present value (*i.e.*, the discounted value) of the future tax payment of $50. Still assuming a 5% interest rate, the present value (*i.e.*, today's cost) of $50 to be paid in a decade is $31. So you should still defer, since you can set aside just $31 now to fund the $50 in the future. By contrast, if your tax rate will be, say, 75% in ten years, the present value of the $75 future tax bill is $46 today. So you'd be better off paying the IRS its $40 right now.

Still, as a rule of thumb, the basic advice for most taxpayers, most of the time, is to take advantage of *tax deferral* when possible:

> Defer income and
> Accelerate deductions
> To cut your tax bill

OK, so this is a terrible haiku. But it's good tax advice!

¶1002 CAPITAL EXPENDITURES AND *INDOPCO, INC. V. COMMISSIONER*

The value of *tax deferral* for the taxpayer has a corresponding cost for the government. The Treasury loses what the taxpayer gains! Correct timing, then, is critical for the accurate measurement of *net income*. The tax law faces a roadblock, though: a problem of (wait for it!) *valuation* often prevents the system from getting the timing right.

In principle, an income tax should recognize changes in asset values as they occur.

> **EXAMPLE 4.** Perry owns a flower shop. He spends $50,000 on a state-of-the-art computer system to take internet orders and track inventory. In Year 1, all is well. The new system does a great job, and it's easy to use. Perry expects that the computer system will retain its value for at least three more years. But in Year 2, he gets a nasty surprise, when an unexpected change in technology makes the computer hardware and software nearly obsolete, reducing its value to $5,000.

The Haig-Simons ideal counsels a market-based approach. In this example, Perry should get no deduction when he buys the computer, because it has lasting value. In Year 1, he has basically exchanged $50,000 cash for a computer worth $50,000: he hasn't made or lost any money yet. But in Year 2, when events chop the market value of Perry's computer by $45,000, he's lost $45,000. Even if he intends to keep the computer and make do, the market price tells us that he's lost $45,000, since that's all Perry could get if he sold the system.

This principled approach is, of course, impossible to put into practice. The tax law cannot observe the change in value of all business assets every year. Instead, the law must adopt rules of thumb and approximations.

The legal doctrine governing "capital expenditures" is one of these rules of thumb. Capital expenditures are business expenses that produce lasting value, and they may not be deducted immediately. Instead, Code Section 263 requires the taxpayer to "capitalize" the expenses, meaning that he builds them into the basis of the relevant business asset.

EXAMPLE 5. Suppose that you run a large law firm, and you notice that the office is looking a little shabby. So you spring for new desks and chairs for all the partners and associates, at a total cost of $100,000. The office certainly looks better, but the tax news is mixed. The $100,000 cost is certainly a business expense, but it isn't immediately deductible, because the chairs and desks will last awhile. Instead, you must capitalize the $100,000 expense into the basis of the desks and chairs. (The Code then permits you to depreciate the assets, or deduct the basis over a set period of a few years.)

The law on capital expenditures is, to put it kindly, highly variable. (To put it less kindly, the law is a mess.) For instance, the costs of repairs are immediately deductible, while the costs of improvements must be capitalized. So if your law firm pays a plumber $50 to fix a leaky bathroom faucet, that's deductible. But if the law firm renovates the bathrooms completely, the costs must be capitalized.

The distinction is easy enough to state — deduct repairs and capitalize improvements. But it's difficult to apply in practice, because the line between repairs and improvements is often unclear. If you really like this kind of stuff, take a look at Rev. Rul. 2001-4,[1] which holds that "heavy maintenance" performed on aircraft may — or may not — be deductible, depending on exactly what is done.

The Supreme Court entered the fray in *Indopco, Inc. v. Commissioner,*[2] a case centering on a corporate acquisition. Unilever (the conglomerate that makes Dove soap and Lipton tea) took over a corporation called National Starch. In the acquisition process, National Starch (later renamed Indopco for some reason) deducted the fees on its tax return, and the IRS objected. The IRS argued that the $3 million in acquisition costs should be capitalized and not deducted immediately.

Indopco, the taxpayer, invoked a rule called the separate asset test. The separate asset test required taxpayers to capitalize the costs of creating a new business asset. For instance, in an earlier case called *Lincoln Savings,*[3] the Supreme Court had held that when a taxpayer spends money to create a separate asset, the expenditures must be capitalized. In that case, federal regulators required a savings and loan to contribute money to a new reserve account. Because the reserve created a separate asset, the contributions were capitalizable rather than deductible, said the Court.

Indopco argued that the holding in *Lincoln Savings* supported a negative inference: if an expenditure does not create a separate asset, then it should be deductible. That's exactly what happened in the National Starch takeover, according to the taxpayer: the legal and investment banking fees facilitated the acquisition, but the taxpayer didn't acquire a separate asset of any kind.

---

1 Rev. Rul. 2001-4, 2001-1 C.B. 295 (2001).

2 503 U.S. 79 (1992).

3 Commissioner v. Lincoln Savings and Loan, 403 U.S. 345 (1971).

(By contrast, Unilever, the acquiring corporation, most certainly did acquire a separate asset—National Starch! So Unilever would capitalize the acquisition costs into the basis of the acquired company.)

The Supreme Court disagreed, pointing out that National Starch had assured its board, shareholders, and the public that the acquisition would produce lasting benefits. It followed, the Court ruled, that Indopco could not deduct the costs of being acquired but must capitalize them.

You might ask, reasonably enough, how Indopco could capitalize the $3 million when there was no identifiable asset to which to capitalize them. National Starch didn't buy anything: it was (to use some poor grammar) bought!

But every business has an intangible asset called goodwill, which is sometimes defined as the value of a going concern. Technically, goodwill is the value of a business above and beyond the value of its identifiable assets. What that means is that a viable business is worth more than the sum of its parts: intangibles like reputation, repeat customers, even a good location all combine to raise the value of a business.

EXAMPLE 6. Frank Pepe Pizzeria Napolitana (Pepe's) in New Haven, Connecticut occupies a modest storefront in the Wooster Square neighborhood. It is jam-packed every night, and the lines extend for blocks on weekend nights. The pizza is truly famous[4] (and it's really, really good—you must try the white clam). If you were to buy Pepe's, you would have to pay more than the cost of the modest building, worn booths, and brick oven. You'd be paying for goodwill, which includes reputation, a loyal customer base, and the American passion for pizza.

Indopco, then, added to the basis in its goodwill the $3 million in acquisition expenses. Unfortunately for Indopco, self-created goodwill isn't amortizable, so the $3 million will simply remain as unused basis until (if ever) Indopco sells all its assets or abandons its business entirely.

¶1003 DEPRECIATION AND *SIMON V. COMMISSIONER*

Another of the tax law's rules of thumb concerns "depreciation." We all know that many things lose value over time. I'm sure your parents, like mine, have warned you never to buy a new car because it loses half its value when you drive it off the lot. (Actually, our families are right. You're better off, in general, buying a low-mileage used car still under warranty. But that's a debate for another time.)

Cars, like other machines, depreciate because of wear and tear. If you're like me, that new car is soon going to have a coat of dust outside and plenty of dog hair and spilled popcorn inside. Random people on the street will key your car's

[4] According to one article, Pepe's is one of the best-known pizzerias in the United States. *See Frank Pepe Pizzeria Napolitana*, Wikipedia entry, available at https://en.wikipedia.org/wiki/Frank_Pepe_Pizzeria_Napoletana.

finish, and urban dwellers have no hesitation about denting your bumper to fit into a tight parallel parking space. Soon enough, that shiny new car will be a thoroughly used car.

Now, the Haig-Simons ideal, just to review, would suggest that the tax law should take notice of depreciation by gauging the precise decline in value of each asset every year. But, as we've already said, the difficulties of *valuation* make that solution impossible.

So, instead, the tax law adopts a set of assumptions about depreciation for assets, including vehicles, machinery, and real estate. In particular, Code Section 168 provides formulas for deducting a percentage of the value of different assets over time. For example, Section 168 provides that nonresidential real property (*e.g.*, an office building) is depreciable over 39 years using the straight-line method. Translating from the original tax jargon, that means that the office building's owner can deduct 1/39th of the basis of the building every year for 39 years.

But please don't amend your tax returns to depreciate your personal car. Code Section 167 provides that depreciation is permissible only for property used in a business or property "held for the production of income," meaning investment activities. So you and I can't depreciate our cars, no matter how scratched and dented they are. But a flower shop, say, can depreciate its delivery van, which is used in its business. And the Hertz car rental company can depreciate its fleet of Fords, because it is in the business of renting cars.

If you think about it for a minute, Section 167's distinction between personal and business use makes good sense. We have seen, over and over, that the income tax must not permit taxpayers to deduct personal consumption. (*See*, particularly, Chapters 2 and 9.) Depreciation on your personal car is just that — personal consumption. It isn't fun, of course, to watch your car depreciate. And it really isn't fun to scrounge up the cash when it's time to replace a worn-out car. But what you are buying is personal transportation — the ability to drive to the movies or to the grocery store. And that isn't deductible.

Now, in general, the formulas in Code Section 168 operate pretty reliably to inform taxpayers how much depreciation to take. But every now and then, a taxpayer spots a legal ambiguity and takes advantage of it.

Consider the case of *Simon v. Commissioner*.[5] Richard and Fiona Simon were (and Fiona Simon still is) part of the New York Philharmonic violin section. To understand the tax case, you need to know a little bit more than you do (unless you are a string player) about violin bows.

The Simons paid $50,000 for two Tourte bows made in the early 19th century. Apparently, old bows sound better than new ones, and the Simons, as high-level classical musicians, needed the best sound possible. But bows, even great ones, wear out if they're heavily played, and the Simons' bows would eventually wear

[5] 68 F.3d 41 (2d Cir. 1995).

out.[6] Still, the Tourte bows had value as antiques even after they were no longer playable, and the Simons were likely to be able to resell the bows (after they had become unplayable by their standards) for $50,000 or even more.

The Simons were professional violinists, and so they depreciated their Tourte bows, just as a flower shop would depreciate its delivery van. But the IRS objected. Noticing that the Tourte bows actually increased in value (as antiques) over time, even after being played out, the IRS argued that the bows were not "property of a character subject to the allowance for depreciation" as required by Section 168 at that time.

The IRS position had some merit. Depreciation, after all, solves a *valuation* problem. The Section 168 formulas approximate (very roughly) the decline in the value of assets over time. The Simons' Tourte bows, unlike modern bows, did not lose value over time. Instead, the Tourte bows became more valuable. As of 1990, the two bows were appraised at a total of $80,000! So the Simons were not worse off each year due to the decline in value of their bows.

But the Second Circuit, like the Tax Court, ruled in favor of the Simons, holding (in effect) that Congress intended a rule of thumb and not an individualized inquiry. The Tourte bows, Judge Winter noted, did suffer "wear and tear" as they were played. And that was enough to satisfy the statutory criteria. No evidence of declining value was needed.

Table 10.2 Tax Deferral in Simon v. Commissioner

Year	Section 168 Deductions	Haig-Simons Income
1	($10,000)	$1,000
2	($10,000)	$1,000
3	($10,000)	$1,000
4	($10,000)	$1,000
5	($10,000)	$1,000
...		$1,000 per year
30	$80,000	$1,000
Total Income	$30,000	$30,000

The *Simon* court noted, too, that Code Section 168 was intended to avoid administrative determinations of value. The statute takes a formulaic approach precisely so that the IRS and taxpayers won't wrangle over how long assets last or how much they decline in value each year.

But if *Simon* is a victory for administrability, it illustrates well how out-of-whack the tax law can get when it declines to engage in *valuation*. The Simons were entitled to deduct $50,000 over a short period — for assets that were increasing in value. The result of this *valuation* error, as Table 10.2 shows, was to

6 If you really want to know quite a bit about how a bow becomes played out, have a look at the Tax Court opinion in *Simon*, 103 T.C. 247 (1994).

grant the Simons massive *tax deferral*: they reported big deductions in the first five years and would report a gain on the sale only much later when the bows were sold. (To make the numbers easy, the table assumes that the Simons took straight-line (proportional) depreciation; that the bows gained $1,000 of value per year; and that the Simons sold their bows in Year 30 for $80,000.)

¶1004 REAL WORLD TRANSACTIONS: BONUS DEPRECIATION AND THE GREAT RECESSION

The tax experts who advise the President and Congress are well aware of the possibility that *valuation* mistakes in the income tax can produce *tax deferral*. Indeed, policy makers often enact accelerated depreciation for the express purpose of creating *tax deferral* and encouraging businesses to buy more plant and equipment.

For instance, when the Great Recession hit in 2008, the President and Congress wanted to use the Tax Code to stimulate the economy. So they worked together to enact "bonus depreciation," which (until recently) offered *extra* depreciation in the first year equal to 50 percent of the cost of certain assets.[7]

> **EXAMPLE 7.** Marianne owned a grocery store. She wanted to update the store and buy new equipment, but the $500,000 price tag seemed daunting. Then her accountant told her about bonus depreciation. She could deduct $250,000 in the *first year*. At Marianne's 40% marginal tax rate, Uncle Sam was, in effect, handing her a check for $100,000. Now, that was a good deal!

Bonus depreciation was intended to get business owners like Marianne to take that step and invest in their businesses. Extra investment, the logic ran, would spur the economy, as Marianne and others like her hired new workers and sold more stuff.

But there has been some debate over whether bonus depreciation actually encourages *more* investment — or, instead, just rewards businesses that would have invested anyway. After all, some Mariannes out there were planning to spend the $500K anyway. They didn't need the $100,000 check from Uncle Sam to get them to invest. For them, the money was just a windfall — and costly to the Treasury.[8]

---

[7] Code Section 168(k).

[8] *See Extension of Bonus Depreciation*, Tax Policy Center, available at http://www.taxpolicycenter.org/taxtopics/conference_bonus_depreciation.cfm.

CHAPTER 11

Losses and the Interest Deduction

Introduction . . . ¶1100
The Interest Deduction . . . ¶1101
Tax Arbitrage and *Knetsch v. U.S.* . . . ¶1102
Hobby Losses, *Storey v. Commissioner,* and *Nickerson v. Commissioner* . . . ¶1103
Real-World Transactions: Wash Sales and Repos . . . ¶1104
Selective Loss Realization and *Fender v. United States* . . . ¶1105

¶1100 INTRODUCTION

By now, you've noticed that a host of deductions are necessary to measure *net income*. Not to be slighted are two special deductions: the interest deduction and the deduction for losses. Both follow the now-familiar pattern. The income tax must permit the deductions in order to measure net, not gross, income, but the catch is that the law often stumbles in determining the amount and timing of deductions.

¶1101 THE INTEREST DEDUCTION

Interest is what a borrower pays to a lender for the privilege of using the lender's money. You can think of borrowing as "renting" money. If you lend me $100, I am renting the money from you. I ultimately have to pay back the $100 and typically will have to pay you "rent" or interest as well. And, just like rent, interest is paid periodically and must be paid throughout the "rental" or borrowing term.

For income tax purposes, interest can be an expense of earning income. And so, in order to define *net income* correctly, the tax permits businesses and investors to deduct their interest expense.

EXAMPLE 1. Suppose that Apple Computer wants to build a new factory. The corporation borrows $20 million at an interest rate of 5%. Apple management knows that the loan will cost 5%—or $1 million—every year. That's the "rental fee" for using the bank's money for a year. When Apple calculates its profits for the year, it can deduct the $1 million under Code Section 163 as a cost of earning income.

That result should make intuitive sense: "renting" money is just as much a cost of doing business as is renting a storefront or paying workers. (Of course, the

$20 million loan itself is not income to Apple, and the $20 million repayment is not deductible. *See* Chapter 7, *supra*.)

By contrast, when individuals borrow to pay for personal consumption, the interest is not deductible. For instance, if you take a trip to Europe and charge the costs to your credit card, the interest you pay to the credit card company is not deductible.

Accordingly, Section 163(h) disallows any deduction for personal interest expense, with one major exception: home mortgage interest. Interest on home mortgages is generally deductible, with a few limitations. For instance, when a taxpayer takes out a mortgage to buy a home, interest is deductible only on the first $1 million of indebtedness.[1] So taxpayers who want to buy really, really big McMansions (or who want to buy more than a one-bedroom apartment in Manhattan) will have to plan to pay nondeductible interest to the extent their mortgage loans exceed $1 million.

¶1102 TAX ARBITRAGE AND *KNETSCH V. U.S.*

Even though the interest deduction is usually appropriate in order to measure *net income*, some taxpayers have figured out how to use the deduction to distort their income—in a downward direction, naturally. The basic technique is called tax arbitrage, and we will see that it can produce *tax deferral* or, in some cases, permanent tax reductions.

The simplest case of tax arbitrage involved taxpayers who borrowed to purchase tax-exempt bonds. (I say "involved," past tense, because Code Section 265(a)(2) now disallows this particular gambit).

EXAMPLE 2. Suppose that a tax-exempt bond sells for $1,000 and pays 10% interest (or $100 annually). (A "tax-exempt" bond is one that pays tax-exempt, or excludable, interest.) That's $100 tax-free every year. Good deal! But the deal gets even better if the taxpayer, Janis, borrows $1,000 to buy the bond—that way, she spends no out-of-pocket cash. Now, you will have spotted that Janis will have to pay interest on the loan, and that will reduce her profit on the bond. Indeed, suppose Janis must pay 10% interest on the loan. In this case, it would seem that Janis's deal is just a wash: if she makes 10% but must pay 10%, then she nets zero.

But here's the trick: *if* Janis can deduct the interest she pays on the loan, she will come out ahead thanks to tax arbitrage. Take a look at Table 11.1, which illustrates why. On a pre-tax basis, Janis takes in $100 and pays $100, leaving zero in her pocket. But because the interest income is tax-exempt, while the deduction is fully allowed, Janis is left with a $100 net tax deduction. If she's in the 40% bracket, she likely has plenty of other income to offset, and so that deduction is worth $40 to her.

---

[1] Code Section 163(h)(3)(b)(ii).

Table 11.1 Tax Arbitrage

	Financial position	Tax position
Income	100	0
Deduction	-100	-100
Net profit	0	-100

Put another way, Uncle Sam is prepared to hand Janis $40 for—doing next to nothing. All Janis has to do is (a) figure out what tax arbitrage is and (b) bear the transaction costs of buying the bond and borrowing the money.

This kind of easy tax arbitrage was once legal (ah! the good old days!), but Section 265(a)(2) closes the loophole by denying an interest deduction for interest paid on debt used to acquire tax-exempt bonds. Still, clever taxpayers have found ways to take advantage of tax arbitrage: the trick is always to distort net income by deducting interest payments while earning tax-exempt or tax-preferred income.

The most infamous case of tax arbitrage involved Karl Knetsch, who purchased what must have seemed a very sweet investment from the Sam Houston Life Insurance Company in 1953.[2] *Knetsch*, like many tax shelter cases, turns on the *substance over form* doctrine. To understand what Karl was purporting to do (but wasn't), it's useful to begin by asking what an annuity is and why people buy them.

An annuity is just a contract between an individual and an insurance company. The individual pays a price (called a "premium") of $X. In exchange, the insurance company promises to make annual payments (hence the term, "annuity") of $Y to the individual for a specified term of years. For instance, I might pay $1 million now to buy an annuity that will pay me $Y per year for twenty years.

Some annuities are deferred annuities: they do not pay out right away but instead begin paying $Y after a lapse of time. For instance, if I buy an annuity at age 50, I might elect to defer payments for 20 years, figuring I won't need the money till I retire. You can imagine, though, that the deferred feature increases the annual payment ($Y) that the taxpayer can receive for a given investment of $X upfront. It's as if you put $X into a bank account. If you leave the money in the account for a while, the interest will compound, and you'll have more to spend later on.

If any of this is confusing, here's a simpler way to see the big picture. An annuity is just an investment, pretty much like a bank account. The individual puts $X into her account, and she will be able to withdraw that amount plus interest. If she starts pulling out her money right away, she'll earn less interest overall than if she, say, keeps the money in the account for 20 years, earning interest, and then pulls out the money.

---

[2] Knetsch v. U.S., 364 U.S. 361 (1960).

A life annuity adds a valuable feature that bank accounts lack: the insurance company promises to continue to pay $Y per year for as long as the individual lives. *Ex ante*, the parties will expect that the total sum paid will return the original investment of $X plus interest. But the life annuity wraps a bet into the package: the life insurance company is betting that the individual will die early, while the individual is betting that she will live long.

So why would an ordinary person want an annuity? You might speculate that annuities are attractive because the interest rate is especially good, but, in fact, the interest rates on annuities is typically lower than the rate available in the marketplace on bank accounts and bonds. That fact suggests that there must be something especially valuable about annuities—something that individuals can't buy if they invest in bank accounts or bonds.

In fact, annuities have three valuable features. First, an annuity shifts reinvestment risk from the individual to the insurance company. The insurance company guarantees an interest rate over a long period, so that the individual will not risk having to reinvest her funds at a low return. Second, an annuity shifts longevity risk to the insurance company too. We usually think of long life as a good thing, but from a financial perspective it's not so great to live to be 100, because you may outlive your savings. An annuity ensures that an individual's money will last as long as she does.

The third valuable feature of annuities is that they produce *tax deferral*. Annuities are taxed under Code Section 72, which contains two favorable rules for annuities. One source of deferral is that annuity payments aren't taxed until the taxpayer receives them. That means that a taxpayer who buys, say, a 20-year deferred annuity does not pay tax until she starts receiving cash in year 20. By contrast, a taxpayer who invests in a bank account or a bond must pay tax every year even if she doesn't pull out any cash.

An extra source of *tax deferral* is that the Code calculates income on annuities using a taxpayer-favorable method. Intuitively, it should make sense that every payment of $Y is a mix of two items: (a) a return of basis and (b) interest income. Financially speaking, the stream of interest income to the taxpayer should be front-loaded, *i.e.*, higher in the early years than in the later years. That's how a bank account would work. But Section 72(b) defers income by treating every payment of $Y as comprising the same mix of return of basis and interest income.

(By this point, you might guess—and you'd be right—that the insurance lobby in Washington is powerful and effective. The plain language of the Code awards valuable *tax deferral* to annuities, and you can bet that life insurance companies charge hefty prices for these tax-favored assets.)

But in the *Knetsch* case, the taxpayer pushed the tax treatment of annuities a step too far. The transactions in *Knetsch* are complex, but it's worth parsing through what the parties did. I've modified the numbers so they're easier to follow. The two parties are Karl Knetsch and the Sam Houston Life Insurance Co, and you can think of the deal as involving three steps.

STEP ONE. Karl borrows $10 million from Sam Houston and uses the money to buy an "annuity bond" (really, just a life annuity). The annuity will start to pay out in 30 years, when Karl is 90.

STEP TWO. Karl's annuity carries a 2.5% interest rate, so it will earn $250,000 in the first year. But Karl's loan carries a higher 3.5% interest rate, so Karl will owe $350,000 to Sam Houston. This would be a bad deal for Karl if tax savings weren't involved: he'd be losing $100K every year!

STEP THREE. The point of the deal is tax arbitrage, which (as you'll remember) is the combination of tax-favored income with deductible interest. Here, the taxable income from the annuity for the first 30 years is zero (because no payments are being received). The interest deduction is $350,000, which is worth quite a bit at Karl's 80% marginal tax rate ($280,000 to be exact).

So the real "villain" in *Knetsch*, the provision that gives rise to the tax shelter, is tax arbitrage, which in turn reflects the tax-favored status of annuities in Section 72. When you first read the case, you might think that Karl and Sam Houston are playing games with nonrecourse debt. The fact that Karl borrows some of the interest payments due may also look fishy. But the nonrecourse debt serves a business function, ensuring that Sam Houston can never claim Knetsch's assets (other than the annuity itself) in repayment of the debt. And when Karl borrows additional amounts to pay his interest obligation, that's just a way of reducing his cash outlay—again, a business objective. All of the tax gain to Karl lies in tax arbitrage—the mismatch between the zero taxable income on the annuity and the fully deductible interest.

To see the point, imagine the counterfactual. If an annuity were taxed like a bank account, then in the first year, Karl would report $250,000 of income and a deduction of $350,000 for a net loss of $100,000. You might think that the $100K loss is a nice tax shelter, but no! It's just an accurate portrayal of Karl's real economic loss on the deal: he is paying $100,000 to Sam Houston every year. It would be irrational for Karl (or anyone) to pay $100K in order to deduct $100K: even at Knetsch's 80% marginal tax rate, he saves only $80K in taxes but is out of pocket $100K.

The Supreme Court nixed the intended tax effects of the deal by deeming it a sham. The majority pointed out that the deal had no purpose other than to secure tax deductions. Karl did not fit the profile of the typical annuity buyer: his annuity would have paid him either $90,000 per month starting at age 90 or (if he continued to borrow the maximum amount against the contract) $43 per month. Neither scenario fit the model of the middle-class person using an annuity to hedge against hard times if he lives too long.

The Court was surely right, in the sense that Knetsch wasn't in this for peace of mind. But the decision still marks an especially aggressive use of the *substance over form* doctrine. After all, the Congress intended to award *tax deferral* to annuity buyers. Karl and Sam Houston didn't concoct these tax benefits out of thin air: they were taking advantage of explicit tax benefits found in the Code. And the contracts between the parties were quite real in the sense that they were binding; you can bet that the parties would enforce the terms should either side default. So the Court's position that the deal was a sham amounts to the assertion, defensible but not obvious, that policy makers intended only to award tax benefits to sincere annuity buyers and not to those motivated by tax arbitrage.

¶1103 HOBBY LOSSES, *STOREY V. COMMISSIONER*, AND *NICKERSON V. COMMISSIONER*

The income tax, as we have seen, must permit taxpayers to deduct business costs in order to tax *net income*. At the same time, the income tax must not permit individuals to deduct the cost of personal consumption. These two mandates are often simple enough to accomplish. If a grocery store, for instance, spends money to pay cashiers and to advertise the weekly special on Diet Coke, there is no question that its expenditures are deductible.

But it can be surprisingly hard for the IRS to tell the difference between a bona fide business and a hobby. The so-called "hobby loss" cases involve a range of activities from horse breeding to truck racing to organic farming.[3] In every case, the taxpayer characterized his or her activities as a business, while the IRS charged that the taxpayer's purported "business" was nothing more than an expensive hobby.

The stakes in a hobby loss case are high for both sides. When a business loses money—that is, when deductions exceed income—the excess deductions ("losses") are fully deductible. But a hobby isn't a business at all: the Code treats net losses as nondeductible personal consumption.

> **EXAMPLE 3.** Suppose that Kaitlin, a law firm associate, is also a world-class runner who runs marathons. In a year, Kaitlin wins $20,000 in prizes but spends $35,000 on travel, training, equipment, and race fees. If her running is a business, she may deduct all her expenses and use her $15,000 in excess deductions to reduce taxes on the salary she earns as a lawyer. But if her running is a hobby, she may not deduct the $15,000 loss.

Code Section 183 provides that hobbyists may use their deductions to offset income from the hobby but that excess losses are not deductible. In the example, Kaitlin the runner can offset her $20,000 in prize money with up to $20,000 in running deductions. But she cannot use the additional $15,000 in deductions. At all. Ever.

---

[3] Morley v. Commissioner, 76 T.C.M. 363 (1998) (permitting deduction for dentist's Arabian horse breeding); Plunkett v. Commissioner, 47 T.C.M. 1439 (1984) (permitting some deductions and denying others and denying architect's deductions related to mud racing and truck pulling); Zdun v. Commissioner, 76 T.C.M. 278 (1998) (denying dentist's deductions related to apple orchard).

The tax treatment of hobbies may at first seem harsh, but consider the mischief that taxpayers could accomplish if hobby losses were deductible. Some people have quite expensive hobbies. Showing horses, for example, can cost hundreds of thousands of dollars. If hobby losses were deductible, then people with fancy hobbies would be better off than people with cheap ones. The horse-show crowd would enjoy tax-deductible consumption that, say, novel readers would not.

The problem, of course, is that one person's hobby is another person's business. There are hobbyists who show horses for fun—and professionals who show horses for profit. And probably nearly everyone who shows horses hopes to win prizes and maybe some money in recognition for their effort.

The now-familiar problem is one of *valuation*. Many businesses are enjoyable at least some of the time. (Chocolate shop, anyone? Maserati dealership?) And many hobbies involve hard work. (Have you ever shoveled out a horse's stall?) The law cannot readily observe the combination of business and personal value produced by a given expenditure. Indeed, it's probably impossible to draw any accurate distinction. So, instead, the law falls back on an all-or-nothing standard: every activity is either 100% business or 100% a hobby.

The legal standard is whether the taxpayer has an honest profit objective. When asked, of course, many hobbyists would say that they had a profit motive. But the law doesn't rely on the taxpayer's testimony. Instead, it looks to the facts and circumstances to determine whether a particular taxpayer conducted his affairs in a businesslike way.

The result is a body of law that is highly variable and seems to turn on whether or not the trial court likes and believes the taxpayer's version. Lee Storey's case provides a good example.[4]

Lee Storey was (and still is) a successful water-rights lawyer in Arizona. In the mid-2000s, she made a documentary film, "Smile Til' It Hurts: The Up With People Story," about the 1960s youth singing group, Up with People.[5] Lee spent countless hours on nights and weekends making the film, and she spent a considerable amount of money. She took film classes, hired experts, and marketed the film. The film earned impressive accolades but, like many documentaries, made virtually no money.

The trouble began when the IRS audited Lee's tax return and disallowed the deductions she had taken for film production costs, ruling them nondeductible hobby losses under Code Section 183. The amounts of money at stake were stunning: the IRS asserted that Lee owed additional taxes totaling more than $250,000.

---

4 Storey v. Commissioner, T.C. Memo 2012-115 (2012).

5 The website for the film can be found at http://www.smiletilithurts.com/index.html.

Any hobby loss case turns on its facts, and the Tax Court in *Storey* consulted the nine-factor test prescribed by the regulations under Section 183.[6] The nine factors are:

(1) the manner in which the taxpayer carries on the activity,
(2) the expertise of the taxpayer or his advisors,
(3) the time and effort expended by the taxpayer in carrying on the activity,
(4) the expectation that assets used in the activity may appreciate in value,
(5) the success of the taxpayer in carrying on other similar or dissimilar activities,
(6) the taxpayer's history of income or losses with respect to the activity,
(7) the amount of occasional profits, if any, which are earned,
(8) the financial status of the taxpayer, and
(9) elements of personal pleasure or recreation.

Some of these factors militated against Lee's claim that filmmaking was a business. She had substantial income from her law practice, for instance, which under factor (8) suggests that a secondary activity may be a hobby. She clearly enjoyed making the film (factor (9)) and made very little money from it (factors (6) and (7)).

Nevertheless, the Tax Court ruled that Lee was engaged in a business, not a hobby, and therefore her expenses were entirely deductible. The court emphasized the businesslike manner in which Lee budgeted, planned, and marketed the film. The court found it persuasive that a film might lose money during a lengthy start-up period, and the opinion notes that the economic downturn in 2008 may have adversely affected the film's profitability. The Tax Court opinion also noted with approval that Lee took measures to learn about filmmaking and hired experts to help.

A dairy farm stood at the center of another hobby loss case, *Nickerson v. Commissioner*.[7] Melvin Nickerson had grown up on a farm but had made his career in advertising in Chicago. Still, when middle age rolled around, he and his wife, Naomi, thought they might someday want to return to the farming life, so they bought a run-down dairy farm in Wisconsin. Melvin drove the ten-hour round trip to the farm most weekends, although Naomi did not. He spent his time on the farm renovating the farmhouse and reviving an abandoned orchard.

Melvin and Naomi reported losses from the farm—about $10,000 per year in mid-1970s dollars (or about $40,000 today). The IRS challenged the losses, contending that the dairy farm was "not engaged in for profit" within the meaning of Code Section 183.

Just as in *Storey*, the courts relied on a multi-factor test. The Tax Court ruled against the Nickersons, finding that they did not operate the farm in a businesslike

---

[6] Regulations Section 1.183-2(b).

[7] 700 F. 2d 402 (7th Cir. 1983).

way and that it was not plausible that Melvin's weekend efforts could revive the "dilapidated" farm. But the Seventh Circuit overturned the Tax Court, an unusual move in such a fact-intensive inquiry. The Court of Appeals found it reasonable that the taxpayers had engaged in a gradual ramp-up of the farm and had incurred losses during a lengthy start-up period.

Nickerson, like *Storey*, illustrates just how thorny *valuation* can be in the hobby-loss context. Unable to look inside the taxpayers' hearts and minds to determine the mix of business value and personal value provided by a film or a farm, the courts are left to apply their own life experience to the facts. The Seventh Circuit bought the story that the Nickersons were "a family of modest means attempting to prepare for a stable financial future." Just as plausibly, however, a court might—as the Tax Court did—see the Nickersons as spending money on a hobby farm that might, someday, serve as a country house or retirement home.

Stepping back, what is notable about Section 183 is that it takes an individualized approach to the *valuation* problem inherent in hobby loss cases. Each taxpayer has the opportunity to prove that her individual situation is sufficiently businesslike to qualify for full deductibility. The result is that the tax system (and taxpayers) incur substantial litigation costs and run the risk of variable decisions by different triers of fact. By contrast, the law fends off *valuation* problems in other contexts with bright-line rules. Some items simply are never deductible, no matter how strong the facts of the individual case: recall the case of Sandra Pevsner, the Yves St. Laurent boutique manager denied a deduction for the cost of fancy dresses she never wore outside work, discussed in Chapter 9.

What makes hobby loss cases difficult is that hobbyists and professionals co-exist in many businesses. The law could conceivably adopt a bright-line rule that certain activities are never businesses, but the result would be to mismeasure the net income of professionals in those fields. Plenty of amateurs produce screenplays, for instance, but many professional writers do too, and we could say the same for showing horses, breeding dogs, and farming. The tax law seems to be stuck making individualized determinations, despite the administrative cost.

Still, Section 183 mitigates these costs a bit by adopting some taxpayer-favorable presumptions. Section 183(d) provides that if an activity produces net profits in three of five years, it is presumed to be engaged in for profit. And, giving a special hug to the horsey set, the Code permits horse racing, breeding, or showing to qualify if the activity is profitable in two years out of seven.

¶1104 REAL-WORLD TRANSACTIONS: WASH SALES AND REPOS

Investors in stocks and securities have to incorporate tax planning into their investment strategies. A tax benefit could increase the payoff to an investment, while a tax penalty could obliterate an expected profit.

Two common transactions in the securities markets are "wash sales" and "repos." Both involve a planned sale and purchase of securities, and they look similar the first time you encounter them. But they're very different in their financial attributes, and different tax rules apply.

> **EXAMPLE 4.** Jesse owns a diversified portfolio of stocks. Among the stocks in his portfolio is GE stock, which he bought for $100 per share two years ago. The GE stock is now worth only $70 per share. Jesse believes the price of GE will likely go up in the future, but he would like to claim his tax loss now. Accordingly, he sells the GE stock, realizing a deductible loss of $30 per share under Code Section 165 (which permits the deduction of losses realized in business or in investment activities). Ten seconds later, Jesse clicks the "buy" button on E-Trade and buys a new chunk of GE at the same price of $70 per share. When the dust clears, Jesse still has GE stock in his portfolio. But he has a valuable tax deduction of $30 and a lower tax basis in the stock of $70 per share.

Jesse's transaction is known as a "wash sale" because the sale of the GE stock is offset, or washed out, by the immediate repurchase of the stock. Technically, the stock he sold and the stock he bought are different shares with different identifying numbers. But in financial terms, his portfolio is unchanged. Jesse has cleverly managed to have his cake and eat it too: he realized a tax loss without having to alter his investment portfolio!

To combat wash sales, Congress enacted Code Section 1091, which disallows losses if the taxpayer purchases substantially identical property within 30 days of the wash sale. Jesse, for instance, would today run afoul of Section 1091. The Code would disallow his $30 per share loss and restore his basis to $100, preserving the loss for later *realization*.

A repurchase agreement, or repo, also features a purchase and sale, but the purpose and the financial impact of the transaction are very different.

> **EXAMPLE 5.** Big Brokerage ("BB") owns a large inventory of U.S. Treasury securities. To raise short-term capital, BB engages in repos or repurchase agreements. In a repo, BB sells a specified quantity of securities (say, with a face amount of $10 million) to a buyer, often an investment fund. The buyer pays, say, $10 million for the securities. BB and the buyer agree to reverse out the transaction in a few days: BB will contract to repurchase the securities at a slightly higher price, say, $10,010,000.

At first glance, a repo seems a lot like a wash sale, since it involves a sale and repurchase. BB, like Jesse in the example above, starts and ends with $10 million of Treasury securities in its portfolio. But a repo isn't aimed at selective loss *realization*. Indeed, BB may have built-in gains rather than losses.

Financially, a repo functions like a borrowing. From BB's perspective, it has received $10 million for a few days. Just as in the case of a loan, BB has to pay back the loan amount ($10 million) plus interest ($10,000). Here, the "interest" is just built into the contractual repurchase price. It follows that the "buyer" in a repo is really a lender. The buyer pays out cash of $10 million in order to earn $10,000 of interest (over a few days).

Seen in this light, repos may seem even more puzzling. Why go through all this rigamarole of "sales" and "repurchases"? Why not call the deal what it is—a loan? The answer is that the repo form is easy and standard, and it offers the buyer/lender excellent collateral for the loan. The repo contract, after all, provides that the buyer can keep the Treasury securities if BB fails to pay the $10,010,000 repurchase price.

The repo market is large and deep, and financial institutions are often active participants, using the market to gain access to short-term credit and to make short-term investments.[8]

Tax-wise, you might suppose that repos are taxed like purchases and sales of securities. Under Code Section 1001, the seller would recognize gain or loss on the initial sale, and the buyer would recognize gain (in our example, $10,000) in the repurchase.

But no! In fact, the IRS has used the *substance over form* doctrine to tax repos as what they really are—short-term loans. The tax law doesn't treat a repo as a *realization* event for BB (unless BB defaults on the loan and the buyer keeps the securities as collateral). Instead, the tax law treats BB as having borrowed $10 million. The $10,000 in interest is deductible to BB and includible by the "buyer."[9]

¶1105 SELECTIVE LOSS REALIZATION AND *FENDER V. UNITED STATES*

The Code permits taxpayers to deduct losses, as long as they are realized in the context of a business or an investment activity. (*See* Code Section 165.) This rule makes eminent good sense. As we've seen, the income tax seeks to tax *net income*, and losses are simply another kind of, well, business or investment expense—a cost of doing business, really.

> **EXAMPLE 6.** Cassandra owns an art gallery. She buys and sells paintings with the objective of making a profit. Sometimes she picks a winner: she recently sold a minor Picasso sketch for a $1 million gain. But other times, she isn't so lucky. Just last month, she lost $300,000 when she bought a painting that turned out to be a fake. But, hey, it happens! Putting these two transactions together, Cassandra's *net income* is $700,000. That's her net profit or, equivalently, her Haig-Simons income.

---

[8] *See* Adam Copeland *et al.*, *Lifting the Veil on the U.S. Bilateral Repo Market*, Liberty Street Economics, Federal Reserve Bank of New York, July 9, 2014, available at http://libertystreeteconomics.newyorkfed.org/2014/07/lifting-the-veil-on-the-us-bilateral-repo-market.html#.VWzLwzc_4ul.

[9] For a discussion of the relevant legal authorities (and an argument that these authorities may be incorrect for some modern repos), *see* William W. Chip, *Are Repos Really Loans?*, Tax Notes, May 13, 2002, available at https://www.cov.com/~/media/files/corporate/publications/2002/05/are-repos-really-loans.ashx.

But you won't be shocked to learn that taxpayers have managed to manipulate even these simple rules to their advantage, using the *realization* requirement. As we saw in Chapters 5 and 6, the *realization* doctrine is a mixed blessing. It sidesteps the *valuation* problem of assigning a market value to taxpayers' assets every year—a big plus. But the *realization* requirement makes it easy for taxpayers to understate their income and achieve *tax deferral*. Policy makers have taken steps to limit *realization* games, but we will see that there is still plenty of room for taxpayers to turn *realization* to their advantage using the Section 165 loss deduction.

One of the easiest routes to *tax deferral* is selective loss *realization*. A taxpayer who has both gains and losses on investments can choose to sell the losers and hold onto the winners. The result is that the taxpayer can use the tax deduction for losses to offset other income now. She can hold off realizing the gains until much later.

> **EXAMPLE 7.** Daniel has a large portfolio of corporate stocks that he has purchased over time. At the end of the taxable year, he has unrealized gains of $10,000 and unrealized losses of $8,000. On a mark-to-market basis, Daniel has made a profit of $2,000. He's doing pretty well! But if he sells only the loss stocks, he will look to Uncle Sam as if he has lost $8,000. He can use that loss to offset other income now.[10] Daniel can hold onto his gains and realize them only later. (If he holds on long enough, he can avoid taxation entirely thanks to the Code Section 1014 basis step-up.) The result is *tax deferral,* homemade and cheap.

This kind of selective loss *realization* is entirely legal. But some taxpayers want more: they would like to claim their tax losses while holding onto their investments. The result is a transaction known as a "wash sale," because it involves transactions that cancel each other out—they produce a wash.

The previous section in this chapter discusses wash sales in detail, but here's a quick refresher. In its simplest form, a wash sale involves selling an asset and buying it back immediately. In our example, Daniel would sell his loss stocks and buy them back immediately in order to claim his loss now while keeping them in his portfolio. Going forward, his basis would be lower, but that's the essence of *tax deferral*: Daniel prefers to claim a deductible tax loss now even if he'll have higher gains (due to her lower basis) later on.

Today, Code Section 1091 limits wash sales by denying a loss deduction if the taxpayer sells and repurchases "substantially identical stock or securities" within 30 days. So, in our example above, the Code would deny Daniel's claimed loss. In effect, Section 1091 overrides Section 165. To claim the loss, Daniel would have to keep the losing stocks out of his portfolio for 30 days. The catch, of course, is that the price of the stock might rise in the meantime, and he would miss out on the upside.

---

[10] He should, however, take note of the capital loss limitations discussed in Chapter 13 at ¶1302.

The lure of wash sales is so powerful that taxpayers have attempted to engineer around the Section 1091 rules. In *Fender v. United States,* [11] the IRS attacked a sale and repurchase of bonds arranged by Harris Fender, described by the court as "an experienced investment banker." Simplifying the facts a bit, a trust for Harris's sons had invested $500,000 in bonds. The bonds had declined in value to $300,000 but could not be easily sold, because they were unrated. Harris Fender finally managed to sell the bonds to the Longview Bank, which paid $300,000 for them.

Now comes the fishy part. At the time of the sale, Harris just happened to hold a 40% ownership stake in the Longview Bank. A couple of weeks later, Harris increased his stake in the bank to 51%. Forty-two days after buying the bonds, the Longview Bank sold them back to the Fender trusts for $300,000 plus 42 days' interest.

The trusts reported a $200,000 loss on the sale of the bonds, but the IRS disallowed the loss as not a "bona fide" loss under Section 165. The Fifth Circuit agreed with the IRS. Harris's relationship with the Longview Bank suggested that the purported sale was really just a favor by the bank. Most damning was the testimony of the bank's president, Norman Taylor, who testified that he understood that the transaction was an accommodation to Harris Fender and that the trusts would repurchase the bonds within 90 days. Props to Norman for honesty!

The takeaway is that Harris was too clever by half. He must have been aware of the wash sale rules of Section 1091, and he probably believed that waiting 42 days would be sufficient. He surely knew about the related-party loss disallowance rules of Section 267, which disallow losses on sales between individuals and corporations, but only if the individual owns more than 50% of the stock. Those rules, too, technically did not apply, since Harris made sure that the sale took place when he owned only 40% of the stock.

But Harris's careful plan foundered when the court applied the *substance over form* doctrine. He had successfully avoided the literal terms of Section 1091 and Section 267. But the prearranged nature of the sale and repurchase led the IRS—and a federal appeals court—to perceive the transaction as artificial.

Expert opinions are mixed on whether Fender is a welcome antidote to taxpayer opportunism or an overly aggressive use of the *substance over form* doctrine. Harris Fender certainly steered his transactions around the rules on wash sales and related-party sales in order to achieve *tax deferral.* Still, it's worth noting that Congress chose to address selective loss *realization* with bright-line rules rather than broad standards. If it is reasonable for taxpayers to rely on bright lines, then the court's approach in *Fender* defeats taxpayers' legitimate expectations about the boundaries of the law.

---

[11] 577 F.2d 934 (5th Cir. 1978).

CHAPTER 12

Whose Income Is It?

Introduction . . . . ¶1200
Marriage and *Druker v. Commissioner* . . . . ¶1201
Real-World Transaction: Dividing Property and Income at Divorce . . . . ¶1202
Assignments of Earned Income: *Lucas v. Earl* . . . . ¶1203
Assignments of Income Using Entities . . . . ¶1204
Assignments of Income from Property:
Blair v. Commissioner and *Helvering v. Horst* . . . . ¶1205

¶1200 INTRODUCTION

To this point, we've focused mostly on the taxation of individuals and businesses. We haven't taken notice of a major social fact: the existence of families. Families take a variety of forms: some people are married, while others cohabit, have roommates or live alone. Some people have children or care for elderly parents. And so on.

The variety of family forms poses a dilemma for the tax law. On the one hand, it is difficult for the law to determine relationships among individuals. It would probably be undesirable (not to mention creepy) if the IRS were to try to sort out the degree of commitment in our various relationships. Not to mention that the legal recognition of family relationships raises deep questions of social justice. The law's definition of marriage, for instance, has been sharply contested over time.[1]

On the other hand, the tax law probably cannot carry out its mission of taxing income if it ignores relationships entirely. Family life can increase—or reduce—the resources at our command. A married couple, for instance, may share a dual income, improving the well-being of both. A parent of young children will find that she has far less disposable income than her childless peers.

In this chapter, we will focus on a core problem of family taxation: *income shifting*, one of our six key concepts. *Income shifting* arises when an individual shares resources with another person, but the law treats the two as separate taxpayers. When family members have different tax rates, it is often easy to shift income to the lower-bracket party. The result is that the family as a unit pays less in total tax—and has more money to spend, at the Treasury's expense.

[1] *See, e.g.*, Obergefell v. Hodges, 576 U.S. __ (June 26, 2015).

Suppose, for example, that you have a two-year-old daughter. The chances are pretty good that she's totally dependent on you. She probably has no income of her own, and the two of you probably share a home, food, transportation, and so on. But if the tax law ignored her age (and your relationship) and treated your two-year-old as a separate taxpayer, she would have a zero marginal tax rate because of her low income.

In that situation, you might be very tempted to shift some income to your daughter to take advantage of that zero marginal tax rate. If you are otherwise in, say, the 40% bracket, you and your daughter (as a family) would gain 40 cents in tax savings for every dollar you shift her way.[2] And, of course, you can shift income without losing control: your two-year-old will spend "her" money in whatever way you direct!

You can think of *income shifting* as moving money from one pocket of your coat to another. You don't much care, since you'll probably spend the money the same way no matter where it is. But if the government taxes the two pockets differently, you'll have a clear reason to shift cash from one pocket to the other.

In fact, the tax law does, somewhat bizarrely, treat your two-year-old daughter as a separate taxpayer. But, since 1986, the law has prevented *income shifting* to young children via the so-called "kiddie tax" in Code Section 1(g). The "kiddie tax" prevents parents from shifting investment income to their kids by taxing children's unearned income at the parents' marginal tax rate. In our example, the two-year-old's income would be taxed at 40%, and so there would be no financial payoff to shifting income to her.

But the kiddie tax addresses only one type of *income shifting*. We shall see that the problem of *income shifting* has motivated a variety of legal doctrines—and that the law has left open many legal opportunities for tax planners to take advantage of *income shifting*.

¶1201 MARRIAGE AND *DRUKER V. COMMISSIONER*

The tax rules for married couples illustrate the centrality of *income shifting* to the taxation of the family. The income tax has tried a variety of different approaches, ranging from ignoring marriage entirely to taxing married and single people very differently. Every change in legal regime has been driven by the perceived need to respond to opportunities for *income shifting*.

In its early years, between 1913 and 1948, the income tax did not tax married individuals differently from single ones. Everyone paid tax based on his or her own income, and so everyone had his (or her) own marginal tax rate. But in that era, many wives did not work outside the home and did not own property. And so most married couples faced a financial incentive to shift income from husband to wife.

[2] You can't, of course, shift all your income to her, because then she'd be in the 40% bracket! But you could shift enough income to her to take advantage of her lower initial tax rate.

At that time, *income shifting* was simple and entirely legal: if the husband transferred title to investment property to his wife, she would be the owner for tax purposes, and the income generated by the assets would be taxed at her (lower) marginal rate. To be sure, some couples weren't willing to shift title to assets to the wife. But the well-advised taxpayer could consult a lawyer and make clever use of trusts and other devices.

The existence of community property law compounded the tax inequities of that period. A few words of background will clarify the issue. Generally speaking, states have two kinds of systems for determining the property rights of married couples. In common-law states, ownership follows title. So if stocks or bonds, for instance, are registered in the husband's name, he is the owner, and any dividends and interest are taxed to him. In community property states, by contrast, the law treats all income earned (and property acquired) during a marriage as owned jointly by husband and wife. The Supreme Court in *Poe v. Seaborn*[3] ruled that community property law accomplished a kind of automatic income shift for couples in those states. Husbands and wives, the court ruled, could split community income 50-50 for tax purposes.

As you can imagine, married residents of community property states rejoiced at the opportunity for tax reduction through *income shifting*, while residents of common-law states fumed. The tax distinction was politically untenable, and, in 1948, the Congress acted. Before 1948, married and single tax filers faced the same tax rate schedule. But beginning in 1948, the tax brackets for married couples were set at twice the level of tax brackets for single filers, and the "marriage bonus" was born! The new tax schedule, in effect, permitted married couples in all 50 states to split their incomes and reduce their taxes.

By the late 1960s, though, social change was in the air, and single people had begun to vent their own resentment at the preferential tax treatment of married couples. With marginal tax brackets as high as 70%,[4] a single man (or woman) in that period could face a much higher tax bill than his (or her) married counterpart.

So, in 1969, Congress acted again, this time to mitigate the tax disadvantage for single people. The new law adjusted the rate schedule so that some married people now faced a marriage penalty—that is, their taxes (as a couple) rose when they marry. Other married couples still received a marriage bonus.

The 1969 marriage penalty created a new aggrieved class of two-earner couples. In the mid-1970s, one such couple, James and Joan Druker, challenged the marriage penalty as unconstitutional under the Equal Protection Clause of the 14th amendment to the U.S. Constitution.[5] The Drukers were married but filed their 1975 and 1976 tax returns as "unmarried."

---

[3] 282 U.S. 101 (1930).

[4] *See* http://www.cch.com/wbot2013/029IncomeTaxRates.asp.

[5] Druker v. Commissioner, 697 F.2d 46 (2d Cir. 1982).

Writing for the Second Circuit, Judge Friendly ruled against the Drukers. Marriage, he agreed, is a fundamental right protected by the Constitution, but the marriage penalty doesn't prevent people from marrying—it just increases the financial cost of marriage. Moreover, the judge noted, the marriage penalty doesn't reflect any congressional animus against the married state. Rather, it reflects the so-called "trilemma," or the impossibility of designing a policy that (1) imposes progressive marginal tax rates, (2) imposes equal taxes on equal-earning married couples, and (3) has no marriage penalty or bonus. Mathematically, Judge Friendly correctly realized, something had to give. Here's why:

> **EXAMPLE 1.** Suppose that Alice and Burt earn $10,000 each, while Charles earns $20,000 and Dan earns $0. In a progressive tax system, C should pay more than A (or B) does. But here's the rub: if Alice and Burt marry, and Charles and Dan marry, the two *couples* will each have $20,000 in income. If the two couples are to pay equal taxes on their equal incomes, then either A and B will have to pay higher taxes (a marriage penalty) or C will have to pay lower taxes (a marriage bonus). Or both.

Continuing the example, there are only two ways to avoid a marriage penalty. One would be to ignore marriage completely. If A, B, C, and D were taxed the same way whether married or single, marriage would be a non-event (tax-wise). But, as we have seen, that approach invites *income shifting*.

The only other solution is to do away with progressive marginal tax rates. A perfectly flat tax would ensure that everyone paid, say, 25% of income in taxes, whether married or single. But a flat tax would raise tax rates on low-income people and so faces obvious fairness objections.

Today, the uneasy compromise continues: the federal income tax imposes marriage penalties on some couples and awards marriage bonuses to others. Taking the long view, we can see that the congressional aversion to *income shifting* continues to rule the day. Taxing married couples as a unit has the downside of producing marriage bonuses and penalties. But it prevents husbands and wives from cutting their taxes by shifting income between spouses.

¶1202 REAL-WORLD TRANSACTION: DIVIDING PROPERTY AND INCOME AT DIVORCE

As if divorce weren't already a stressful event, the tax law ups the stakes. The rules governing transfers of property and income at divorce set traps for the unwary but offer a prize to the well-advised—the legal opportunity to reduce taxes via *income shifting*.

Family law may require divorcing couples to make three kinds of financial transfers. Property settlements involve the division of marital property. Alimony (sometimes called spousal support) is paid by one former spouse to the other, usually for a limited period as the parties adjust to earning their own way in the marketplace. And child support is paid by one parent to the other, usually until a child is 18 or 21.

Three income tax rules govern these transfers. First, Section 1041 governs the transfer of property between spouses (and former spouses as part of a divorce settlement), creating a carryover basis regime that is similar to Section 1015 (gifts), except that a divorcing couple can transfer losses as well as gains. (By contrast, ordinary gifts can shift gains but not losses, as Chapter 3 discusses.) Second, Section 71 provides that alimony (spousal support) is deductible by the payor and includable in the income of the recipient. Third, Section 71 carves out child support from the deduction/inclusion regime. Instead, child support is not deductible to the payor and not includable to the recipient.

Taken together, these rules make tax planning very salient to divorce. A well-advised couple can use the rules to shift income to their mutual advantage, and it's all perfectly legal. But without good tax advice, a divorcing couple can fall into a tax trap.

To illustrate the potential for tax savings via *income shifting*, begin with Section 1041. As we saw in Chapter 3's discussion of gifts, a carryover basis regime can shift income from the transferor to the recipient, and Section 1041 (unlike Section 1015) permits loss-shifting as well.

EXAMPLE 2. Erin owns Apple stock with a basis of $2,000 and a fair market value of $10,000. She also owns Microsoft stock with a basis of $15,000 and a fair market value of $10,000. In other words, Erin has appreciated and depreciated stock in her portfolio.

A naïve division of Erin's property would look only at fair market values. Both the Apple stock and the Microsoft stock are worth $10,000, and so if the parties intend to sell the stock (or consider the two to be equivalent investments), they might be indifferent about who takes which stock. But that naïve approach would be a mistake, because it ignores the tax features of each stock. The Apple stock has a built-in gain of $8,000, while the Microsoft stock has a built-in loss of $5,000.

A more sophisticated approach to tax planning would shift the taxable gain and loss to the party that places the highest value on each. The gain, obviously enough, should go to the lower-bracket party. The loss, by contrast, is of greatest value to the higher-bracket party.

So, in our example, Erin and her soon-to-be ex-spouse should compare their marginal tax rates. To see the opportunity, suppose that, after the divorce, Erin will be in the 40% bracket, while her spouse will be in the 0% bracket. If the spouse takes the Apple stock, he (or she) can sell the stock and pocket all $10,000, since the tax on the gain will be zero. If Erin takes the Microsoft stock, she can pocket $10,000 and make use of the $5,000 loss, which is worth $2,000 to her (at her 40% marginal tax rate).

Under this scenario, the parties walk away with $22,000 between them, after taxes. By contrast, if Erin takes the Apple stock and her spouse takes the Microsoft, $3,200, or 40% of her $8,000 gain, they would have only $16,800 after taxes. Erin would owe the Treasury. Erin's spouse would net $10,000, but the loss would go unused. In total, the two would pocket only $16,800, much less.

In this sense, *income shifting* can be a win-win game. If the parties understand that they can split $22,000 rather than $16,800, then they can divide up assets so that everyone benefits. (In this case, the tax plan requires that Erin take all the Microsoft stock and the spouse take all the Apple stock. But they likely have tax-neutral assets (like a bank account) that could be used to offer a little extra money to Erin's spouse to even up the division of assets.)

The tax rules on alimony and child support also permit *income shifting* between divorced spouses, although taking advantage of the income shift takes some planning and may require compromises. The key is Section 71, which defines alimony in subsections (b) and (c). Among other things, alimony (for tax purposes) must cease at the death of the recipient spouse and must not constitute child support.

These rules offer two opportunities for *income shifting*. The first is an election found in the statute itself: parties that prefer to have alimony made nondeductible (and nonincludable) can do so under Section 71(b)(1)(B). This treatment might be advantageous if the payor has a lower marginal tax rate than the payee. That's an unusual situation, to be sure, since the richer spouse usually pays alimony and has a higher marginal tax rate. But perhaps the richer spouse has business losses or other deductions that leave her in a low tax bracket.

In the more typical case, the payor has a higher marginal tax rate. In that scenario, alimony is tax-favored relative to child support, because the income will be deducted at the payor's high rate and included at the recipient's low rate. The tax planner's trick here—and it may involve some compromises by the parties—is to maximize alimony and minimize child support. If the parties agree, they can both benefit from having more after-tax income to split between them.

For instance, continuing the example of Erin, it would be most tax-advantageous for the parties if payments by Erin to her ex-spouse are considered alimony for tax purposes. The alimony deduction is worth quite a bit to Erin in the 40% bracket, while the inclusion will not be costly to Erin's ex-spouse (who, by hypothesis, will still be in the 0% bracket after including the alimony).

Of course, the parties may not be willing to jump through the statutory hoops, which include a requirement that alimony must cease at the death of the recipient and that alimony must not cease at a time related to a child's attaining a certain age, marrying, dying, or leaving school.[6]

But tax planning at divorce needn't take an all-or-nothing form. In most cases, it is possible to create a mix of alimony and child support that meets the parties' needs. The critical point to understand is that both parties can benefit

---

[6] Code Section 71(c)(2).

from *income shifting*, because it minimizes the total tax bill and maximizes the pool of after-tax funds available to split.

The downside, of course, is that the tax rules on alimony and child support, like the tax rules on property settlement, can disadvantage unsophisticated parties. A divorcing spouse who bargained for, say, $50,000 per year in alimony, will find that she has much less after paying taxes due. The big lesson then is: don't let your friends or clients get divorced without thinking through the tax angle.

¶1203 ASSIGNMENTS OF EARNED INCOME: *LUCAS V. EARL*

Income shifting within the family is so attractive as a tax strategy that taxpayers have pushed the boundaries of the law again and again. The courts have responded with a doctrine known as the "assignments of income" rules. These decisions, taken together, permit *income shifting* if taxpayers are willing (and able) to part with a sufficient ownership interest.

The leading case on earned income, *Lucas v. Earl*, takes a hard line against the shifting of earned income within the family.[7] Guy and Ella Earl, wealthy Californians, had entered into a contract that treated all income and property as jointly owned. The Earls took the position that the contract should control the allocation of their income for tax purposes, with the result that Guy and Ella should each be taxed on half of Guy's earnings as a lawyer.

The tax years at issue in the case were 1920 and 1921. Recall that during this period, married couples were taxed as separate individuals and that income-splitting (having each spouse taxed on half of total income) would minimize the couple's total tax bill. The Earls thought they had attained a kind of tax nirvana.

The IRS, you will not be shocked to learn, disagreed. The government treated the contract as valid under California law but asserted that Guy should still be taxed on 100% of his earnings.

The Earls' argument for income-splitting had considerable force. The income tax, as you know, seeks to tax people on the resources they have at their command. The Earls' contract irrevocably gave half of Guy's income to Ella. Typically, the tax law respects contractual allocations. For instance, if you and a classmate go into partnership together and agree to split your income 50-50, then you'll each be taxed on half your income—no matter who brings in the clients!

But the Supreme Court simply didn't buy that the husband-wife contract should be treated like a business partnership. The Court ruled for the IRS, treating the Earls' contract as an invalid assignment of income. Justice Holmes's short opinion is conclusory: he reads the income tax as seeking to tax salaries "to those who earned them" and not to respect "anticipatory arrangements and contracts" that attempt to shift income away from the earner. Guy earned the salary by working as a lawyer; therefore, under Holmes's rationale, he must be taxed on it.

---

[7] 281 U.S. 111 (1930).

Holmes's analysis suggests why a business partnership can split earnings for tax purposes, but a husband-wife contract cannot. In a business partnership, the partners are making an arm's length agreement to engage in a joint venture. Presumably, both partners will work to bring in business, and both are willing to take the chance that, in any given year, one partner will be more successful than the other. If, over time, one partner consistently does better at bringing in business, you'd expect arm's length parties to readjust their deal. By contrast, the husband-wife contract is a nonmarket arrangement within the family. There was no expectation that Ella would work (although she apparently had property income), and the parties certainly did not have adverse economic interests.

The most unfortunate part of the *Earl* opinion is Holmes's fruit-and-tree metaphor: he writes that "no distinction can be taken according to the motives leading to the arrangement by which the fruits are attributed to a different tree from that on which they grew." We shall see that sorting out the "fruit" from the "trees" in later cases posed a puzzle for several judges.

Still, the opinion in *Earl* seems forceful enough to prevent the shifting of earned income. If earnings must be taxed to the earner, then it would seem impossible to shift salary from one family member to another. And, in fact, the courts have held this line. In *Armantrout v. Commissioner*,[8] for example, the Seventh Circuit included in a father's income a tuition benefit granted to his children by his employer. The court rejected the father's argument that the children should be taxed because they received the money. Instead, the court treated the scholarship like any other fringe benefit—as part of the father's salary.

But it would be over-reading *Earl* to conclude that the shifting of earned income is never possible, as we shall now see.

¶1204 ASSIGNMENTS OF INCOME USING ENTITIES

Wholly-owned corporations have, historically, proved an attractive vehicle for *income shifting*. Unlike family members, corporations have no mind of their own: if you're the sole shareholder, the corporation has to do as you say. When a corporation also has a lower marginal tax rate, it can make tax sense to shift income to the corporation.

Under today's tax rates, the strategy of shifting income to domestic (that is, United States) corporations rarely makes sense. As of 2014, the top individual rate is about 40%, while the top corporate rate is 35%. A casual glance might suggest that people should shift lots of income to corporations to capture that 5% rate differential. But keep in mind that corporate income is taxed twice: once at the corporate rate and once at the shareholder's dividend rate. Congress has set the tax rate on dividends at a fairly low level (by historical standards): most dividends from domestic corporations are taxed at a maximum rate of 20%. But,

8 570 F. 2d 210 (7th Cir. 1978).

even so, it makes little sense to shift income to a U.S. corporation right now: if the corporation earns $100, it will pay tax of $35, leaving $65 to distribute. Once the (40% bracket) shareholder pays tax on that amount, she'll have only $52 left—less than if she earned the $100 directly and kept $60 after taxes.

But in past years, the corporate tax rate was low enough, compared to the individual tax rate, to make *income shifting* to domestic corporations worthwhile. It was even more attractive to shift income to *foreign* corporations with a very low or zero tax rate.

For instance, in *Johnson v. Commissioner*,[9] a professional basketball player, Charles Johnson, sought to shift income to his wholly-owned foreign corporation. Simplifying a bit, Johnson formed a Panama corporation and executed a contract that assigned to the corporation all his earnings from basketball. Under the contract, the Panama corporation would pay Johnson a modest salary of $18,000 per year) and would retain the rest of his earnings as profit.

Johnson's tax plan, and other arrangements like it, attempted to shift income to an entity taxed at a lower rate. If successful, Johnson could defer U.S. taxes until he withdrew the money years later.

The IRS, however, took a dim view of the arrangement and challenged it under *Lucas v. Earl*.[10] The Service argued that Johnson, and not the corporation, was the true earner of the income. Thus, under *Earl*, all of the basketball earnings should be taxed directly to Johnson rather than to the Panama corporation.

The court in *Johnson* spotted the hitch in the IRS argument. Corporations (and other entities) don't really perform services: only human beings do. Even a household name like Apple Computer doesn't act in the world directly: Apple Computer is just a pile of legal documents. Instead, it is the employees of Apple that create, make, and sell computers, iPads and iPhones. Taking *Lucas v. Earl* literally, the tax law would have to attribute all of Apple's earnings to its employees!

The problem of *income shifting* thus poses a special puzzle in the case of entities. The law surely wants people to make use of entities to pool capital, labor and risk, and so the law ought to recognize the entity's existence. At the same time, the law dislikes the shifting of income by individuals to corporate alter egos as a tax dodge.

The *Johnson* court might have responded by looking through to substance and disregarding form. It was pretty clear, after all, that Johnson had no reason to have a Panama entity—other than to reduce his taxes. But the *Johnson* court declined to invoke the *substance over form* doctrine. Instead, it ruled for the IRS on purely formal grounds. Johnson's employer, the Golden State Warriors, had refused to contract directly with the Panama corporation. Instead, the team insisted on remaining in contractual privity with Charles Johnson, who then assigned his rights to the corporation. That lack of privity, the court held,

---

9 78 T.C. 882 (1982).

10 Lucas v. Earl, 281 U.S. 111 (1930).

precluded the shifting of income to the corporation. Johnson was the "tree," the court found—not because he was the one playing basketball, but because he was the one who formally signed the contract with the Warriors.

Although Johnson marks an IRS victory, it provides a roadmap for successful *income shifting* using entities. As long as taxpayers get the formalities right, they can shift income. Thus, Charles Laughton, the actor, was able to shift income to an alter-ego corporation, because the corporation was in privity with the film studios who sought Laughton's services.[11]

¶1205 ASSIGNMENTS OF INCOME FROM PROPERTY: *BLAIR V. COMMISSIONER* AND *HELVERING V. HORST*

Cases like *Earl* and *Johnson* involve earned income, which is what most taxpayers have. But the super-rich (and even the comfortably rich) also have property income. The income tax law permits widespread *income shifting* for property income, provided that the taxpayer follows the rules.

There are two key differences between earnings of human beings and earnings from property. First, humans are mortal, and their earnings die with them. Thus, the tax law can tax the earner during his or her lifetime, and the problem of shifting earned income, well, exits this world with the earner. But property outlasts human lives. At the owner's death, if not before, the income from property must shift to someone. Second, the law recognizes human beings and property as separate, meaning that I can transfer my property to you if I choose to do so. But the law does not permit transfers of earning power or "human capital": I cannot irrevocably sell my earning power to you. (An employment contract purchases certain services and may entitle the holder to damages if the employee fails to perform, but we do not think of the contract holder as the "owner" of the person's earning power, and the law will not grant specific performance.)

So the tax law simply must provide for the shifting of property income. The basic rule is that property income shifts with ownership of the property. Suppose, for instance, that you own a $1,000 bond paying 10% interest. If you give that bond to your daughter, then she (and not you) will be taxed on the interest income from the bond after the date of the gift. Simple enough. But harder questions arise when property owners give a lesser property interest than the simple transfer in our example.

One hard case arose in *Blair v. Commissioner*.[12] Edward Blair was the life tenant of a trust established by his father. As the holder of a life interest, Edward was entitled to any income produced by the property in the trust, and he would receive the income for as long as he lived. But Edward could not direct the investment of the property (called the "corpus" of the trust by trusts and estates lawyers),

---

[11] Laughton v. Commissioner, 40 B.T.A. 101 (1939).

[12] 300 U.S. 5 (1937).

and he could not dispose of the property and spend the proceeds. Someone else (called the "remainderman") would receive the corpus after Edward's death.

At some point, Edward decided to give his kids some money. Surely acting on the advice of counsel, he didn't just pull out his wallet and fork over some cash. Instead, he signed an instrument directing the trustee of the trust to pay $9,000 per year to Edward's kids for the entire term of his interest. That is, as long as Edward lived, that portion of his trust income would be paid directly to his kids. Edward did not report the $9,000 on his income tax return: he took the position that the kids (and not he) should be taxed on that sum.

We can surmise that Edward's kids were in a lower tax bracket than he was, because the IRS challenged this arrangement. The IRS argued that the assignment of income was ineffective. Citing *Lucas v. Earl*,[13] the Service argued that the income belonged to Edward and that he could not shift his tax liability by contract.

The Supreme Court disagreed and ruled for Edward. The court distinguished *Earl* on the ground that earned income is different than income from property: "The tax here is not upon earnings." But the Court declined to explain why (and how) the difference between earnings and property should matter. The opinion did state that, "There is here no question of evasion." But that is, er, less than helpful, because the Blairs were surely evading taxes in exactly the same way the Earls were—by *shifting income*.

On a first read, *Blair* seems logical enough. The assignment, made by contract, seems to resemble a property interest, and indeed, the Court concludes, "The interest was present property alienable like any other.... The beneficiary may thus transfer a part of his interest as well as the whole..." So, it would seem that taxpayers can readily shift income from property as long as they transfer, well, property.

But that simple statement, it turns out, doesn't accurately describe the law. Later cases muddied the water by invalidating assignments of income involving property. The confusion is so thick that even very smart people have a hard time distinguishing *Blair* from other assignment of income cases.

Consider *Helvering v. Horst*.[14] Horst owned a bearer bond with interest coupons. Bearer bonds are pretty much extinct in the United States today, but they used to be quite common. Bearer bonds physically divided a bond into its principal and interest payments (called coupons). Each coupon says something like "Pay to bearer the sum of $100 on or after December 1, 2014." The holder of the bond coupon, then, could take the coupon to any bank, and the bank would pay them $100 (less a fee, naturally), no questions asked. (A historical aside: bearer bonds, as you can imagine, were fantastic for money laundering and tax evasion, since they aided the flow of cash without identification. In the 1980s, the United States took steps to require U.S. bonds to be registered to their owners, rather than in bearer form.)

---

[13] Lucas v. Earl, 281 U.S. 111 (1930).

[14] 311 U.S. 112 (1940).

Horst decided to give his son a gift in the form of several coupons soon to mature, and he probably thought this was canny tax planning. A gift in cash would (under the rules of Code Section 102) not shift income from him to his son. But an assignment of interest income definitely would.

Not so fast. The IRS took the position that dad, and not his son, should be taxed on the coupons, even though the son collected the money. The *Horst* case went all the way to the Supreme Court and, in 1940, the Court ruled for the IRS: the assignment of income was ineffective for tax purposes.

How can we reconcile *Horst* with *Blair*? It's a question for the ages. The coupons in *Horst* were property, certainly, just as was the assigned interest in the trust income in *Blair*. And yet the shift in property in *Blair* also shifted taxable income, while the shift in ownership in *Horst* did not.

The opinion in *Horst* is, to put it kindly, not terribly helpful. The court goes into great length about how the dad had realized the value of the coupons in giving them to his son. The court's point is valid enough: whenever someone gives a gift of $100, we can assume that the value of the gift to the donor is at least $100 (or else she'd keep the money). But Papa Blair, as much as Papa Horst, "realized" the value of his gift in much the same way: it must have been worth it to Blair to give the $9,000 to his kids—or else he wouldn't have done so.

The best theory for reconciling the three cases—*Earl*, *Blair*, and *Horst*—seems to involve some notion of control. All three men made formally irrevocable transfers; they formally gave up control of the income they shifted. But Guy Earl retained control of his earning power: he could still choose his clients and even stop working altogether. The father in Horst, too, kept considerable control. By giving away only coupons that would mature quite soon, Horst kept his future options open. In future years, Dad could consider his tax position (and his son's) and decide how much to shift. In contrast, Edward Blair gave up a portion of his life interest for his entire lifetime. The assignment granted $9,000 per year to his kids for as long as Edward himself collected any money — for the rest of his life.

The idea of control sheds new light on the fruit and tree metaphor that sprouted up in *Earl*. The simple fruit/tree distinction is, well, overripe. If the "tree" is capital or human capital, and the "fruit" is income, then all three guys—Earl, Horst, and Blair—gave away fruit. But we can complicate the metaphor to capture some idea of control. After all, Earl and Horst also owned (and kept) the trees, while Edward Blair didn't own the tree. As a life beneficiary of the trust, Edward had an entitlement to income (fruit) only—and no power to control or dispose of the underlying corpus (the tree). So in fruit-and-tree terms, the rule is something like this: if you own the tree, you have to give away the branch on which the fruit grows. But if all you own is a share of the fruit, you can give away part of your share, as long as you give it away every year. This is still a pretty awful metaphor, but at least it tracks the cases a little more closely.

Still, even though the idea of control sheds some light on the assignment of income problem, it isn't obvious how the IRS and courts should determine how much "control" a donor retains. One can imagine a facts and circumstances control test, which would empower courts to consult "life in all its fullness."[15] But the courts, wisely enough, rejected that route. Instead, they developed a "carve out" test, which looks only to the structure of the interests given and retained.

The "carve out" test asks whether the donor has assigned a stream of payments that is coextensive (in time) with the donor's own interest. Thus, Edward Blair, for instance, had a lifetime stream of income, and he gave away a lifetime stream of income. That passes the carve-out test.

By contrast, the dad in *Horst* did "carve out." He had a stream of interest and principal payments extending into the future, and he assigned only the coupons that would mature soon. If you picture the stream of payments as extending horizontally across time, Horst "carved out" a few payments, after which the whole stream of payments would revert to him. It's that reversion in time that makes *Horst* a carve-out case.

Lucas v. Earl is also a carve-out case if you imagine Guy Earl's *human* capital as producing a (potential) stream of cash over time. Because no one can assign his human capital to another person, he definitionally keeps a reversion in his human capital. (The analogy would be a bond owner who assigns the interest payments on her bond but keeps the principal payment.)

This formal distinction has a certain logic, and yet, if you're finding all of this bizarre, you're right. The carve-out cases turn on a distinction between interest and principal that finance theory has long ago rejected. To a business analyst, a cash flow is simply a cash flow. The legal label "principal" or "interest" has no financial significance (except to the extent the legal label affects the lender's or borrower's risk or remedies).

Recognizing the fungibility of cash flows, Code Section 1286 now governs the taxation of transactions like *Horst* that involve "stripped" bonds. A stripped bond arises when the ownership of principal and interest is separated, as in the assignment of coupons in *Horst*. Section 1286 makes use of the insight that all cash flows have a present value. The statute assigns a present value to each payment due on the bond (whether principal or interest). The bond owner who (like Horst) assigns interest payments to someone else by gift must allocate his basis between the retained and assigned interests based on their relative fair market values. The recipient of the assigned interest takes a carryover basis based on that allocation. The donor and donee then accrue interest income as the value of their respective interests accrete over time.

EXAMPLE 3. Harriet bought for $1,000 a one-year bond with a principal amount of $1,000 and an interest rate of 10%. One year before the bond matures, Harriet assigns

---

[15] See Chapter 8, which discusses Welch v. Helvering, 290 U.S. 111 (1933).

the interest payment of $100 to her daughter. Under Code Section 1286, Harriet allocates her basis of $1,000 between the retained principal payment and the assigned interest payment of $100. At a 10% discount rate, the present value of the $1,000 payment to be received in one year is $909, and the present value of the $100 is $91. One year later, when Harriet receives $1,000, her gain of $91 will be treated as interest income. When the daughter receives $100, her gain of $9 will also be treated as interest income. The effect of Section 1286 is to allocate the total interest income of $100 between Harriet and her daughter, split $91 and $9.

But Section 1286 applies only to bonds and not to other property interests. For those, the assignment of income cases remain good law. Which means that tax lawyers must, upon occasion, don their garden gloves and sift through the scattered metaphors of fruit and tree.

CHAPTER 13

Capital Gains and Losses

Introduction . . . . . . ¶1300
The Preferential Rate . . . . . . ¶1301
The Capital Loss Limitation . . . . . . ¶1302
Real-World Transactions: Sale of a Closely-Held Business . . . . . . ¶1303
What Is a Capital Asset? . . . . . . ¶1304
Real-World Transaction: Stocks and Bonds . . . . . . ¶1305
Conversion and *Bramblett v. Commissioner* . . . . . . ¶1306

¶1300 INTRODUCTION

The term "capital gains" may have a familiar ring. It's the kind of term people toss out at cocktail parties and at the Thanksgiving table. Depending on your family, you may hear, "If only they'd cut the capital gains rate, this economy would be humming." Or, "The capital gains rate is a total giveaway to the rich." (Or you may just hear chewing sounds and "Pass the gravy.") There is, in fact, a lively debate over the desirability of special low rates on capital gains. Whether a low capital gains rate spurs economic growth or just rewards rich people is, indeed, central to the empirical and normative controversy.[1]

But, for good or ill, capital gains and losses have been part of the tax law for decades and will likely persist. Capital treatment of gains and losses, we will see, reflect an effort to address problems of *valuation*, *realization* and *tax deferral*. But like many legal rules, capital gains and losses solve some problems but create others.

Here's a really quick introduction. Certain assets, called "capital assets," produce capital gain or capital loss when sold. Very generally, capital assets (which are defined more precisely in Code Section 1221) are assets held for investment rather than for sale to customers. Thus, Microsoft stock held by an investor is a capital asset. Cans of peas on a grocery store's shelves are not. (Non-capital assets are called "ordinary" assets and produce ordinary gain and loss when sold.)

Capital treatment of gains or losses has two (and only two) consequences. First, some capital gains are eligible for a special, low tax rate under Section

[1] For one law professor's take on the problem, see Chris Sanchirico, *'Common Sense' Aside, What Do We Really Know About Capital Income Taxes and Growth?*, Tax Vox blog, Tax Policy Center, March 15, 2013, available at http://taxvox.taxpolicycenter.org/2013/03/15/common-sense-aside-what-do-we-really-know-about-capital-income-taxes-and-growth/.

1(h). The favored category consists of capital gains on assets held more than one year. As of 2015, the top rate on capital gains is 20%, compared to about 40% for ordinary income. (Remember: any income or loss that is not capital is "ordinary.") Second, all capital losses are subject to the capital loss limitation in Code Section 1211. Very generally, capital losses can be deducted only to the extent of capital gains and cannot be deducted against ordinary income. (There is a modest relief rule for individuals, who can deduct a whopping $3,000 per year of capital gains against their ordinary income.)

Before we dive into the details, you might want to make a cautionary note on terminology. The term "capital gain" has a specific, technical meaning in the tax law. (For those who simply cannot wait, the definition resides in Code Section 1222.) But it's easy to get confused if you try to import ordinary language into the mix. For example, not all types of capital produce capital gains (plant and equipment, for instance, are not capital assets in the tax sense.) And many types of capital income (to borrow a term from economics) are not capital gains.

In fact, the term "capital gain" is a tax-law fiction, a made-up creation found only in tax. It isn't related to—or found in—economics, finance, or even accounting (other than tax accounting). And, to compound the confusion, capital gains have nothing to do with other uses of the term "capital" in the tax law: in particular, capital gains have nothing—zero—to do with capital expenditures. As Chapter 10 discusses, capital expenditures arise when a taxpayer spends money in ways that produce lasting benefits for her business (or investment strategy). Capital gains and losses come about when the taxpayer sells property. And a taxpayer can claim capital gains treatment whether or not she has made any capital expenditures.

Having established what capital gains are not, we can now turn to the task of determining what they are.

¶1301 THE PREFERENTIAL RATE

The big prize in the capital gains world is the preferential rate, but the prize goes only to some capital gains and not to all of them. Working your way through the Code is painful, but beneficial, like running. And, just as in running, a roadmap will help. (OK, enough with the analogy!)

The preferential rate itself appears in Code Section 1(h). The rates on capital gains are progressive, and they mirror the taxpayer's ordinary income bracket. Thus, for instance, in 2014, someone with income in the 10% or 15% ordinary income bracket would pay a capital gains rate of 0%. The top rate on capital gains is 20%, and it applies to income that would be taxed at 39.6% if it were ordinary.

But the preferential rate applies only to "net capital gain" (adjusted for a few other items in Section 1(h)(3)), and—unhelpfully—section 1(h) does not define that term for us. The key, it turns out, is Section 1222, which, simplifying a little, tells us that net capital gain is the excess of long-term capital gains over short-term capital losses. Reading further in Section 1222, you'll see that the critical dividing line is twelve months—the holding period that demarcates "long-term" and "short-term" capital gains.

Boiling all this down, the critical point to remember is this: only long-term capital gains (gains on assets held for more than 12 months) are taxed at the preferential rate. Short-term capital gains are taxed at the same rates as ordinary income.

EXAMPLE 1. Monique has enough earned income to place her in the 39.6% tax bracket. In 2014, she sells Microsoft stock for a gain of $10,000 and sells Apple stock for a gain of $10,000. She bought the Microsoft stock ten years ago and the Apple stock last week.

The Microsoft gain is a long-term capital gain. Given that Monique's ordinary tax bracket is 39.6%, her capital gains bracket will be 20%. So she will owe $2,000 to Uncle Sam on that transaction. The Apple gain, by contrast, is a short-term capital gain. Monique will pay tax on that gain at her ordinary marginal tax rate of 39.6%. So she will owe the Treasury about $4,000—twice as much!

Section 1222 contains a number of mechanical netting rules for determining net capital gain. But their purpose is straightforward. They essentially "basket" or aggregate capital gains and losses to ensure that the preferential rate applies only to, well, the net long-term capital gain.

EXAMPLE 2. Alex has a long-term capital gain of $25,000 and a long-term capital loss of $12,000. The rules of Section 1222 subtract the loss from his gain, so that the preferential rate applies only to the $13,000 net gain. (The result would be the same, incidentally, if Alex's loss were a short-term capital loss.)[2]

By now, you may—justifiably—feel frustrated by the complex web of capital gains rules. What is the point of all this? What are capital gains *for*? The answer lies in three of our six core concepts: *valuation*, *realization*, and *tax deferral*. The capital gains rate preference attempts to mitigate a set of pathologies in the tax law. (Whether the cure is worse than the ills it addresses is an open question.)

To see the connection, recall the origins of the *realization* doctrine. A true Haig-Simons income tax (as Chapter 1 discusses), would tax individuals on the change in the value of their assets each year. But concerns about *valuation* and liquidity led the drafters of the tax law to adopt the *realization* requirement instead, with the result that individuals pay tax on gains only when they sell their assets.

And the *realization* doctrine, as we have seen, permits taxpayers to engage in *tax deferral*. Someone who owns appreciated stock can, quite legally, put off taxation indefinitely, as long as she is willing to hold onto the stock. So the realization requirement avoids the difficulties of *valuation* but at the cost of awarding taxpayers the legal opportunity for tax deferral.

Tax deferral, as we have seen, costs the Treasury billions of dollars every year. So it might seem odd that the law grafts on an additional tax preference for

[2] See Code Section 1222(11).

capital gains! A taxpayer holding, say, Microsoft stock, can not only defer her taxes indefinitely, but if and when she decides to sell, she will pay half the normal tax rate (like Monique in the example above).

But this seemingly crazy result has a logical motivation. The *realization* requirement, it turns out, creates two more problems for the tax law, and it is these problems that the capital gains rate preference seeks to address.

The first is the problem of lock-in, which is a by-product of *tax deferral.* As Chapter 6 explains, the *realization* requirement encourages taxpayers to defer realizing gains. Thanks to the time value of money, taxpayers have every incentive to defer *realization* as long as possible: the longer the deferral period, the lower the present value of the tax. Indeed, if taxpayers can hold onto assets until death, their heirs can claim a stepped-up basis under Code Section 1014 (discussed in Chapter 5), thus avoiding any income tax on the gain. Ever.

Tax deferral not only costs the Treasury money, but from an economic perspective, it has an even more pernicious effect: it tends to "lock in" taxpayers to their existing investments. Lock-in is inefficient, an economist would say, because it alters the way people behave. When the tax law discourages investors from changing their investments, it slows the flow of capital to more productive assets. Thanks to the *realization* requirement, then, the tax law subsidizes stasis and discourages the movement of capital toward higher-valued uses.

EXAMPLE 3. Barry owns Microsoft stock, which he bought for $150 and is now worth $250. Looking ahead, Barry thinks that Apple stock would be a better bet. He estimates that he could earn (before taxes) a profit with a present value of $35 if he switched to investing in Apple. But selling the Microsoft stock would trigger the *realization* of $100 of gain. And if Barry is in the 40% tax bracket, the tax of $40 would outweigh the $35 he could gain by reinvesting. So Barry is locked in.

We can use Barry's situation to illustrate why the capital gains rate preference helps. By cutting Barry's tax rate on stock gains in half (from 40% to 20%), the tax law reduces lock-in. Barry will now, if he's rational, sell his Microsoft stock and reinvest in Apple, because the tax cost of $20 now is less than the potential profit of $35.

The distinction between long-term capital gains and everything else should now begin to make sense. Code Section 1221 defines a capital asset by excluding certain categories of assets. The big exclusion is in Section 1221(a)(1), which treats inventory as producing ordinary income and not capital gains. If you think about why, the idea of lock-in is fairly helpful. People who buy and sell assets quickly are, by definition, not locked in. Think about a grocery store, for example. Safeway could, in theory, obtain tax deferral if it held onto its inventory a long time before selling. But no one wants five-year-old lettuce or twenty-year-old peanut butter. So tax deferral just isn't a tax strategy that Safeway can use for its inventory. Accordingly, Section 1221(a)(1) excludes inventory from capital gains treatment.

Pursuing this line of thinking, we can also make sense of why short-term capital gains do not qualify for the preferential rate. Short-term gains are realized by people who apparently are not locked in. By definition, the taxpayer has held the asset for 12 months or less. Active stock traders, who "churn" their portfolios with frequent buying and selling, also are not using tax deferral as a tax strategy. And so the 12-month dividing line between long- and short-term capital gains denies them the preferential rate as well.

The long-term capital gains rate thus combats the negative effects of one tax preference (*tax deferral*) by enacting another (the low rate on capital gains). Congress might, of course, have adopted a different approach. Repealing Section 1014 would fight lock-in, for instance. Still, lock-in provides one core rationale for the preferential rate on capital gains.

The preferential rate on long-term capital gains also addresses a second tax problem attributable to the *realization* requirement: bunching. Bunching arises when a taxpayer realizes a large gain, which pushes his income into higher tax brackets than if he had been taxed all at once. Put another way, the realization requirement, combined with progressive marginal tax rates, can overtax people because it makes them look richer (in the year of realization) than they really are.

EXAMPLE 4. Kristin is single and earns $75,000 per year as a computer programmer. She bought Apple stock twenty years ago for $5,000, and it is now worth $205,000. When Kristin sells the Apple stock, her salary plus the gain of $200,000 will amount to $275,000, pushing her from the 25% tax bracket into the 33% bracket.[3]

The problem with bunching, then, is that it makes Kristin look as if—for one year—she is quite well off. But, in fact, she has had no sudden good fortune. Instead, the gain accrued over twenty years, at an average of $10,000 per year. So an accurate picture of Kristin's financial status would put her at $85,000 per year for the last 20 years, still squarely within the 25% rate bracket.

The capital gains rate preference addresses bunching in a rough-cut way by lowering the tax rate on long-term gains. In Kristin's case, the realization of gain on her Apple stock will still push her up through the tax brackets, but the capital gains preference will operate at every level, so that the gain will be taxed at 15%.

Understanding the capital gains preference as a response to bunching also helps explain why the Code excludes some gains from capital treatment. Returning once again to the Safeway example, a grocery store is unlikely to suffer bunching on its inventory. Why? Because the business, to be profitable, must sell its inventory frequently. And so Section 1221(a)(1) excludes inventory from capital asset status.

---

[3] Updated tax brackets are found in Rev. Proc. 2014-61, available at http://www.irs.gov/pub/irs-drop/rp-14-61.pdf.

The bunching rationale also helps illuminate why short-term capital gains do not qualify for the preferential rate. By definition, bunching occurs only when gains accrue over more than one year. So someone lucky enough to buy and sell at a gain within a year cannot complain that her income has been taxed at the wrong marginal tax rate because it accrued over a long period.

The bunching and lock-in rationales offer some support for the capital gains rate preference, and they illuminate the connections to *valuation*, *realization*, and *tax deferral*. But it would be too far a stretch to suppose that the low rate on capital gains is a well-tailored solution to either problem. The capital gains rules are bright-line rules, not standards. And they provide a tax cut to broad categories of taxpayers and classes of assets, some of which are neither locked in nor "bunched."

> **EXAMPLE 5.** Serge is single and earns $450,000 per year, placing him in the 39.6% marginal tax rate bracket. He typically holds investments for no more than a year or so, preferring to rebalance his portfolio roughly once per year. Still, Serge can follow a tax-advantageous *realization* strategy without altering his plans (much). He holds stocks with gains for one year and one day to qualify for the long-term capital gains rate preference.

Serge will qualify for the 20% capital gains rate cut even though he isn't particularly locked in (given his short investment horizon) and doesn't suffer bunching (because he is already in the top rate bracket).

¶1302 THE CAPITAL LOSS LIMITATION

The capital gains rate preference is the glamorous half of the capital gains rules. It gets all the press—good and bad—and all the attention. But the humbler capital loss limitation is at least as important for tax planning, and it merits sustained attention.

It would be natural to suppose that the capital gains limitation is the price taxpayers have to pay for the capital gains rate preference; some kind of quid pro quo. But that natural assumption would also be a mistake. In fact, the capital loss limitation should exist even if there were no capital gains preference. (And, indeed, it did persist even in the late 1980s, when the tax law imposed the same rate of tax on capital gains and ordinary income.)

The capital gains loss limitation responds to the problem of selective loss *realization*. Recall that in Chapters 5 and 6, we saw that the *realization* requirement motivates a simple mantra for tax planning: hold gains and sell losses. We also saw that the strategy is especially valuable for wealthy taxpayers with diversified portfolios, who often can "cherry-pick" losses from their portfolios near year-end.

EXAMPLE 6. Vicky has a portfolio of 30 different stocks, purchased at different times. Overall, she has gained $50,000 on her investments. Nice! But, among the individual stocks, some have gained value while others have lost value. In fact, she has a total of $150,000 in gains and $100,000 in losses.

Purely from a tax perspective (and supposing for the moment that there is no capital loss limitation), Vicky should hold the gain stocks and sell the loss stocks. To be sure, Vicky may face some real-world constraints on that strategy if her investments are illiquid or have a risk-return profile not easily replicated by other investments. (Recall the wash sale rules of Code Section 1091, discussed in Chapter 11, which prohibit taxpayers from claiming a loss if they sell and reinvest in the same property within a short period). But many Vickys in the world will find it easy enough to "cherry pick" tax losses.

To cabin this strategy, the capital loss limitation in Code Section 1211 restricts the deductibility of capital losses. Capital losses may be deducted only against capital gains (plus, in the case of an individual, $3,000 of ordinary income). The limitation will prevent Vicky from cherry-picking losses from her investment portfolio to shelter ordinary income. Vicky can, however, cherry-pick losses to offset any capital gains she realizes. For instance, if Vicky realizes $40,000 in capital gains in order to reshuffle her portfolio a bit, she can—easily and legally—sell stocks that will produce a total of $40,000 in capital losses.

The capital loss limitation, then, limits but does not defeat selective loss *realization*. Wealthy taxpayers with diversified portfolios will still tend to follow the mantra: hold gains and sell losses. But they will amend their strategy to incorporate the knowledge that capital losses can be used only to offset capital gains (plus $3,000).

The dark side of the capital loss limitation is that it can prevent taxpayers from deducting real economic losses.

EXAMPLE 7. Terence invested his life savings of $100,000 in a mutual fund in 2007. After the market crash of 2008, Terence's portfolio was worth only $25,000. Terence sold the mutual fund shares in 2009. But he has no capital gains, and so Section 1211 prevents him from deducting his $75,000 capital loss (beyond the $3,000 annual deduction against ordinary income permitted by Section 1211(b)(1)).

Like many bright-line rules in the Code, Code Section 1211 is under- and over-inclusive. The Vickys of the world can still cherry pick losses to offset their capital gains, while the Terences of the world are overtaxed, because they cannot deduct real investment losses.

Code Section 1212 mitigates the hardship of nondeductible capital losses by permitting an indefinite carryforward, which just means that unused losses roll over to the next taxable year. In our example, Terence can deduct $3,000 of his loss against ordinary income this year. Next year, he will have a $72,000 capital loss carryover, and if he still has no capital gains, he will be able to deduct another $3,000. His loss going into year 3 would be $69,000. At this rate, it will take him 25 years to deduct his loss! Although some deduction is better than no deduction, in present value terms, the deferred tax loss is worth only a fraction of the real loss Terence suffered.

¶1303 REAL-WORLD TRANSACTIONS: SALE OF A CLOSELY-HELD BUSINESS

The rules on capital gains and losses govern the sale of any asset, from small to large, and they are often important in mergers and acquisitions.

Begin with the simplest transaction (from a tax perspective), a sale of stock. Suppose that a big corporation like General Electric (GE) agreed to sell a subsidiary to an acquirer. General Electric would realize gain or loss, depending on the relationship of its basis to the amount realized on sale. The gain or loss would be capital, because the stock is a capital asset under Section 1221. That is, the stock is property, and it does not fall into any of the statutory exclusions. For example, GE is not a dealer in stocks; the stock is not a depreciable asset; and so on.

The sale of the assets of a business (rather than the stock in a corporation) is usually more complicated from a tax point of view, because it involves separate calculations of gain and loss on each asset of the business. The character of the gain or loss (capital or ordinary) will depend on the nature of each asset.

EXAMPLE 8. Stuart owns an unincorporated grocery store called "Gourmet to Go." Ready to retire, Stuart sells the business's assets to Paula for $500,000. The purchase price includes the building as well as all equipment and inventory. The purchase price also gives Paula the right to continue to use the "Gourmet to Go" name.

In one sense, Stuart has sold Paula just one asset, a grocery business. But in another sense, Stuart has sold a collection of different assets, including real estate, inventory, and intangibles. The distinction matters, in part, because it determines the character of the gain or loss Stuart will realize.

The tax law adopts the second view and treats the transaction as the sale of all the separate assets that, together, constitute the grocery store. A special Code provision (Section 1060, if you must know) requires Stuart and Paula to allocate the $500,000 purchase price among the various assets, including the "goodwill" of the store, which is the value of the business above the value of its hard assets.

EXAMPLE 9. Continuing the example of Stuart and Paula, suppose that the allocation looks like this:

Asset	Allocated Purchase Price	Stuart's Basis	Stuart's Gain or Loss
Building	$300,000	$325,000	-$25,000
Inventory	$150,000	$140,000	$10,000
Goodwill	$50,000	$0	$50,000

The allocation of the purchase price serves two functions. The first is to determine the seller's gain or loss on each asset and to ensure that each item takes the appropriate character. For instance, the character of Stuart's $25,000 loss on the building will be determined under Code Section 1231 (which governs real property used in a business). His $10,000 inventory gain is ordinary under Section 1221(a)(1). And goodwill is a capital asset (because it is not excluded by any of the Section 1221 categories), and so his gain is capital.

The second function of the purchase price allocation is to determine the purchaser's basis. Paula's basis in the building, for instance, will be $300,000. The inventory will take a basis in Paula's hands of $150,000. And the goodwill's basis will be $50,000, which Paula can amortize over 15 years under Code Section 197.

As you can imagine, the taxation of real-world mergers and acquisitions is more complicated. Corporate taxation introduces new wrinkles, and real businesses have hundreds or thousands of assets, not just three. Still, these basic principles form the bedrock of the tax rules that apply even to mega-bucks transactions.

¶1304 WHAT IS A CAPITAL ASSET?

Most of the legal complexity in the field of capital gains arises from the capital asset definition. Code Section 1221 appears, at first glance, to provide a set of bright-line rules. Reading down the list, we see that inventory, certain property used in business, and other items are not capital assets. But hidden in Section 1221(a)(1) is a distinction that has proved difficult for the IRS and the courts to implement with any certainty at all: the distinction between assets held for investment and assets held for sale to customers.

In simple cases, of course, the distinction is clear. When Safeway stocks its shelves with fresh carrots, it intends to sell them to customers. The result is that the carrots are not capital assets, thanks to Section 1221(a)(1), which excludes inventory. When an individual investor buys 100 shares of Apple stock, the stock is a capital asset, because it is not "held for sale to customers in the ordinary course of business." That is, it is an investment asset.

But the line between holding for sale and holding for investment is far murkier for real estate. Real estate investors often have mixed or dual motives. Suppose, for instance, that you spot a "For Sale" sign on 100 acres located a few miles out of town. The price is reasonable, and you are willing to take the bet that the town will expand and that, someday, the land will be worth even more. You probably don't know, at that early stage, just how things will play out. It could be that you'll just hold the land for a few years and resell it. Or, if the town really booms, you could see yourself hiring a lawyer who could divide up the land into home sites or parcels for shopping centers. Depending on how things go for you in the next few years, there's even a chance that you could come up with the capital to build homes or a mall on the land yourself.

The problem is that Section 1221 deals very poorly with mixed motives. Section 1221 requires a unitary purpose for each asset: it must be held for sale to customers, used in the trade or business, or held for investment. But your plans encompass, probabilistically, all three options. You might sell home sites, build and operate a mall, or resell the property without any development at all. Eventually, of course, you will choose one route. But if you sell in the meantime, it will be difficult for the law to determine whether the property is a capital asset.

This legal uncertainty isn't just an academic hypothetical. We saw exactly this problem in the famous case of *Malat v. Riddell*.[4] In *Malat*, the taxpayer was a member of a partnership that bought and developed rental properties. The partnership had bought farmland in Inglewood, California. Initially, William Malat and the other partners reported capital gains on sales of real estate. But the partnership's plans changed over time. The partners initially intended to build garden apartments, but they needed financing and a zoning change for that plan to work. When they couldn't obtain financing, they tried an alternative development plan, but that one failed too.

The course of business, like true love, never does run smooth![5] In one last try, the partners decided to subdivide and sell individual home sites, but they retained some land, still hoping to develop commercial properties. At that point, the partners had a falling out, and they decided to sell the remaining parcels to "get out and be done with it."

The taxpayer-partners reported the sales of home sites as ordinary income, but they reported the sale of the remaining land as capital gains. The IRS, scenting money to be had, took the position that all the gains were ordinary, and the District Court and the Court of Appeals ruled for the IRS. Still, it was clear that the taxpayers had mixed motives. Consider this testimony from William, responding to a question about what the partnership intended to do with the property if zoning or financing became problematic:

> [W]e felt that we had made a good buy on the property as far as price is concerned, so that if we couldn't do anything in the way of zoning, we would sell the whole thing off in bulk. We wouldn't get hurt.[6]

The Court of Appeals struggled to fit the facts into the Code's presumption that taxpayers have just one motive. The judges took note that the partnership was

---

4 383 U.S. 569 (1966). Additional facts are found in the Court of Appeals opinion, Malat v. Riddell, 347 F.2d 23 (9th Cir. 1965).

5 William Shakespeare, *A Midsummer Night's Dream,* Act 1, Scene 1 (Lysander) (on love, not business).

6 Malat v. Riddell, 347 F.2d 23, 28 (9th Cir. 1965).

in the business of developing land, not investing in it. And the court concluded that most of the partners' alternative plans involved selling in some fashion or other, so that the final sale was part of the purpose of selling, rather than holding for investment.

But the Supreme Court reversed and remanded, holding that the lower courts had misapplied the law. The Court consulted the dictionary and directed the lower courts to determine which purpose was primary or "of first importance." Easy enough to say, but hard to do. Pity the poor trial court judge to whom the case was assigned for retrial! The Court's directive required the judge to tease out which of many motives was "primary."

The sad but predictable outcome is that well-advised taxpayers with well-paid lawyers have been able to use the *Malat* test to their advantage. Taxpayers with mixed motives who sell at a gain will, of course, emphasize their investment motive, while taxpayers who sell at a loss will highlight their purpose of selling.

The courts have tried to offer some guidelines for determining motive, but with limited success. Capital asset cases involving real estate are still surprisingly indeterminate. The famous quotation, often repeated in judicial opinions, is, "If a client asks in any but an extreme case whether, in your opinion, his sale will result in capital capital gain, your answer should probably be, 'I don't know, and no one else in town can tell you.' "[7]

Byram v. United States[8] illustrates the Bizarro World of capital asset cases involving real estate. John Byram sold seven pieces of real property in 1973, reaping a profit of $2.5 million. Six of the seven properties were held for short periods, from six to nine months, just long enough to qualify for long-term capital gains treatment under the law at that time. The IRS took the position that Byram held the properties for sale to customers in the ordinary course of business and, thus, their sale produced ordinary income under Code Section 1221(a)(1). John, of course, disagreed.

The *Byram* opinion, like most of the real-estate capital asset opinions, is long, detailed, and agonized. The court makes use of a seven-factor test,[9] which weighs:

(1) the nature and purpose of the acquisition of the property and the duration of the ownership;
(2) the extent and nature of the taxpayer's efforts to sell the property;
(3) the number, extent, continuity and substantiality of the sales;
(4) the extent of subdividing, developing, and advertising to increase sales;
(5) the use of a business office for the sale of the property;

---

[7] The quotation apparently originated in an older edition of the Mertens treatise and has been repeated many times. 3B Mertens *Law of Federal Income Taxation,* Zimet & Weiss Rev., Sec. 22.138, n. 69, pp. 623, 624. See, e.g., Cole v. Usry, 294 F. 2d 426, 427 n. 3 (5th Cir. 1961), Thompson v. Commissioner, 322 F. 2d 122, 123 n. 2 (5th Cir. 1963), Byram v. U.S. 705 F.2d 1418, 1418 (5th Cir. 1983).

[8] 705 F.2d 1418 (5th Cir. 1983).

[9] *Byram,* supra, citing *U.S. v. Winthrop*, 417 F.2d 905, 910 (5th Cir. 1969).

(6) the character and degree of supervision or control exercised by the taxpayer over any representative selling the property; and
(7) the time and effort the taxpayer habitually devoted to the sales.

John Byram, it turned out, looked pretty much like an investor based on these tests. He made little or no effort to sell the properties. He didn't advertise or use real estate brokers. He didn't develop or improve the properties, and he didn't have an office. Apparently, Byram just had a really good eye for real estate. And the court rejected the IRS's argument that the third factor, the number of sales, could be controlling: seven sales in a year, the court concluded, was still within the realm of investing rather than selling to customers.

You might think the court's conclusion is reasonable enough, given the premise that all seven factors must be considered. But the *Byram* decision is infamous because the holding seems at odds with the common-sense interpretation of the facts. John sold 22 properties over a three-year period, grossing over $9 million and netting a profit of nearly $3.5 million. In 2014 dollars, those figures are—hold on—$48 million and $19 million. So the Fifth Circuit bought the story that a guy who constantly bought and sold properties, and who churned through nearly $50 million in real estate over three years, was just an investor. It seems unlikely that Byram was suffering much from lock-in or bunching, since his business model involved fairly rapid turnover. So something seems wrong with that picture, and yet it is the law.

¶1305 REAL-WORLD TRANSACTION: STOCKS AND BONDS

The capital gains rate preference and capital loss limitation shape tax planning for investors. Indeed, they motivate another simple mantra:

Capital gains good, capital losses bad.[10]

What this slogan means is that, if the taxpayer has room to choose, capital gains are always preferable. If they're long-term, they qualify for a preferential rate. Even if they're short-term, they can be used to soak up capital losses. Capital losses, by contrast, are generally a tax negative. A taxpayer with abundant capital gains won't mind capital losses, but anyone else may find herself with nondeductible or deferred losses.

The ideal investment asset, then, would combine capital gains on the upside with ordinary losses on the downside. In fact, Congress has granted something like that status to certain business assets in Code Section 1231. (Section 1231 applies

---

[10] The allusion is to George Orwell's *Animal Farm*, in which the sheep chant, "Four legs good, two legs bad." Unlike the sheeps' chant, however, this slogan is useful in tax planning.

to assets that are used in the trade or business, are held for more than one year, and either are depreciable or are real estate.) But investment assets do not qualify for Section 1231, and, in fact, most investments are, by design, capital assets.

Still, the mix of ordinary income and capital gain and loss varies from asset to asset. To see the variability, consider three common investment assets: stocks, bonds, and real estate.

Stocks are capital assets in the hands of investors, because they are not held for sale to customers (Section 1221). So appreciation and depreciation in the value of stocks produce capital gain and capital loss. Dividends on U.S. stocks often qualify for a special tax break. Under Section 1(h)(11), dividends are taxed at the long-term capital gains rate. But dividends do not count as capital gains for purposes of the Section 1211 capital loss limitation. So, unlike true capital gains, they cannot absorb excess capital losses.

Bonds held by investors are capital assets too, and so gain or loss on these assets can be capital. But the capital character of gain and loss may be modified by rules that treat discount and premium on bonds as interest income (in the case of discount) or reductions in interest income (in the case of premium).[11]

EXAMPLE 10. Harry buys a bond issued by General Electric for $82. The bond does not pay stated interest, but the principal, due in two years, is $100. This is an original issue discount, or OID, bond. Code Section 1272 treats the $18 difference between the issue price and the principal amount as interest, not capital gain. Harry must include the OID in income as it accrues, even though he will not receive cash until the bond matures in two years.

The OID rules capture the reality that the discounted price Harry pays for the bond reflects the time value of money. Implicitly, when GE sells Harry the bond, it is promising to pay him about 10% per year on his initial investment of $82. The OID rules aim to create parity between discounted obligations (sometimes called "zero coupon bonds") and interest-bearing obligations.

Still, bonds remain capital assets and so may produce capital gain or loss. Gains and losses on OID bonds are fairly complicated, so take an easier example.

EXAMPLE 11. Imogen buys a bond from General Motors for $1,000. The bond pays 10% interest ($100) annually and will be repaid in five years for $1,000. Imogen must treat the $100 of interest income as ordinary income. But if she sells the bond for $1200, her $200 gain will be capital gain. If she sells the bond for $975, the $25 loss will be capital loss.

[11] Code Section 1272 governs original issue discount; Section 1276 governs market discount; and Section 171 provides a deduction for amortizable bond premium.

¶1306 CONVERSION AND *BRAMBLETT V. COMMISSIONER*

Taxpayers have shown their usual ingenuity in crafting transactions that take advantage of the capital gains rate preference. Tax planners use the term "conversion" to describe deals that can convert ordinary income to capital gains.

Bramblett v. Commissioner[12] offers a clever example. Richard Bramblett and three other investors decided to invest in land in Mesquite, Texas with the idea of developing commercial and residential properties. But the investors structured their venture in a curious way. They formed a partnership (Mesquite East) and a corporation (Town East). Both entities were owned by the four investors in equal proportions. But the two entities split the tasks of development. Simplifying a bit, the partnership borrowed money and held title to the land up to the point the investors decided to begin development. The partnership then sold the land to the corporation at a price determined by appraisers. The corporation then developed the land and sold it to buyers.

The key to understanding the transaction in *Bramblett* is to consider how the investors would have been taxed had they used just one entity. Imagine a single entity that buys land, holds it, develops it, and sells it. Land held in this way is an ordinary asset and not a capital asset. Why? Because it is held for sale to customers in the ordinary course of business and, thus, is excluded from capital asset status under Code Section 1221(a)(1). Had Bramblett and his co-investors structured their venture this way, their profits would have been 100% ordinary income.

The two entities, Bramblett hoped, would enable the venture to convert some of its ordinary income to capital gain. Recall that the *Byram* case (discussed in ¶1304, above) establishes a multi-factor test for determining whether real estate is a capital asset. As long as the entity holding the real estate conducts minimal activity, lacks an office, doesn't advertise, and engages in few land sales, the land will retain its capital character.

You can now see why Bramblett used two entities. Mesquite East, the partnership, was entirely passive. It didn't develop the land, advertise, have an office or otherwise carry on business. Of course, Mesquite East didn't need to! It had a captive customer in Town East, which bought all of the land when the time was right. But Mesquite East was engineered by tax planners to meet the *Byram* tests for capital asset status.

The result, Bramblett hoped, was that the investors' profits would be split between Mesquite East and Town East, with the portion attributable to Mesquite East taxable at long-term capital gains rates. The financial stakes were high: at that time, the top marginal tax rate on ordinary income was 50%, while the top rate on capital gains was just 20%.

The IRS challenged the transaction, but in the end Bramblett and his co-venturers won. The Fifth Circuit ruled that Mesquite East met the *Byram* criteria

---

12 960 F. 2d 526 (5th Cir. 1992).

handily. The Fifth Circuit also rejected the IRS claim that the activities of the corporation should be attributed to the partnership. (The IRS theory would have imputed Town East's development and sales to Mesquite East, with the result that all income would have been ordinary.)

The Fifth Circuit also rejected the IRS view that *substance over form* could justify attributing the corporate activity to the partnership. The parties had an independent business reason for using two entities, the court noted: the incorporation of the development branch of the business shielded the parties from unlimited liability. Moreover, the court noted, the transactions appeared to be made at arm's length values, and the parties followed all business and legal formalities.

The decision in *Bramblett* is narrowly defensible but frustratingly formalist in its approach. The overlapping ownership of the two entities ensured that they would act in concert. The parties could have achieved limited liability by conducting Mesquite East's investment operations through Town East. And it isn't true that the entities observed all formalities: Town East failed to make required interest payments on the promissory notes given to Mesquite East upon the "purchase" of the land.

Taking the long view, though, the court's approach in *Bramblett* reflects a tension in the tax law between formalism and substance. The *substance over form* principle is powerful in taxation, and it prevailed in cases like *Knetsch* and *Fender* (both discussed in Chapter 11, *supra*). But the tax law also respects the legal existence of entities and adopts the legal fiction that they act independently of their owners. These fictions are obviously unrealistic: legal entities like partnerships and corporations have no ability to act except through the decisions of their owners. And yet, these fictions lie at the heart of corporate and partnership taxation.

So the tax planners in *Bramblett* were both clever and careful. They cleverly took advantage of the law's hesitation to disregard legal entities. They were careful to follow most of the necessary formalities for forming and operating two distinct legal entities. And, in a crucial step, they obtained an appraisal to determine the price at which the related parties would sell and buy property.

The lesson? Neatness counts, just as your second-grade teacher told you.

CHAPTER 14

Tax Shelters

Introduction . . . ¶1400
Estate of Franklin . . . ¶1401
Frank Lyon Co. v. U.S. . . . ¶1402
ACM Partnership v. Commissioner . . . ¶1403

¶1400 INTRODUCTION

You've nearly completed our tax marathon! At this stage, you know so much that you can begin to put all six concepts together to analyze tax shelters—that is, some of the complicated transactions taxpayers have dreamed up to minimize their taxes—and how the IRS has responded.

¶1401 *ESTATE OF FRANKLIN*

Estate of Franklin[1] is one of the most notorious tax shelter cases in the tax law canon. The transaction illustrates the opportunities for *tax deferral* and *income shifting* that arise when taxpayers take advantage of the *valuation* uncertainties inherent in seller financing and nonrecourse debt.

Wayne and Joan Romney owned and operated the Thunderbird Inn, an Arizona motel. We can assume they were content enough until a tax shelter promoter came their way and offered what must have seemed the deal of a lifetime. The proposed transaction worked this way. The Romneys would sell the Thunderbird Inn for $1.2 million to a group of East Coast investors called, ominously, the Associates. The investors had no interest in running the motel, and so they would simultaneously lease it back to the Romneys. The Romneys would retain decision-making authority and could run the motel as they chose.

The documents provided that the Romneys would lend the Associates the $1.2 million purchase price—critically, on a nonrecourse basis. (Recall that non-recourse debt limits the creditors' (here, the Romneys') remedies to foreclosure on the property.) Every month, the Associates, as borrowers, would owe principal and interest payments of about $9,000 to the Romneys. But the Romneys, recall, had become lessees, and so they owed monthly rent payments of $9,000 to the

[1] Estate of Franklin v. Commissioner, 544 F.2d 1045 (9th Cir. 1976). Franklin was one of the partners in Associates, and since he died before the case was resolved, his estate is the named taxpayer.

Associates. What a coincidence! The debt service offset the rents, so no monthly payments ever changed hands.

In fact, the only cash that changed hands was an upfront cash payment by the Associates to the Romneys of $75,000 (termed "prepaid interest" in the documents). The final term of the deal was critical. At the end of 10 years, the Associates would owe a balloon payment of about $1 million. If the Associates failed to pay their nonrecourse debt, then the Romneys would foreclose.

Now, at first glance, you might think that this is a shady deal. But, in some respects, the *Estate of Franklin* transaction resembles a lot of commercial real estate deals. Seller financing is quite common, especially in real estate, where owner-sellers may have better information about their properties than an outside lender can acquire. Sale-leasebacks are also common: they provide a means for building owners to diversify their investment portfolio (by selling the building and reinvesting elsewhere) while remaining physically in the same office space.

What was shady, it turns out, was the purchase price stated for the Thunderbird Inn. The purchase price of $1.2 million, the Ninth Circuit found, overstated the fair market value of the motel by 100%. The Thunderbird Inn, bought and sold for that inflated price, was really worth only $600,000.

Now, at first glance, the overvaluation seems preposterous. There seems to be no possible reason why a bunch of East Coast investors would come to Arizona and buy a little motel for twice its value. But it turns out that the *valuation* overstatement enabled the Associates to claim massive tax benefits that would shelter their other income.

Here's how the Associates thought the transaction would benefit them. The (inflated) purchase price of $1.2 million would support large, accelerated depreciation deductions. The Associates were likely wealthy, facing high marginal tax rates, so that the deductions were really valuable. Of course, the Associates didn't really want to buy the Thunderbird Inn, and the Romneys didn't really want to sell it. But the inflated purchase price helped with that problem too. When the 10-year balloon payment came due, the wildly overstated price would ensure that the Associates would walk away from their nonrecourse debt, leaving the motel right back where it started—with the Romneys.

From the Romneys' perspective, the deal must've looked like $75,000 in cash for—absolutely nothing. They would "lease back" their own motel on terms that left them completely free to manage it as they liked. After 10 years, the Associates would default, and title to the motel would return to the Romneys. In the (very) unlikely event that the motel was worth more than $1 million after 10 years had passed, the Associates might go ahead and pay. But in that case, the Romneys had made a profit of 100% over the value of their motel!

The big loser in the deal was the U.S. Treasury. The high-bracket Associates would shelter their high incomes with inflated depreciation deductions—that's why deals like this came to be known as tax shelters. The deal offered significant *tax deferral*—big depreciation deductions now, offset (if at all) by gain later on.[2]

Now, you might suppose that the Treasury recouped some of its money because the Romneys would no longer be able to claim depreciation deductions. (Only the owner of a building can depreciate it; the sale-leaseback turned the Romneys into lessees.) But the Romneys were likely in a far lower tax bracket than the Associates, meaning that the deal took advantage of *income shifting*—or really, deduction shifting—as well. (It's also likely that the Romneys had a much lower basis in the motel than the inflated basis the Associates claimed.)

The *Estate of Franklin* tax shelter stands in for a whole generation of overvaluation shelters. Like *Estate of Franklin*, these shelters relied on nonrecourse debt and *valuation* misstatements to generate huge tax deductions for the nominal "purchasers" of assets. As Michael Graetz recounts, everything from farms to chinchillas to really bad movies were sold in just this way during the tax shelter heyday of the 1960s and 1970s.[3]

Nonrecourse debt, and specifically, nonrecourse seller financing, is the key to overvaluation shelters. The depreciation deductions alone would not motivate Associates to pay $1.2 million in cold, hard cash for a motel worth $600,000. A cash deal simply couldn't work; no investor would pay $1 in cash for an extra deduction worth—by definition—less than $1. Even at the very high 70% marginal tax rate at that time, the Associates would not be willing to pay $1 in cash to gain 70 cents in deductions.

So the nonrecourse debt was key. It ensured that the Associates would never be called upon to pay the $1.2 million in cash. Instead, they would only have to give up ownership of the motel—which they didn't want any way!

Seller financing was also key. No bank would lend $1.2 million on a nonrecourse basis for the purchase of a property worth $600,000. (The loan would be underwater from the moment it was made!) But the Romneys, who were very happy to keep the motel in the end, could "sell" the property to the Associates for pretty much any stated purchase price, *since there was no cash loan involved.* Indeed, overvaluation served the Romneys' goal, which was to pocket the $75,000 "prepaid interest" money while running virtually zero risk that the Associates would ever follow through and pay the rest of the purchase price for the motel!

---

[2] The Associates potentially faced gain upon foreclosure, measured by the excess of the unpaid nonrecourse debt over their adjusted basis in the motel. Gain calculated in this way would offset the initial depreciation deductions taken. But the legal basis for this result, Commissioner v. Tufts, 461 U.S. 300 (1983) (discussed in Chapter 7), was not solidified until 1983. At the time of the transaction in Estate of Franklin, the Associates may have taken the position that they would have no gain on foreclosure. But even if the Associates followed what would someday be known as the Tufts rule, they still would have achieved *tax deferral* by deducting depreciation early and including the offsetting gain much later.

[3] Michael J. Graetz, *The Decline (and Fall?) of the Income Tax* (1997).

Given these facts, the only amazing feature of the *Estate of Franklin* deal is that the parties set the value at $1.2 million. Why not call it a $2 million or $3 million motel? The deal would have been just as (un)real at those prices.

The Ninth Circuit opinion spots the *valuation* problem and makes it the centerpiece of its holding. The taxpayers, ruled the court, were not entitled to depreciation deductions because the overvaluation of the property deprived them of any investment in it. The court cannily spotted that the Associates were unlikely (in the end) to pay off the $1.2 million. Accordingly, the court decided, the Associates should not be entitled to depreciate the property. Following a similar rationale, the court disallowed interest deductions on the purported loan, holding that the overvaluation made it unlikely that, in the end, the Romneys would truly lend (or the Associates repay) any money.

The opinion in *Estate of Franklin* is a classic example of *substance over form* analysis in tax. The court isn't bound to respect the formal terms of the deal but instead inquires into what is, objectively speaking, likely to happen if the parties pursue their own best interests. Here, the Associates didn't really want to buy, and the Romneys didn't want to sell, and the inflated purchase price helped ensure that the Thunderbird Inn likely wouldn't change hands. It would be absurd, the court's decision implies, to respect an "investment" made on such terms.

¶1402 *FRANK LYON CO. V. U.S.*

Frank Lyon Co. v. U.S.,[4] like many of the tax shelter cases, turns on the *substance over form* doctrine. To understand the *substance over form* claim lodged by the IRS against the taxpayer, put yourself in the position of a real estate developer. Suppose that you have spotted a prime piece of vacant property. The property is for sale for $1 million, and you think that for an additional $4 million, you could build a profitable shopping center. But you don't have the money on hand, so you need to put together a financing plan. What you need, obviously enough, is someone to lend you all (or most) of the $5 million.

There are two ways to structure the deal. The first, and most intuitive, is a classic loan. You buy the property and borrow the $5 million from the bank. The relationship in that case is clear enough. You are the owner; the bank is the lender. And, when you rent out the stores, the stores will be your tenants. You will use the rents to pay off the loan.

The second way to structure the deal is a lease. It's only a little more complicated and will get you to pretty much the same financial deal in the end. The first step is to persuade someone else to buy the property, build the shopping center, and then lease it to you. This arrangement works just fine from your perspective: you would be able to rent out the stores and use the rents you collect to pay the rent you owe to the owner.

---

[4] 435 U.S. 561 (1978).

In both cases, someone else (the bank in the loan example, the landlord in the lease example) fronts the $5 million necessary to build the shopping center. And in both cases, your profit is the difference between the rents you collect and the amounts you owe to a third party (again, either the bank or the landlord).

You might object that the two kinds of deals will offer you very different management rights. If you build the shopping center yourself, for instance, you can design it from the ground up, choosing the layout, the quality of materials, and so on. Surely the landlord in the second deal structure won't give you the same hands-on control.

But, in fact, it's fairly common in commercial real estate for a tenant to sign a very long-term lease that gives him substantial control over what is built. (You may have seen commercial real estate signs that say, "Will Build to Suit.") The landlord may put some limits on what can be built to ensure that it's a sensible plan. But keep in mind that the bank in the first deal structure is likely to do the same. That is, even though you own the property outright, the bank will only lend you the money if you agree to use it in certain ways. Why? Because both the bank and the lender are laying out millions of dollars, and if your business goes badly, they will be left holding the bag.

The key point is that borrowing and renting are different legal categories, sure, but in financial terms, they can closely resemble each other, especially when the custom of the industry permits substantial customization of the terms of both loans and leases. This is very much true in commercial real estate, where lenders get heavily involved in development plans, and where landlords grant tenants substantial rights and responsibilities for building and running large projects.

None of this malleability worries financial types. Any bank or borrower, landlord or tenant, will not be particularly fixated on how a deal is labelled. Instead, they will focus on the substance of the deal, and particularly on two aspects: (1) cash flows and (2) risks. Cash flows include payments on loans, tenant rents, and insurance proceeds. Risks include upside (if the project does well, who profits?) and downside (if the project does poorly or closes, who loses what?). Real estate lawyers spend their time negotiating complex deals like these.

But the malleability of loan and lease transactions causes mischief in the tax law, because the law imposes different rules on the two. Many of the payments involved are deductible (like interest and rent) in either case. But the elephant in the room is depreciation: an owner may deduct depreciation, while a tenant may not.

The result is that depreciation deductions represent a valuable tax goodie that sophisticated parties will bargain over. Depreciation is especially valuable when marginal tax rates are high and depreciation is accelerated. And depreciation deductions may be more valuable to one party than to others. Recall that the value of a depreciation rises with the marginal tax rate. So a profitable business will have far more use for depreciation deductions than, say, a tax-exempt organization with a zero marginal tax rate.

Putting together the value of depreciation and the malleability of deal structures, how would you expect sophisticated parties to act? Pretty clearly, they will structure their deals to locate depreciation in the hands of the highest bidder. And that means locating ownership in those hands. You would expect, then, to see tax planners structuring deals that treat the highest-bracket party as the "owner" or "landlord," even if the other terms of the deal grant that party very little control over designing and running the development.

The deal in *Frank Lyon* takes exactly this form. The terms of the deal are complicated, and the Supreme Court's opinion is hard to read. But we can summarize the important features of the deal by simplifying a bit and by breaking it down into three components:

(1) *The Sale.* Worthen Bank wanted to build a new office building for $8 million, but the bank regulators refused to grant permission. (You have to wonder whether perhaps Worthen didn't lobby too hard, given the advantages of having regulators "force" them into a lease!) So Worthen looked around for a deal partner willing to construct and own the building and lease it to Worthen. In fact, Worthen initiated a national bidding process, which drew firms like Goldman Sachs. Ultimately, a local appliance dealer, Frank Lyon Co., won the right to buy the property and lease it back to Lyon. Lyon put in about $500,000 of its own cash and borrowed the other $7.5 million from New York Life.

(2) *The Leaseback.* Worthen negotiated a stunningly favorable building lease with Lyon as part of the package deal. For the first 25 years, Worthen would pay Lyon just enough to pay off the loan to New York Life. For the 40 years after that, Worthen would have the option (but not the obligation) to extend its lease at a rent of $300,000 per year. Worthen still owned the land underneath the building and profited from the terms of the ground lease. The ground rents were low during the first 25 years in order to give Lyon time and money to pay off the loan to New York Life. But in the next 50 years, the ground rents rose sharply, from the initial $50,000 to $250,000 per year. When you net out the ground rents Worthen would receive from the building rents it would pay, you see that Worthen was entitled to rent the building for that 40-year period for rents as low as $50,000 per year, a fraction of the original rents. To be sure, the building would then be more than 25 years old. But the terms of the deal locked in a likely bargain for Worthen. And if, when the time came, the deal wasn't sweet enough, Worthen could walk away (and still collect its ground rents).

(3) *The Purchase Options.* Worthen also negotiated the right (but not the obligation) to purchase the building during the first 25 years. The option price is revealing. It was apparently equal to the unpaid balance of the New York Life loan plus a repayment of Lyon's $500,000 investment and 6% interest. Put another way, although Lyon was the nominal owner of the building, Worthen possessed the right to step into Lyon's financial shoes at any time.

Worthen and Lyon documented the deal (and treated it for tax purposes) with Lyon as the owner and Worthen the tenant. The result, of course, was that depreciation deductions—eventually, all $8 million—would go to Lyon.

But the IRS asserted that Worthen, not Lyon, was the owner of the building. Invoking the *substance over form* doctrine, the IRS treated Lyon as just a lender of money ($500,000, to be exact) to Worthen, the true owner. The result: the IRS denied depreciation (and interest) deductions to Lyon. And to add insult, the IRS imputed interest income to Lyon based on a 6% implied return on its $500,000 loan.

Looking at the terms of the deal, there was more than a little logic to the IRS position. The terms of the lease and the purchase option gave Lyon very little potential to profit, while Worthen, the nominal tenant, had very favorable lease terms and options granting it substantial upside if the building appreciated.

Taking a broader view, the problem in *Frank Lyon* has its roots in freedom of contract. Contractual freedom gives the parties to any transaction the power to tailor the terms of the deal to fit their needs. When industry norms permit customization—and when tax benefits invite it—the result is that the labels "lease" and "loan" can lose all economic meaning. The parties to the *Frank Lyon* deal labelled Worthen the tenant and Lyon the owner. But they could, just as accurately, have termed Worthen the owner and Lyon a lender.

The Supreme Court in *Frank Lyon* confronted a massive legal problem. The tax law's distinction between leases and loans was (and is) economic nonsense, and it permitted sophisticated parties to craft deals that would award tax benefits to the highest bidder. But the justices might have felt themselves poorly positioned to impose a regime of economic substance. The Court as an institution just isn't capable of analyzing the economy-wide ramifications of such a major alteration in the tax law. Not to mention that the separation of powers constrains the court from doing anything more than ruling for or against the IRS. The Court could not—even if it wanted to—take on the task of crafting a sophisticated new rule system for allocating tax benefits among transacting parties.

So, instead, the Court sought a defensible middle ground. Frank Lyon Co. could be treated as the owner of the building *for tax purposes*, the Court held, if it bore some of the benefits and burdens of ownership. Analyzing the transaction, the Court noted that Lyon bore downside risk. Lyon could find itself in a tough financial position if Worthen defaulted on the lease, leaving Lyon to pay off the New York Life loan on its own. And Lyon could lose money if the real estate market turned sour and Worthen declined to extend its lease, leaving Lyon to find another tenant in a shaky real estate market.

These downside risks, the Supreme Court held, gave the transaction enough substance to support Lyon's claim of ownership for tax purposes. Lyon thus was entitled to take depreciation deductions on the building and interest deductions on the New York Life loan.

The decision in *Frank Lyon* left many tax experts dissatisfied because it left intact a taxpayers' capacity to structure flexible deals that award tax benefits to the highest bidder. As long as the nominal owner stood to lose money under certain scenarios (however economically improbable), the arrangement would pass legal muster.

But perhaps that outcome is what the Supreme Court intended. It managed to decide the case in a way that didn't roil the economic waters—much. And so the Court essentially punted, leaving it up to the Congress to act, if it chose, to bring the tax law closer to economic reality. So far, the Congress hasn't taken up the opportunity to rationalize the taxation of leasing and loans. *Frank Lyon* remains good law today.

¶1403 *ACM PARTNERSHIP V. COMMISSIONER*

The transaction in *ACM Partnership v. Commissioner*[5] aimed to produce *tax deferral*. By this stage in this book, you won't be shocked to learn that the shelter took advantage of a gap in the law caused by a *valuation* problem. The ACM transaction is complex, involving multiple parties, international tax rules, offsetting transactions, an installment sale, and a notional principal contract. But a little legal and transactional background will set the stage.

ACM turned on a provision of the income tax called the installment sale rules, so let's begin there. The income tax has long awarded *tax deferral* to installment sales, which are contracts that permit a buyer to pay for her purchase over time. Code Section 453 permits sellers in an installment sale to report gain over time, as cash is received, rather than upfront, when the buyer and seller sign the sales contract.

> **EXAMPLE 1.** Sarah has a car with a basis of $9,000. She sells Ian the car for $12,000 and agrees to accept three annual payments of $4,000 each. Absent the installment sale rules, Sarah would have gain equal to $3,000 on the day she and Ian sign the contract.[6] After all, the sale is a realization event. But the tax law gives Sarah a break; the installment sale rules permit her to recognize her gain over time as payments come in. In the simplest case, she would allocate her basis ratably to each of the three payments, so she would recover 1/3, or $3,000 of basis each time. Thus, she would recognize gain of $1,000 (payment of $4,000 over allocated basis of $3,000) each year.[7]

The installment sale rules serve several functions. For one thing, they make it easy for individuals and small companies to account for sales over time. The installment sale rules also avoid the *valuation* problem that the law would confront if it tried to tax installment sales immediately. In principle, the amount realized would be the fair market value of the buyer's obligation (not its face amount). In the Sarah-Ian example, for instance, Ian's credit may be poor, or interest rates

---

5 157 F. 3d 231 (3d Cir. 1998).

6 For simplicity, the example ignores the time value of money: that is, three annual payments of $4,000 would have a fair market value less than $12,000 when discounted.

7 Note that Code Section 453 does not apply to dealers or to sales of inventory. Also note that Section 483 would require the seller to break out and report separately the interest component on the sale.

may be high. In either case, his obligation to pay $12,000 would be worth less than that on Day One.

For decades, the installment sale rules drifted along, a sleepy backwater in the tax law, a simple, even friendly, tax break for small transactions and individual taxpayers. But the rules weren't limited by their terms to small transactions or small taxpayers, and bigger fish took notice of a feeding opportunity.

A tempting target, and the centerpiece of *ACM Partnership*, was the basis rule applicable to contingent installment sales. To see why this rule was needed, consider a simple example.

> **EXAMPLE 2.** Dr. Sam Smith, a small-town dentist, has just turned 70 and would like to retire. He has a basis of $100,000 in his practice and feels that it should be attractive to another dentist. Dr. Jenna Jones, a young dentist just out of school, would like to buy Sam's practice. But Jenna isn't sure how much the practice is worth, and Sam can't promise that all his patients will remain with the practice after he leaves. So Sam and Jenna agree to a very common deal: Jenna will pay Sam nothing upfront but, over the next 5 years, Jenna will pay Sam 25% of her annual revenues. The logic is simple: if the practice does well, Sam will profit along with Jenna for 5 years. But if the practice turns out not to be worth very much in that period, Sam won't collect much either.

A contingent installment sale solves a business problem—the uncertain value of the asset being sold. But the *valuation* uncertainty also poses a problem for the tax law. In a normal installment sale, the law can measure gain based on the total contract payments. (In the Sarah-Ian example above, the contract payments totaled $12,000, so everyone knew that Sarah's gain would be $3,000 eventually.) By contrast, in the contingent installment sale, no one will know the seller's gain until the contract payments eventually are made.

The Code Section 453 regulations at the time of *ACM Partnership* attempted to solve the problem by allocating the seller's basis ratably over time. In the Sam-Jenna example above, the regulations would have required Sam to divide his $100,000 basis by five (because payments are due once a year for five years). Sam would then have recognized gain or loss each year, based on the difference between the payment received and his allocated basis of $20,000.

IRS regulation writers are pretty smart, and they try to think through whether their rules might open up opportunities for tax planning. So the authors of the contingent installment sale regulations, included the proviso that the IRS could require an alternate method of basis recovery if the general rule would "substantially and inappropriately accelerate recovery of basis."[8] The tax authorities knew

---

[8] Regulation Section 15a.453-1(c)(7)(iii), (former) Temporary Income Tax Regulations. found at 46 Fed. Reg. 10716. The final regulations, Regulation Section 15a.453-1(c)(3), retain the ratable basis allocation rule but with two refinements. First, the rule does not permit taxpayers to claim a loss in any period; any unused basis is carried forward to a subsequent period. Second, Regulation Section 15a.453-1(c)(7) contains elaborate rules that authorize the IRS to redetermine basis allocations if the ratable allocation rule "substantially and inappropriately" defers or accelerates basis recovery.

that tax planning often seeks *tax deferral*, and fast recovery of basis is one way to achieve it. But the regulation writers overlooked the possibility that taxpayers might deliberately postpone basis recovery. After all, such a possibility makes little sense: who on earth would want to recover less basis and thereby generate more taxable income early on?

Enter ACM Partnership and the financial firm Merrill Lynch. Tax experts at Merrill had figured out how to use the installment sale rules to produce a deductible capital loss but with little or no risk of a real economic loss.[9] Merrill reached out to a number of clients, and one that took the plunge was Colgate, the toothpaste company. Colgate had realized a $100 million capital gain on the sale of stock in a subsidiary, and so Colgate was intrigued by Merrill's promise of an immediate capital loss that would offset the gain, reducing the net tax to zero.

Merrill's plan relied on three features of the tax law. The first was the contingent installment sale rules, which we have already met. The second was the U.S. rules on international taxation. Under U.S. tax law, generally speaking, a non-U.S. person is not taxable on capital gains on stock and securities, even if the securities are issued by U.S. companies and traded on U.S. markets.[10]

The third feature of the tax law that made the deal in *ACM Partnership* possible was the rules governing partnership taxation. Partnerships are pass-through entities, meaning that they do not pay tax as entities, the way corporations do. Instead, a partnership's income (and loss) for any year flow through to the partners for that year.

Merrill put the three rules together to create a transaction that involved a partnership between a nontaxable foreign entity and Colgate, the fully-taxable U.S. client. (Merrill itself also joined the partnership as an accommodation party.) The deal involved a series of financial transactions that would deliberately accelerate gain—right into the hands of the nontaxable foreign party. The foreign firm would exit the scene after the initial gain had begun to give way to corresponding losses. These losses would be captured by the remaining partner—Colgate!

Simplifying a bit, the transactions worked this way:

Merrill and Colgate formed ACM partnership with Algemene Bank Nederland, N.V. ("ABN"), a Dutch bank. Initially, ABN owned 90% of the partnership, meaning that 90% of any income or loss would flow through to ABN. Colgate owned 9%, and Merrill owned 1%. Acting according to plan, ACM purchased $180 million in securities. A very short time later, ACM turned around and sold the securities for $180 million.

You might think, reasonably enough, that ACM had made neither a profit nor a loss on the deal: that's what buying for $180 and selling for $180 usually produces. But keep in mind that the installment sale rules ignored actual market

9 Under the rules of partnership taxation, the loss would eventually be matched by an offsetting gain, when the parties liquidated the partnership or sold their partnership interests. But the gain could be deferred as long as the partnership remained in existence. *See* Code Section 731.

10 There are exceptions to this rule, but they are not relevant here. *See* Code Sections 871, 881 and 897.

values and, instead, imposed arbitrary rules of thumb. To take advantage of the contingent installment sale rules, Merrill instructed ACM to make use of a financial device called a notional principal contract.

A notional principal contract is a common financial transaction, and there's nothing (necessarily) fishy about it. A notional principal contract is essentially a financial bet. The contract specifies the timing and amount of payments to be made by each party. The amount of each party's payment is either fixed upfront or made contingent on some measurable index (*e.g.*, an index of stock prices, interest rates, or currency exchange rates). Unlike a debt instrument, which obligates one party to lend and the other to repay a principal amount, a notional principal contract (as its name suggests) does not require the lending or repayment of principal. Instead, the notional principal amount is a reference point for calculating payments due by one or both parties.

EXAMPLE 3. Bank A and Firm B enter into a notional principal contract. Pursuant to the contract, A pays B the sum of $15 million at the inception of the contract. In return, B must pay A four annual payments, beginning one year from the inception of the contract. Each payment will equal the product of (a) a notional principal amount of $100 million and (b) an interest rate index (say, LIBOR, or the London Interbank Offered Rate).[11]

So, for example, if LIBOR stands at 5% one year from the contract date, B must pay A $5 million (5% times the notional principal amount of $100 million). Neither B nor A will ever pay the $100 million; it is a reference figure only.

In the business world, notional principal contracts are particularly useful for hedging. Suppose, for example, that your business has borrowed money from a bank at a floating interest rate. (A floating interest rate means that the interest rate changes along with market interest rates.) You are (or should be!) worried that interest rates will rise, because if they do, your payments to the bank would rise too. To hedge (reduce) your risk, you might enter into a notional principal contract. The contract would require you to pay an upfront sum and, in return, you would receive payments based on the floating interest rate. We would say that the notional principal contract has hedged your exposure to interest rates: if interest rates rise, you will owe the bank more money, but you will also receive a higher payment on the notional principal contract.

But the notional principal contract in *ACM Partnership* was a different animal. It enabled the parties to create a contingent installment sale. Recall that ACM Partnership purchased securities for $180 million. It then sold them for a package of consideration worth $180. But the trick was that the consideration ACM received consisted of $140 million in cash plus a notional principal contract that

[11] Investopedia defines LIBOR as "a benchmark rate that some of the world's leading banks charge each other for short-term loans." http://www.investopedia.com/terms/l/libor.asp.

provided for six annual payments pegged to LIBOR. The investment bankers valued the notional principal contract at $40 million. (That is why ACM accepted the contract plus $140 million in cash in exchange for $180 million in securities).

According to the installment sale regulations, ACM's sale was a contingent installment sale, because the amount of the payments was uncertain. No one knew exactly what LIBOR would be in each future year. Following the tax regulations to the letter, ACM divided its basis of $180 million into six equal components of $30 million each. The trick was that there was a serious mismatch between the level stream of basis recovery and the extremely front-loaded stream of payments. The result was a massive (and artificial) acceleration of gain—followed by an equally massive (and equally artificial) offsetting loss.

Table 14.1 Gain and Loss in ACM Partnership

Year	Basis	Amount Realized	Gain (Loss)
1	30	140	110
2	30	8	-22
3	30	8	-22
4	30	8	-22
5	30	8	-22
6	30	8	-22
TOTALS	180	180	0

As Table 14.1 shows, the tax planners intended to produce a massive gain of $110 million in Year 1, followed by an equally massive loss totalling $110 million in years 2 through 5.

In the early days, ABN, the Dutch bank, took a brief but central role in the tax drama. In Year 1, ABN was a 90% partner, and, accordingly, 90% of the $110 million gain was allocated to it. But ABN, being a foreign corporation (from the U.S. perspective), was not taxable on the gain.

In a stunning coincidence, ABN just happened to sell its stake in ACM Partnership to Colgate just after the close of Year 1. (Yes, this is sarcasm. The sale was a key part of the plan!) By Year 2, Colgate owned 99% of ACM Partnership, and so Colgate reported 99% of the $110 million loss in Years 2-5.

Whew! Whatever you think about the legality of the deal in *ACM Partnership*, you must admit that it was clever and audacious. The IRS certainly thought it was too clever by half. The Service audited ACM Partnership (and several similar deals sponsored by Merrill Lynch) and invoked the *substance over form* doctrine to disallow any tax effects of the purchase and sale of securities for $180 million.

The Third Circuit ruled for the IRS, holding that the purported installment sale lacked economic substance. The Court's opinion goes through the objective and subjective versions of the economic substance test, and both (according to the Court) point in the same direction. Taking an objective perspective, the

Third Circuit noted that the purchase and sale of securities had only "nominal, incidental effects" on ACM's economic position. The purported loss, the court ruled, was not a *bona fide* loss.

From a subjective point of view, the court found that Colgate had shown little concern about the economic risk and return of the transactions and had focused instead on the tax benefits it would produce. Colgate agreed to pay $3 million in transaction costs, the court noted, for a transaction that would produce zero profit on a pre-tax basis. (The court noted that ACM Partnership had reinvested its cash in Colgate debt, an investment that might have served a business purpose. But that that investment, the court ruled, was separate and independent from the contingent installment sale and its tax benefits.)

In the end, Merrill's clever tax scheme cost its client, Colgate, a bundle in taxes. Still, even though the IRS won the case, it's worth noting that some of the taxpayer's legal arguments were not baseless. First, the taxpayer relied on the IRS's own regulations in structuring its transactions. The IRS argued, and the court agreed, that the *substance over form* doctrine should override the installment sale regulations. But the regulations did purport to offer bright-line rules on which the taxpayer could rely. Second, the taxpayer invoked *Cottage Savings*[12] (discussed in Chapter 6), and it is interesting to consider the contrast between the two cases. *Cottage Savings* held that purely formal differences are sufficient to trigger a realization event. ACM Partnership argued that, in similar fashion, the formalities of its transactions should be respected in calculating its tax liabilities.

Whether ACM Partnership's arguments should have won or lost, they do pose serious and enduring questions about the balance between rules and standards—and substance and form in the tax law.

[12] Cottage Savings Association v. Commissioner, 499 U.S. 554 (1991).

APPENDIX A

A Glossary of Tax and Business Jargon

I've written this book to be as jargon-free as possible. Not all judges and clients, however, will follow suit. And every field of law has its own language. So, to help you as you navigate the law, here are definitions for common tax and business terms.

Accelerated depreciation: See depreciation.

Annuity: An annuity is a contract between an issuer (almost always a life insurance company) and a buyer. In the simplest case of a single-premium life annuity, the buyer pays a lump sum upfront in return for an annual stream of payments that will last her entire life. For example, 70-year-old Rosemary might pay Genworth Life Insurance Company $1 million today in return for an annual payment of $100,000 for as long as she lives. The annuity represents a bet on (i) how long Rosemary will live, and (ii) what kind of investment return can be earned in the marketplace. If Rosemary lives till 90, the insurance company may well lose money on the bet. If she dies before 80 or so, the insurance company wins the bet. Why do people buy annuities? The answer lies in risk-shifting. Rosemary should buy the annuity only if she is willing to pay (an often high) price to shift to the insurance company the risks that (i) she will live an unusually long life, and (ii) investment returns may fall.

Average tax rate: Total income tax liability divided by total taxable income. Average tax rates are used to measure overall tax burden on an individual, a family, or a group of taxpayers. See Chapter 2.

Bonds (synonym: *debentures*): A bond is a debt instrument. The bond issuer is the borrower, and the bond holder is the lender. The bond buyer lends money to the bond issuer, typically a business or government entity. The bond issuer pays the holder interest and will repay the principal at maturity.

Corporate stock: An equity or residual interest in a corporation. In a corporate liquidation, stockholders receive what is left after all corporate debts have been paid. The result is that stockholders receive a variable return—more if the corporation is profitable, and possibly nothing at all if the corporation loses money. For example, suppose that X Corporation has $1 million in cash (and no other assets) after paying off all its debts. A stockholder holding 10% of the single class of common stock would receive 10% of the assets of the corporation upon liquidation—here, $100,000.

Credit (also *tax credit*): A dollar amount subtracted from the taxpayer's tax liability. For example, if Sean's initial tax liability for the year is $10,000, but he is entitled to a $500 tax credit because he installed energy-efficient windows, his tax liability is reduced by $500, and he owes the IRS only $9,500.

Creditor (synonym: *debt holder*): A creditor is a lender.

Debt: Debt is the borrowing of money. The lender (or creditor) provides money to (or funds the purchase of goods by) the borrower. The terms of the debt establish the interest rate, the date for repayment of the principal, and the remedies for nonpayment.

Debtor (synonym: *debt issuer*): A debtor is a borrower.

Deduction: An amount subtracted from income. For instance, if Angela has $50,000 of income and is permitted an additional deduction of $1,000, her income falls to $49,000.

Depreciation: A periodic (usually annual) deduction that reflects the predicted decline in the value of an asset due to wear and tear. For instance, if David buys a delivery van for his flower shop for $20,000, and the van is expected to last 10 years, the tax law might permit David to deduct one-tenth (or $2,000) of the original cost of the van every year for 10 years. *Straight-line depreciation* permits the taxpayer to deduct a level amount per year over the predicted life of the asset (as in the example of David's delivery van). *Accelerated depreciation* awards deductions at a faster rate than straight-line. Acceleration can take the form of a front-loaded depreciation schedule or a (deliberately) too-short asset life, or both. For instance, the tax law might permit David to deduct the $20,000 cost of his van over just five years, with $10,000 deducted in the first year, $5,000 in the second, $2,500 in the third, and $1,250 in the fourth and fifth years. Accelerated depreciation produces *tax deferral.*

Discounted value (or *discounted present value*): See present value.

Dividend: A distribution of property (usually cash) to holders of corporate stock in their capacity as stockholders. Dividends are often expressed on a per-share basis and are paid to all shareholders as of a publicly-announced record date. Suppose, for example, that Microsoft announces a 25-cent dividend, payable to holders of record as of May 1. That means that Annie, who owns 100 shares on that date, will soon receive a check from Microsoft for $25 (*i.e.,* 25 cents multiplied by 100 shares).

Equity: Generally, an ownership interest, with two common uses. (1) An equity owner in a business owns the residual claim; the contrast in that context is to a debtholder. For instance, if Sara owns all the common stock in a corporation, while Derek owns only a debt obligation of the corporation, we would say that Sarah holds equity, while Derek holds debt. (2) A property owner's equity in her property equals the fair market value of the property less any outstanding debt. Equivalently, equity is the amount the owner could keep if she sold the property and paid off all debt obligations related to the property. For example, if Donald Trump buys Trump Tower for $100 million and borrows $80 million from Big Bank to finance the purchase, we would say that Donald has equity in the building of $20 million. If the value of Trump Tower rises to $105 million (and the amount of debt remains constant), we'd say that The Donald now has equity of $25 million.

Exclusion: An amount not included in income. For instance, if Barry earns $50,000 in cash salary and receives on-site meals worth $1,000, section 119 may permit him to exclude (not include) the $1,000, so that he reports only $50,000 on his tax return instead of $51,000. See Chapter 3.

Fringe benefits: Goodies provided by employers to their workers, like free lunch at the office or stand-by airline tickets. See Chapter 3.

Gain: The difference between the amount realized on a sale and the taxpayer's basis in the asset. See Chapter 5.

Goodwill: In a business setting, goodwill is sometimes called "going concern value," or the value of an ongoing business. More precisely, goodwill is the excess of the fair market value of a business over the value of its tangible (and identifiable intangible) assets. Think about it this way. Suppose you want to buy a successful local coffee shop, Perk Up, and the price is $1 million. What are you getting for your money? The coffee shop has many assets that could be listed on paper: you'd be buying a building, some tables and chairs, an inventory of coffee, and the "Perk Up" logo and brand name. But those assets might be worth only, say, $400,000. So why would you pay $1 million? The answer is intuitive when you think about the difference between a going business, on the one hand, and a defunct coffee shop, on the other. You're paying the extra $600,000 because of the goodwill associated with the business. Perk Up is successful because it has (say) friendly customer service, reliably good coffee, clean bathrooms, and a large fan base among students at the local college. Goodwill isn't tangible, but it is very real. The value of any going business often exceeds the value of its assets by a considerable amount.

Income shifting: Taxpayers can reduce their tax bill if they can shift taxable income from a person with a high marginal tax rate to a person with a low marginal tax rate. If Asla and Brian are an unmarried couple, and if Asla has a 40% marginal rate, while Brian has a 0% marginal rate, they could save a bundle in taxes if they could legally attribute the money to Brian. Income shifting is explained in detail in Chapter 1.

Interest: The amount paid by a borrower to a lender as compensation for the use of money for a period. The interest rate is expressed as a percentage of the borrowed amount per time period (e.g., five percent per year).

Life insurance: Life insurance is a contract between an individual and a life insurance company. The individual pays a premium, usually annually and in cash. In return, the life insurance company promises to pay a set benefit if the insured person dies during the policy period.

Long position: A person takes a long position in an asset (often, corporate stock) when she holds the asset or has an obligation to buy the asset at a set price. The owner of 1,000 shares of GE stock thus has a long position in GE. So does the person who has signed a forward contract (basically, an advance purchase agreement) to buy GE stock for a fixed price at a fixed future time. If Marlin, for example, has agreed to buy 1,000 shares of GE at $100 per share on January 1 of next year, she will benefit financially if the stock price rises above $100 and will lose financially if the stock price falls below that level.

Loss: The term "loss" has two meanings in tax: (1) A loss on the sale or other disposition of an asset, measured by the difference between basis and amount realized. (See Chapter 5) (2) The excess of deductions related to an activity over income related to the activity. A business, for example, might be said to operate at a loss if its deductible expenses exceed the income it produces.

Marginal tax rate: The tax rate applied to the next dollar of income or deduction. Marginal tax rates are used in tax planning. See Chapter 2.

Mortgage (*mortgagor, mortgagee*): A mortgage is the name for a loan that is secured by a particular piece of property. The *mortgagor* is the property owner, who gives the *mortgagee* (a bank, or in seller-financing, the seller of the property), a security interest in the property. A security interest allows the creditor (mortgagee) to *foreclose* (or take ownership of the property) if the mortgagor does not pay the debt. The terms of the mortgage typically allow the creditor to foreclose quickly, without first pursuing a lengthy course of other legal remedies; and they typically give the creditor *first priority* claim to the asset in the event of bankruptcy (a valuable right, if the debtor's total debts exceed her assets). A mortgagor typically cannot sell the property without paying off the debt or arranging for assumption of the debt by the buyer of the property.

Net income: The income tax seeks to tax net income rather than gross income; that is, the taxpayer's economic gains net of the costs of earning those gains. Mechanically, deductions transform gross income into net income. Exclusions ensure that items used in the production of income are not (mistakenly) counted as income. Chapters 2, 8, 9, and 11 consider problems of determining net income.

Nonrecourse debt (contrast: *recourse debt*): A debtor borrows money on a nonrecourse basis when the lender agrees that its only remedy (if the borrower fails to pay) is to take possession of a particular piece of property. Put another way, nonrecourse debt is always secured by specific property, and the lender's only recourse (upon default) is to foreclose on the property. For instance, if Natalie borrows $1 million on a nonrecourse basis to buy land, and if Natalie fails to pay off the debt (or simply decides not to pay), the lender's only recourse is to take possession of the land. If the land is worth less than $1 million, the lender is stuck with the loss. Nonrecourse debt may initially sound like a really bad deal from the lender's point of view. In contrast to recourse debt, the nonrecourse lender *bears the downside risk*—the risk that the property's value will fall. So why would a lender take this risk? The answer is that the lender is presumably compensated for the risk in some way: she gets a higher interest rate on the loan or (if she is the seller of property) a higher price for the property.

OID (*original issue discount*): Original issue discount is, financially speaking, just another way for debtors to pay interest to creditors. But the interest is built into the terms of the deal (specifically, the amount borrowed and the amount to be repaid) rather than being payable in cash periodically. For instance, suppose that Bigcorp. wants to borrow $100 million to build a new factory. A typical loan would bear stated interest at a market rate, say, 5%, so that Bigcorp. would pay the bank $5 million in interest per year and, at the end of the loan, would repay the principal of $100 million. But suppose that Bigcorp. wants to backload cash payments; perhaps the new factory will take awhile to build and become profitable. Bigcorp. could issue its debt at a discount, borrowing $100 million and paying zero interest but promising to repay (in 10 years) a larger sum, say, $160 million. This apparently "interest-free" loan isn't interest-free at all: it turns out that a promise to pay $160 million in 10 years is equivalent (roughly) to paying 5% all along on the initial $100 million!

Options (also *put options and call options*): An option is the right but not the obligation to engage in a specified transaction during a fixed time period and at a set price. If Fran holds an option to buy Greenacre, for example, she has the right, but not the obligation, to purchase the property. The option contract typically will specify the price Fran must pay (e.g., $1 million) and the date on which the option expires (e.g., one year from the date of the option contract). Up to the date of expiration, Fran can choose to exercise the option (by paying the $1 million). If she lets the option expire (or "lapse"), the contract simply terminates, with no further obligation by either party. A *call option* is (like Fran's option) the option to buy property. A *put option* is the option to sell property. For example, if Barry thinks that the value of Apple stock will fall below its current price of $50, he might enter into a put option giving him the legal right (but not the obligation) to sell Apple stock at $50. If the stock price falls to $40, Barry can exercise the option and force the other party, in effect, to overpay by $10. Of course, if the stock price remains at or above $50, Barry's put option is worthless, and he will let it expire.

Phantom Income: Taxable income that is not matched by a cash flow. Taxpayers dislike phantom income, because it creates tax liability without generating the cash needed to pay the tax.

Present value (also *discounted present value*): Present value is a financial calculation that permits investors to compare amounts of money received at different times. The underlying idea is that money can always be invested at some interest rate, so that a given sum today will grow to a bigger sum tomorrow. How much the investment grows over time depends on (i) the interest rate and (ii) the time period involved. For example, if you put $100 in a 5% bank account today and leave it there for 10 years, it will grow to $163. Working backwards, in effect, we would say that the present value of $163 to be received in 10 years is $100!

Progressive (contrast *regressive*): A tax system is progressive if, on average, richer persons pay a higher share of their income than poorer ones do.

Realization (also *realization requirement*): Realization is the tax rule that postpones the measurement of income from an investment until the taxpayer sells. Put another way, the realization requirement gives taxpayers the legal authorization to ignore (for tax purposes) their economic gains and losses until they decide to sell. If, for instance, Marta buys Microsoft stock for $10,000, and it grows (over a decade) to $25,000, the tax law takes no notice of her good fortune (or business acumen) unless and until Marta sells the stock. Chapters 1 and 6 discuss the connections among realization, valuation, and tax deferral.

Recourse debt (contrast *nonrecourse debt*): A person borrows money on a recourse basis when she agrees that the lender can, if necessary, sue for the sale of any (and all) of the borrower's assets in the event that the borrower does not pay. That is, the lender has full recourse to all of the borrower's assets. For instance, suppose that Simon borrows $100,000 from a bank in order to open a new restaurant, and the debt is recourse debt. If Simon's restaurant fails, and he can't pay off the $100,000, then the bank can legally demand that Simon sell his other assets, including (say) his investment portfolio and (in some states) even his home.

Regressive (contrast *progressive*): A tax system is regressive if, on average, poorer persons pay a higher share of their income than richer ones do. For instance, a head tax of a flat $50 per person would be regressive, because the $50 tax payment represents a higher share of the income of a poor person than of a rich person. For Roberta, who earns $100,000 per year, the $50 would be a bit of a nuisance but quickly forgotten. For Paula, who earns just $10,000 per year, the $50 might seriously cut into her grocery budget.

Seller financing: In seller financing, the seller of property "takes back" a note (debt obligation) from the buyer in lieu of cash. Suppose that the price of Blackacre is $1 million. I might sell it to you for $1 million in cash. Or I might (if we can negotiate acceptable terms) accept instead your *promise to pay* $1 million on a fixed schedule, plus interest at an agreed-upon rate. The latter transaction is seller financing: the seller stands in dual capacity as seller of the property and lender of the purchase price.

Short position: A person takes a short position in an asset (often, corporate stock) when she has an obligation to sell the asset to another person at a set price. If, for example, Luke has contracted with Laura to sell her 1,000 shares of Apple stock for $50 per share on January 1 of next year, we say that Luke is "short" (or "has shorted") Apple stock. A short position represents a bet that the price of the asset will fall. In that sense, a short position is the opposite of a long position, because the holder of the position will profit if the stock price falls. If, on January 1, Apple stock is selling in the marketplace for just $40, Luke will be very happy about his contract, because he can spend $40 to buy each share and immediately resell for $50—a profit of $10 per share! If, on the other hand, Apple is trading for $75, then Luke will be sad, and Laura very happy, because she can buy Apple on the cheap from Luke for $50 and resell in the market for a profit of $25 per share!

Stock: See corporate stock.

Stockholder (also *shareholder*): an owner of corporate stock.

Stock dividend: The terms *dividend* and *stock dividend* are *not* interchangeable. A dividend is the generic term for any distribution of property by a corporation with respect to stock. A "stock dividend" is a term of art meaning the distribution of [additional] shares of stock with respect to shareholders' original holdings.

For example, if Aislynn owns 200 shares of IBM stock, and IBM declares a 1:1 (one-for-one) stock dividend, the corporation will issue to her 200 more shares. When the dust settles, IBM has twice as many outstanding shares, but each shareholder's proportional interest remains the same (at least, until some begin buying or selling shares).

Substance over form: The substance over form doctrine permits the IRS and the courts (but not, generally, the taxpayer) to tax a transaction in accordance with its economic attributes—rather than according to the form it takes. The substance over form doctrine is often invoked to combat tax shelters (Chapter 14) but arises pervasively in tax as the IRS combats taxpayer opportunism.

Tax credit: See credit.

Tax deduction: See deduction.

Tax deferral: Taxpayers engage in tax deferral when they devise strategies that permit them (legally) to put off paying their taxes until later. All else equal, most taxpayers would prefer to pay $100 to the IRS later rather than now. As long as the tax bill remains $100 (and doesn't grow due to interest or penalties), the taxpayer benefits, because she can invest the money in the meantime. In effect, tax deferral is an interest-free loan from the IRS to the taxpayer. Chapters 1 and 10 go into more detail.

Tax loss: See loss.

Valuation: Valuation occurs when the tax law requires taxpayers to determine how much income they have received. Valuation issues arise pervasively in the tax law, in contexts ranging from the business-personal distinction (see Chapters 2, 8, and 9) to income from property (see Chapters 5 and 6) to issues of borrowing, capitalization, depreciation, and losses (see Chapters 7, 10 and 11).

APPENDIX B

How to Answer an Issue-Spotter Exam Question

Students sometimes feel at sea when they confront an issue-spotter question in law school. College, it may seem, doesn't prepare us very well for this kind of professional exercise. None of my college exams involved stuff like estoppel, motions to dismiss, or the realization requirement.

But, in fact, a good issue-spotter exam just follows the rules for any good essay. The three key elements are structure, legal judgment, and quality of expression. This section will discuss each in turn and will provide examples. For obvious reasons, the examples here focus on tax, but the insights should be more generally applicable.

I should add that professors differ. But if, like many of my Yale students, you have received no (other) guidance at all on how to write an exam, I hope this will be useful.

STRUCTURE

Begin with structure. Try to channel your best English teacher here—you know, the one who was tough but fair and helped you learn to write really well. Every good essay should have a thesis, should prove its thesis in an organized way, and should provide evidence for its assertions. A law school exam should follow the same model.

A thesis, in this context, is a clear and concise statement of what the issues are and how you will resolve them. Doing this is, of course, harder than it sounds. Typically, you will need to do your legal analysis first (in outline form or by jotting notes for yourself) and then go back and come up with a concise thesis. Please don't take the reader along for a ramble through the issues, thinking out loud. Instead, this is a moment for you to be the teacher: be organized and clear about where you are going.

For example, consider the issue-spotter question below, taken from one of my past exams at Harvard. (This happens to be a short answer question, but a longer issue-spotter just involves more issues.)

> *Pierre graduated from the Harvard Law School in 2004. From 2004 through April 2008, he worked at a corporate law firm as a litigator. His work consisted of defending products liability cases (i.e., lawsuits alleging that his clients made defective products). In 2007-08, Pierre earned an LLM in International Law from NYU Law School (attending night and weekend classes). In May 2008, Pierre took a job with the State Department negotiating international human rights treaties. Can Pierre deduct on his federal income tax return the tuition he paid to Harvard? To NYU? Please offer Pierre some brief advice.*

A good answer would open by spotting the issue, relating it to the facts given, making reference to the relevant law, and giving a summary of the conclusions.

> The issue is whether Pierre's tuition payments to Harvard and to NYU may be deducted under section 162, must be capitalized under section 263, or are nondeductible under section 262. I conclude that Pierre may not deduct his Harvard tuition but has a reasonable (though not uncontestable) case for deducting his NYU tuition.

The answer would then go on and, in an organized way, discuss and address each issue.

A middling answer would dive right in without orienting the reader to the issues or the writer's legal conclusions. For instance:

> The question is about Pierre, who paid tuition to Harvard and NYU and probably would like to deduct his tuition on his tax return. Let's see if he can.
>
> The answer then proceeds to spot issues in no particular order and address them piecemeal without cluing in the reader where it's going.

Another mistake is to open with the case law without orienting the essay to the facts given. For example:

> The main case on point here would be *Wassenaar v. Commissioner,* which held that a student could not deduct the costs of his LLM in taxation. Wassenaar had gone to law school and then went right to his LLM program.

The body of the essay should present the analysis in an organized way. The particular organization you choose should be driven by the issues, but the structure should be visible to the reader. In this issue-spotter, for instance, there is a question about the Harvard tuition and the NYU tuition, and so a logical organization would consider the Harvard tuition issue first and the NYU tuition issue second.

The body of the essay should also invoke relevant legal authorities. For example:

> The Harvard tuition is not deductible since the J.D. qualifies graduates for the (new) trade or business of being a lawyer. See Regulation Section 1.162-5(b).

A lesser answer might omit the authority or rely instead on secondary sources:

> I don't think Pierre can deduct the Harvard tuition. See Casebook at p. xx.[1]

---

[1] It's fine to use the casebook and even to cite to the casebook if you reproduce its material verbatim, but please take the time to read what it says. Then look at the Code or the case and cite that. After all, your textbook isn't, er, legal authority! Cite to relevant cases by name, just as you would in a brief or memo.

LEGAL JUDGMENT

An issue-spotter should not only use good legal judgment but should demonstrate that judgment for the reader. The difference lies in the exposition: your task is to show and to explain your reasoning and to be clear about the judgments you are making and their justification.

A common mistake is to jump to a conclusion without portraying much of your reasoning. The conclusion may be correct, but it lacks the connections to the law and to the facts that will persuade your reader. For instance, a middling answer would state the issues and then simply say:

> The tuition Pierre paid for the LLM at NYU falls into a gray area in the law. Pierre's facts are better than those in *Wassenaar,* so I'm pretty sure he can take the deduction. It's worth a try anyway.

A better answer would explain how you've analyzed the relevant law:

> Pierre's LLM tuition falls into a gray area. Unlike Wassenaar, Pierre was clearly engaged in the practice of law before he attended NYU. But under Regulation Section 1.162-5(b)(3), the key issue is whether the LLM qualified Pierre for a new trade or business or provided the minimum qualifications for his profession.
>
> The norms of the profession should be relevant in determining the status of the LLM. In legal practice circles, being an international lawyer (or, even more narrowly, a human-rights treaty negotiator) is a different specialty from corporate litigation, but it is still recognized as the practice of law and may be done by people with the same legal training. Thus, Pierre might argue that "being a lawyer" is a single trade or business, as did the taxpayer in *Ruehmann*. Importantly, under professional norms, an LLM in international law is not generally a minimum requirement for practicing international human rights law; it is helpful but not necessary for any licensing requirement.
>
> Given these professional norms, I conclude that Pierre has a good chance of success on the merits if the matter were litigated. But, as a matter of caution, I would want Pierre to be aware of cases holding that being a tax lawyer is a new trade. See Johnson v. United States, 332 F. Supp. 906 (E.D.La. 1971) (lawyer could not deduct the cost of an LLM in taxation because it prepared him for the new business of being a tax lawyer) (summarized in Casebook at 312). I believe that the *Johnson* precedent is distinguishable, because the tax law is a notoriously complex field and because many tax lawyers obtain an LLM as they enter the tax field. Still, the Johnson precedent suggests that this remains a gray area.

Note that this answer sticks closely to the facts of the issue spotter. It relates the case law and regulations to the question at hand. It does not fall into the trap of reciting the facts and analysis in relevant cases at length, which will tempt the reader to think that you are cutting and pasting the case briefs from your outline. For instance, a middling answer might say:

> One case on point is *Wassenaar*. In *Wassenaar*, the taxpayer attended law school and then, after just one summer, attended NYU for an LLM. The court in *Wassenaar* analyzed whether the taxpayer's past employment in non-legal jobs could qualify as being engaged in the provision of services for compensation. The court also analyzed whether the taxpayer's work on the law journal and as a summer associate could qualify as performing legal work for compensation. The court put great weight on the fact that Wassenaar had not produced legal work as an attorney. The fact that Wassenaar was not a member of the bar before attending NYU was also dispositive.

This summary of Wassenaar isn't incorrect, but it *tells* the reader about the case rather than *applying* the case to the facts at hand.

A related mistake is the grand summary of the law, which—once again—will make the reader suspect that you are repeating what's in your outline:

> The question of the deductibility of educational expenses is one that has occupied considerable time in the federal courts. Section 162 provides that a taxpayer may deduct ordinary and necessary business expenses, while Section 263 (as interpreted by *Indopco*) provides that a taxpayer must capitalize expenses that provide a lasting benefit. Adding to the mix, Section 262 disallows any deduction for personal consumption expenditures.
>
> Higher education expenses tend to confound the tax law because they mix business purpose with personal edification, and they produce lasting benefits over time....

This wouldn't be a terrible opening to, say, a chapter on educational expense deductions, but it isn't a precise way to address an issue-spotter. (NB: a policy question or a synthetic question calling for broad comment on the law might benefit from a bigger summary of the law; use your judgment.)

Another common mistake is the waffling answer. For example:

> Pierre might win his case or lose his case. Compared to Wassenaar, he had a much more solid track record as a practicing lawyer, and he had much more practice experience than the victorious taxpayer in *Ruehmann*. Still, there is the *Johnson* case, which held that being a tax lawyer is a new trade or business, so Pierre could lose if a judge put more weight on that case.

This answer applies the cases to the facts at hand but doesn't reach a resolution. By contrast, the answer above suggested an approach—consulting professional norms—that would enable a firmer answer, albeit one that is cautiously hedged. If you don't see the difference between the model answer and the waffle, ask yourself this: if you were the (non-lawyer) client, which answer would be more helpful to you?

Finally, your answer must deploy good judgment about what is important. If issues are small and easily-resolved, say so. Then spend your time on the hard issues. For instance, it is obvious that Pierre's Harvard tuition is nondeductible. Definitely say so, but do it crisply and move on. You could spend pages and pages on why the JD is nondeductible, but it's not a live issue. The LLM, by contrast, is a live issue with an uncertain resolution.

QUALITY OF EXPRESSION

Words are the tools of the law, and you will be judged on how well you use them. Writing well, even under time pressure, is a professional skill that is critical for practitioners, judges, and academics. Once again, your best English teacher had it right:

- Use active, not passive verbs when you can.
- Use parallel constructions when appropriate.
- Choose vivid and precise language, but use adjectives and adverbs sparingly.
- Deploy appropriate transitions so that you communicate structure to the reader.

And so on. The best exams are a pleasure to read. You don't have to be James Joyce (and please don't try!), but clear, precise expression reveals clear, precise thinking.

At the other end of the scale, poor spelling and grammar will definitely lose points. The occasional typo is not a big deal, but repeated mistakes suggest a lack of professional care. Issue-spotters are typically time-pressured exams, so (once again) you'll have to use your judgment in allocating your time between substance and exposition.

APPENDIX C

Roadmaps to Major Casebooks

Many federal income tax courses roughly follow the order of topics in this book, and most casebooks contain most of the cases discussed here. But every professor has his or her own ideas. I have two suggestions to help you coordinate your particular course with this book.

My first suggestion is to make use of the topic index. When your course covers, say, the taxation of gifts, you can look in the index to see that this book covers gifts in Chapter 3. Reading this book before you read the casebook might, just might, help the casebook make more sense, even if the particular cases I have chosen are slightly different from the ones in your casebook.

My second suggestion is to use the casebook-specific tables presented below. The three tables cross-reference the cases in this book to the order of presentation in three leading casebooks: Graetz and Schenk; Bankman, Shaviro, and Stark; and Freeland, Lathrope, Lind, and Stephens.

Table A.1 Cross-References to Michael Graetz and Deborah Schenk, Federal Income Taxation (7th Ed. 2013)

Casebook Chapter	Case	Chapter in this Book
2	Old Colony Trust Co.	4
	U.S. v. Gotcher	2
	Commissioner v. Duberstein	3
	Hort v. Commissioner	5, 13
	Cesarini v. U.S.	6
	Eisner v. Macomber	6
	Cottage Savings Association v. Commissioner	6
	Zarin v. Commissioner	7
	Estate of Franklin v. Commissioner	14
3	Welch v. Helvering	8
	Exacto Spring v. Commissioner	8
	Pevsner v. Commissioner	9
	Hantzis v. Commissioner	9
	Moss v. Commissioner	9
	Indopco v. Commissioner	10
	Knetsch v. U.S.	11
	Storey v. Commissioner	11
	Frank Lyon Co. v. U.S.	14

Casebook Chapter	Case	Chapter in this Book
4	Druker v. Commissioner	12
	Farid-Es-Sultaneh v. Commissioner	5
	Lucas v. Earl	12
	Blair v. Commissioner	12
	Helvering v. Horst	12
	Johnson v. Commissioner	12
5	Bramblett v. Commissioner	13
	Hort v. Commissioner	5, 13
8	ACM Partnership v. Commissioner	14

Table A.2 Cross-references to Joseph Bankman, Daniel Shaviro, and Kirk Stark, Federal Income Taxation (16th ed. 2012)

Casebook Chapter	Case	Chapter in this Book
2	Benaglia v. Commissioner	2
	Turner v. Commissioner	6
	Commissioner v. Duberstein	3
	Inaja Land Co. v. Commissioner	5
	U.S. v. Kirby Lumber Co.	7
	Zarin v. Commissioner	7
	Commissioner v. Tufts	7
3	Eisner v. Macomber	6
	Cottage Savings Association v. Commissioner	6
	Burnet v. Logan	5
	Farid-Es- Sultanah v. Commissioner	5
5	Nickerson v. Commissioner	11
	Moss v. Commissioner	9
	Smith v. Commissioner	9
	Commissioner v. Flowers	9
	Hantzis v. Commissioner	9
	Pevsner v. Commissioner	9
6	Indopco v. Commissioner	10
	Welch v. Helvering	8
	Estate of Franklin v. Commissioner	14
7	Lucas v. Earl	12
	Blair v. Commissioner	12
	Helvering v. Horst	12
8	Hort v. Commissioner	5, 13

APPENDIX C

Table A.3 Cross-references to James Freeland, Daniel Lathrope, Stephen Lind, and Richard Stephens, Fundamentals of Federal Income Taxation (16th ed., 2011)

Casebook Chapter	Case or Topic	Chapter in this Book
2	Cesarini v. U.S.	6
	Old Colony Trust Co.	4
3	Commissioner v. Duberstein	3
4	Exclusions for Fringe Benefits and Meals and Lodging	2
6	Farid-Es-Sultaneh v. Commissioner	5
	Commissioner v. Tufts	7
8	U.S. v. Kirby Lumber Co.	7
	Zarin v. Commissioner	7
10	Tax Aspects of Divorce	12
12	Lucas v. Earl	12
	Helvering v. Horst	12
	Blair v. Commissioner	12
13	Johnson v. Commissioner	12
14	Welch v. Helvering	8
	Indopco v. Commissioner	10
	Exacto Spring Corp. v. Commissioner	8
17	Activities Not Engaged in for Profit	11
21	Malat v. Riddell	13
	Hort v. Commissioner	5,13
24	Burnet v. Logan	5
26	Like-Kind Exchanges	6

Case Table

All references are to paragraph (¶) numbers.

ACM Partnership v. Commissioner, 157 F.3d 231 (3d Cir. 1998) ... 1403

Armantrout v. Commissioner, 570 F.2d 210 (7th Cir. 1978) ... 1203

Benaglia v. Commissioner, 36 BTA 838 (1937) ... 203, 204, 205, 302

Blair v. Commissioner, 300 U.S. 5 (1937) ... 1205

Bramblett v. Commissioner, 960 F.2d 526 5th Cir. 1992) ... 1306

Brewer Quality Homes, Inc. v. Commissioner, 122 Fed. Appx. 88 (5th Cir. 2004) (unpublished op.) ... 804

Burnet v. Logan, 283 U.S. 404 (1931) ... 504

Byram v. United States, 705 F.2d 1418 (5th Cir. 1983) ... 1304

Cesarini v. United States, 296 F. Supp. 3d (N.D. Ohio 1969) ... 602

Christey v. United States, 841 F.2d 809 (8th Cir. 1988) ... 203

Cole v. Usry, 294 F.2d 426, 427 n.3 (5th Cir. 1961) ... 1304

Coombs v. Commissioner, 608 F.2d 1269 (9th Cir. 1979) ... 902

Cottage Savings Association v. Commissioner, 499 U.S. 554 (1991) ... 103, 604, 1403

Dexsil Corp. v. Commissioner, 147 F.3d 96 (2d Cir. 1998) ... 804

Druker v. Commissioner, 697 F.2d 46 (2d Cir. 1982) ... 1201

Duberstein v. Commissioner, 265 F.2d 28 (1959) ... 302

Duberstein, Commissioner v., 363 U.S. 278 (1960) ... 301

Eberl's Claim Service, Inc. v. Commissioner, 249 F.3d 994 (10th Cir. 2001) ... 804

Eisner v. Macomber, 252 U.S. 189 (1920) ... 603, 604

Exacto Spring Corporation v. Commissioner, 196 F.3d 833 (7th Cir. 1999) ... 102, 803, 804

Farid-Es-Sultaneh v. Commissioner, 160 F.2d 812 (2d Cir. 1947) ... 507

Fender v. United States, 577 F.2d 934 (5th Cir. 1978) ... 1105, 1306

Flowers, Commissioner v., 326 U.S. 465 (1946) ... 902

Frank Lyon Co. v. U.S., 435 U.S. 561 (1978) ... 1402

Franklin, Estate of v. Commissioner, 544 F.2d 1045 (9th Cir. 1976) ... 1401

Gotcher, U.S. v., 401 F.2d 118 (5th Cir.1968) ... 203, 204, 205

Haffner's Service Stations, Inc. v. Commissioner, 326 F.3d 1 (1st Cir. 2003) ... 804

Hantzis v. Commissioner, 638 F.2d 248 (1st Cir. 1981) ... 902

Helvering v. Horst, 311 U.S. 112 (1940) ... 1205

Hort v. Commissioner, 313 U.S. 28 (1941) ... 503

Inaja Land Co. v. Commissioner, 9 T.C. 727 (1947) ... 504

Indopco, Inc. v. Commissioner, 503 U.S. 79 (1992) ... 1002

Johnson v. Commissioner, 78 T.C. 882 (1982) ... 1204

Kirby Lumber Co., U.S. v., 284 U.S. 1 (1931) ... 702, 703

Knetsch v. U.S., 364 U.S. 361 (1960) ... 1102, 1306

Kowalski, Commissioner v., 434 U.S. 77 (1977) ... 203, 204

Laughton v. Commissioner, 40 B.T.A. 101 (1939) ... 1204

Lincoln Savings and Loan, Commissioner v., 403 U.S. 345 (1971) ... 1002

Lucas v. Earl, 281 U.S. 111 (1930) ... 1203, 1204, 1205

Malat v. Riddell, 347 F.2d 23 (9th Cir. 1965) ... 1304

Malat v. Riddell, 383 U.S. 569 (1966) ... 1304

Metro Leasing and Development Corp. v. Commissioner, 376 F.3d 1015 (9th Cir. 2004) ... 804

Morley v. Commissioner, 76 T.C.M. 363 (1998) ... 1103

Moss v. Commissioner, 758 F.2d 211, 212 (7th Cir. 1985) ... 901

Moss v. Commissioner, 80 T.C. 1073 (1983) ... 901

Nickerson v. Commissioner, 700 F.2d 402 (7th Cir. 1983) ... 1103

Obergefell v. Hodges, 576 U.S. ___ (June 26, 2015) ... 1200
Old Colony Trust Co. v. Commissioner, 279 U.S. 716 (1929) ... 404
Pevsner v. Commissioner, 628 F.2d 467 (5th Cir. 1980) ... 904
Plunkett v. Commissioner, 47 T.C.M. 1439 (1984) ... 1103
Poe v. Seaborn, 282 U.S. 101 (1930) ... 1201
Settimo v. Commissioner, T.C. Memo. 2006-261 (2006) ... 905
Simon v. Commissioner, 68 F.3d 41 (2d Cir. 1995) ... 1003
Simon, 103 T.C. 247 (1994) ... 1003
Smith v. Commissioner, 40 B.T.A. 1038 (1939) ... 905
Storey v. Commissioner, T.C. Memo. 2012-115 (2012) ... 1103
Thompson v. Commissioner, 322 F.2d 122, 123 n.2 (5th Cir.1963) ... 1304
Tufts, Commissioner v., 461 U.S. 300 (1983) ... 704, 1401
Turner v. Commissioner, 13 T.C.M. 462 (1954) ... 602
Welch v. Helvering, 290 U.S. 111 (1933). ... 802, 1205
Windsor, U.S. v., 570 U.S. __, 133 S.Ct. 2675 (2013) ... 1200
Winters v. Commissioner, 468 F.2d 778 (1972) ... 302
Winthrop, U.S. v., 417 F.2d 905, 910 (5th Cir. 1969) ... 1304
Zarin v. Commissioner, 916 F.2d 110 (3d Cir.1990), rev'g, 92 T.C.1084 (1989) ... 703
Zdun v. Commissioner, 76 T.C.M. 278 (1998) ... 1103

Table of Code, Regulations and Rulings

All references are to paragraph (¶) numbers.

Code Sections

1 ... 401
1(g) ... 301, 1200
1(h) ... 1300, 1301
1(h)(3) ... 1301
1(h)(11) ... 1305
21 ... 905
25A ... 402.02
36B ... 204
42 ... 402.01
61 ... 201, 202, 302, 602
61(a) ... 703
61(a)(12) ... 702, 705
67 ... 801
71 ... 1202
71(b)(1)(B) ... 1202
71(c)(2) ... 1202
72 ... 504, 1102
72(b) ... 1102
74 ... 602
83 ... 202
83(a) ... 202
102 ... 300, 301, 302, 505, 1205
102(c) ... 302, 303
105 ... 204
106 ... 204
108 ... 705
108(a) ... 705
108(b) ... 705
108(b)(2)(E) ... 705
108(d)(2) ... 705
108(d)(3) ... 705
108(e)(5) ... 703
119 ... 203, 204, 205
119(d) ... 203
132 ... 205
132(a)(1) ... 205
132(a)(5) ... 205
132(d) ... 801
132(e) ... 205
132(e)(1) ... 205
132(e)(2) ... 205
132(f)(2)(B) ... 205
132(f)(6) ... 205
162 ... 302, 801, 802, 901, 902, 905
162(a) ... 801
162(a)(1) ... 803
162(a)(2) ... 902
163 ... 1101
163(h) ... 1101
163(h)(3)(b)(ii) ... 1101
165 ... 1104, 1105
167 ... 1003
168 ... 402.01, 1003
168(k) ... 1004
171 ... 1305
172 ... 604
183 ... 1103
183(d) ... 1103
197 ... 1303
221 ... 402.02
262 ... 300
263 ... 1002
265(a)(2) ... 1102
267 ... 1105
274(b) ... 302, 303
274(n) ... 901
453 ... 504, 1403
483 ... 1403
731 ... 1403
871 ... 1403
881 ... 1403
897 ... 1403
1001 ... 501, 502, 504, 505, 603, 604, 605, 704, 1104
1012 ... 501, 503, 504, 507, 601
1014 ... 503, 505, 506, 507, 605, 1105, 1301
1015 ... 505, 506, 605, 1202
1015(a) ... 505
1016 ... 704
1031 ... 104, 606
1031(b) ... 606
1031(e) ... 606
1041 ... 507, 1202
1060 ... 502, 1303
1091 ... 605, 1104, 1105, 1302
1211 ... 1300, 1302, 1305
1211(b)(1) ... 1302
1212 ... 1302
1221 ... 1300, 1301, 1303, 1304, 1305
1221(a)(1) ... 1301, 1303, 1304, 1306
1222 ... 1300, 1301
1222(11) ... 1301
1231 ... 1303, 1305
1272 ... 1305
1276 ... 1305
1286 ... 1205
2001 ... 506
4980H ... 204
4980I ... 204

Regulation Sections

1.61-14(a) ... 602
1.183-2(b) ... 1103
1.1001-2(c) ... 704
1.1001-3 ... 605
1.1012-1 ... 504
1.1031-1(c) ... 606
15a.453-1(c)(3) ... 1403
15a.453-1(c)(7) ... 1403

Rulings

Rev. Proc. 2013-35 ... 506
Rev. Proc. 2014-61 ... 1301
Rev. Rul. 2001-4 ... 1002

Index

All references are to paragraph (¶) numbers.

A

Accelerated depreciation
- defined, Appendix A
- for tax deferral, 1004
- as tax shelter, 1401, 1402

***ACM Partnership v. Commissioner*, 1403**

Acquisitions, corporate, 502, 1002

Airline tickets, tax-free, 205

Alimony, 1202

Allocation
- basis, 504
- purchase price, 1303

American Opportunity Credit, 402.02

Amount realized, defined, 501

Annuity
- deferred, 1102
- defined, Appendix A
- features, 1102
- life annuity, 1102
- tax arbitrage, 1102
- tax deferral of, 1102

Assets
- capital assets
  - defined, 1304
  - description of, 1300
  - held for investment, 1304
  - motives, 1304
- depreciation of, 1003. *See also* Depreciation
- gifts of depreciated assets, 506
- separate asset test, 1002

Assignments of earned income, 1203

Assignments of income from property, 1205

Average tax rates
- defined, 401, 403, Appendix A
- distribution and, 403
- examples, 401
- progressive rates, 401
- regressive rates, 401
- for the top 1% of households, 403
- uses for, 403

B

Bankruptcy, tax planning for, 705. *See also* Cancellation of indebtedness

Barter, 103

Basis
- allocation, 504
- corporate stock, 502
- defined, 501
- gifts and bequests, 505, 506
- gradual basis recovery, 503
- inherited property, 503
- overview, 501
- pre-nuptial agreements, 507
- recovery, 503
- stepped-down, 505
- stepped-up, 505, 506
- timing of basis recovery, 503

Bearer bonds, 1205

Bequests. *See* Gifts and bequests

***Blair v. Commissioner*, 1205**

Bonds
- assignments of income from, 1205
- basis recovery, 503
- bearer bonds, 1205
- cancellation of indebtedness, 702
- capital gains rate preference, 1305
- capital loss limitation, 1305
- defined, 702, Appendix A
- interest on debt to acquire tax-exempt bonds, 1102
- stripped, 1205

Bonus depreciation, 104, 1004

Bonuses
- signing bonuses and gross up for taxes, 405
- as taxable compensation, 303

Borrowed funds
- bankruptcy and insolvency, tax planning for, 705
- cancellated debt, value of, 703
- cancellation of indebtedness, 702
- debt, defined, Appendix A
- disputed debt, 703
- enforceability of debt, 703
- mortgage interest deduction, 1101
- nonrecourse debt, 704, 1401, Appendix A
- purchase agreement, 701

substance over form, 1402
time value of money, 706
valuation and exclusion of, 701
valuation problems, 700

***Bramblett v. Commissioner*, 1306**

Bunching, 1301

Business deductions
child care, 905
commuting, 902
disguised dividends and gifts, 804
double tax on corporate income, 803
Exacto Spring Corporation v. Commissioner, 803
exclusions, 801
meals, 901, 903
net income, 801
overview, 800
personal expenses vs., 802
Welch v. Helvering, 802
work clothing, 904

Business input, valuation of, 203

Business trips, 203

C

Call options, Appendix A

Cancellation of indebtedness
tax planning for bankruptcy and insolvency, 705
U.S. v. Kirby Lumber Co., 702
value of cancelled debt, 703

Capital assets
defined, 1304
description of, 1300
held for investment, 1304
motives, 1304

Capital expenditures, 1002

Capital gains
closely-held business, sale of, 1303
conversion, 1306
defined, 1300
income tax planning, 506
lock-in, 1301
long-term, 1301
netting rules, 1301
preferential rate, 1300, 1305, 1306
short-term, 1301
tax treatment of, 1300
year-end stock trading, 605

Capital losses
closely-held business, sale of, 1303
limitation, 1300, 1302
tax treatment of, 1300

Capitalization
capital expenditures, 1002
timing and valuation, 1002

Carve out, 1205

Case law
ACM Partnership v. Commissioner, 1403
Blair v. Commissioner, 1205
Bramblett v. Commissioner, 1306
Cottage Savings Association v. Commissioner, 604
Druker v. Commissioner, 1201
Duberstein v. Commissioner, 302
Eisner v. Macomber, 603
Exacto Spring Corporation v. Commissioner, 803
Farid-Es-Sultaneh v. Commissioner, 507
Fender v. United States, 1105
Flowers; Commissioner v., 902
Frank Lyon Co. v. U.S., 1402
Franklin, Estate of, 1401
Helvering v. Horst, 1205
Hort v. Commissioner, 503
Inaja Land Co. v. Commissioner, 504
Indopco, Inc. v. Commissioner, 1002
Knetsch v. U.S., 1102
Lucas v. Earl, 1203
Moss v. Commissioner, 901
Nickerson v. Commissioner, 1103
Old Colony Trust v. Commissioner, 404
Pevsner v. Commissioner, 904
roadmaps, Appendix C
Simon v. Commissioner, 1003
Smith v. Commissioner, 905
Storey v. Commissioner, 1103
Tufts; Commissioner v., 704
U.S. v. Kirby Lumber Co., 702
Welch v. Helvering, 802
Zarin v. Commissioner, 703

Cash flow, 1205, 1402

Chapter 11 bankruptcy, 705

Child care expenses, 905

Child support, 1202

Closely-held business
disguised dividends and gifts, 804
sale of, 1303

Clothing, deduction for, 904

Code Section 102, 301, 302

Code Section 108(e)(5), 703

Code Section 132, 205

Community property, 1201

Commuting, 902

Compensation. *See* Salary

Contingent installment sale, 1403

Contracts
contractual freedom, 1402
notional principal contract, 1403

Control of income shifted, 1205

Conversion of ordinary income to capital gains, 1306

Corporations
acquisitions, 502, 1002
assignments of income, 1204
corporate stock, 103, 502, Appendix A
defined, 502
disguised dividends and gifts, 804
double tax on corporate income, 803
income shifting, 106

***Cottage Savings Association v. Commissioner,* 604**

Coupons, assignments of, 1205

Credit. *See* Tax credit

Creditor, defined, Appendix A

D

Debentures, defined, Appendix A. *See also* Bonds

Debt. *See also* Borrowed funds
defined, Appendix A
disputed, 703
recourse, 704, Appendix A

Debt holder, defined, Appendix A

Debt issuer, 702, Appendix A

Debtor, defined, Appendix A

Deductions. *See* Tax deductions

Default of loans, 702

Deferral of taxes. *See* Tax deferral

Deferred annuity, 1102

Depreciation
accelerated. *See* Accelerated depreciation
of assets, 1003
for basis recovery, 503
bonus depreciation, 104, 1004
defined, 402.01, Appendix A
depreciated assets, gifts of, 506
loans vs. leases, 1402
on overvalued property, 1401
real estate, 402.01
straight-line, 1003, Appendix A
tax deferral and, 104, 1003, 1401
vehicles, 1003

Depression, basis recovery during, 503

Discounted present value, 1001, Appendix A

Discounted value, 1001, Appendix A

Dispositions. *See* Sale or other disposition

Disputed debt, 703

Distribution and the average tax rate, 403

Diversification of investments, 605

Dividends
defined, Appendix A
disguised, 804
nondeductibility of, and double tax, 803
realization of, 603
stock dividends, 603, Appendix A
taxed at long-term capital gains rate, 1305

Divorce
alimony, 1202
child support, 1202
dividing property and income at, 1202

Dollar measurement convention of valuation
overview, 201
stock valuation, 202

Double tax on corporate income, 803

***Druker v. Commissioner*, 1201**

***Duberstein v. Commissioner*, 302**

E

Earned income, assignments of, 1203

Earned income tax credit (EITC), 402.01

Education
American Opportunity Credit, 402.02
Lifelong Learning Tax Credit, 402.02
student loan interest, 402.02
value of tax breaks for, 402.02

***Eisner v. Macomber,* 603**

EITC (earned income tax credit), 402.01

Employer-provided health insurance, 204

Entities
assignments of income using, 1204
conversion of ordinary income to capital gains, 1306

Equal Protection Clause, 1201

Equity, 803, Appendix A

Estate planning
gains and losses, 506
income tax and, 506

***Exacto Spring Corporation v. Commissioner,* 803**

Exclusion
borrowed funds, 701
debt relief, 705

deduction vs., 801
defined, Appendix A
employer-provided health insurance, 204
fringe benefits, 203, 205
gifts and bequests, 300, 301, 302, 303
inventory, 1301
meals, 205

Expenses
business vs. personal, 102, 802
capital, 1002
child care, 905
meals. *See* Meals
work clothing, 904

F

Family businesses, disguised dividends and gifts, 804

Family Dollar Stores, Inc., 502

Family taxation
assignments of income from property, 1205
assignments of income using entities, 1204
community property, 1201
dividing property and income at divorce, 1202
earned income, assignments of, 1203
income shifting, 1200, 1201
marriage bonus, 1201
marriage penalty, 1201

***Farid-Es-Sultaneh v. Commissioner*, 507**

Farming as a hobby loss, 1103

***Fender v. United States*, 1105**

FICA tax, 100

Filmmaking as a hobby loss, 1103

First priority claim, Appendix A

Floating interest rate, 1403

***Flowers; Commissioner v.*, 902**

Foreclosure
defined, 704, Appendix A
nonrecourse debt, 704, 1401

Form 1040, categories of income, 201

Fourteenth Amendment, 1201

***Frank Lyon Co. v. U.S.*, 1402**

***Franklin, Estate of*, 1401**

Fraud vs. tax planning, 804

Fringe benefits
business costs as net income exclusions, 801
Code Section 132 exclusions, 205
defined, Appendix A
exclusions, 203, 205
as tax-free compensation, 203
valuation of, 203, Appendix 2-1

Fruit and tree metaphor, 1204, 1205

G

Gains and losses
basis allocation, 504
basis concept, 501
basis recovery, 503
capital. *See* Capital gains
corporate acquisitions, 502
estate planning and the income tax, 506
gain, defined, Appendix A
gift and bequest basis, 505
mark-to-market measurement, 601
overview, 500
prenuptial agreements and basis, 507
year-by-year measurement, 601

Gambling, and cancellation of debt, 703

Gift cards, tax-free, 205

Gifts and bequests
appreciated property, 506
basis rules, 505
bonuses, 303
business gifts, 302, 303
depreciated assets, 506
disguised, 804
Duberstein v. Commissioner, 302
gift tax and income tax, 506. *See also* Estate planning
income shifting, 301, 505
overview, 300
taxing of, 302
tips, 303

Goodwill
closely-held business, sale of, 1303
defined, 502, 1002, 1303, Appendix A
examples, 1002

Great Depression, basis recovery during, 503

Great Recession
bonus depreciation, 104, 1004
causing bankruptcy and insolvency, 705
mortgage defaults, 702

Gross up for taxes, 405

H

Haig-Simons (uses approach) definition of income
borrowed funds, 701
borrowing and the time value of money, 706

capital expenditures, 1002
capital gains, 1301
depreciation, 1003
fringe benefits, 203
gains and losses, 500
overview, 201
realization, 601
stock and stock options, 202
valuation conventions, 201, 202
work clothing, 904

Health insurance, employer-provided, 204

***Helvering v. Horst,* 1205**

Hobby losses, 1103
multi-factor test, 1103
as personal consumption, 1103
valuation of, 1103

Horses, hobby losses and, 1103

***Hort v. Commissioner,* 503**

Human capital, 1205

I

***Inaja Land Co. v. Commissioner,* 504**

Incidence of tax benefits, 903

Income
assignments from property, 1205
categories of
overview, 201
stock and stock options, 202
conventions
categories of income, 201, 202
dollar measurement, 201, 202
Haig-Simons (uses approach) definition of income, 201, 202
defined, 100
difficulty in defining, 100
dividing, at divorce, 1202
legal ambiguity of, 100
measurement problem of, 201
ordinary, 1300
ordinary income converted to capital gains, 1306
phantom, Appendix A
as tool for public policy, 100

Income shifting
assignments of earned income, 1203
control of the income, 1205
corporations, 106, 1204
defined, 106, Appendix A
divorce, dividing property and income at, 1202
family taxation
marriage, 1201
overview, 1200
gifts and bequests, 301, 505
for individuals, 106
overvaluation shelters, 1401
overview, 106
progressive tax rates, 106
property income, 1205

Income tax
equality of, 200
estate planning and, 506
overview, 100
Sixteenth Amendment, 603

Income-splitting, 1203

Independent investor test, 803

***Indopco, Inc. v. Commissioner,* 1002**

Inherited property, basis of, 503

Insolvency, tax planning for, 705

Installment sale rules, 1403

Insurance
annuities, 1102
employer-provided health insurance, 204
life insurance, 1402, Appendix A

Intangibles. *See* Goodwill

Interest
deductions
borrowing and the time value of money, 706
floating rate, 1403
mortgage, 1101
overview, 1101
tax arbitrage, 1102
defined, 1101, Appendix A
repurchase agreement (repo), 1104

Internal Revenue Service (IRS)
substance over form tool, 105
"tax upon a tax," 404, 405

International taxation, 1403

Inventory
bunching, 1301
as excluded capital, 1304
exclusion from capital gains treatment, 1301
sale of closely-held business, 1303
tax deferral, 1301
using borrowed funds to purchase, 700

Investments
capital assets held for, 1304
conversion of ordinary income to capital gains, 1306
diversification, 605
independent investor test, 803
tax deduction for real estate, 402.01

Issue-spotter exam question
legal judgment, Appendix B
quality of expression, Appendix B
structure, Appendix B

J

Joint venture
assignments of earned income, 1203
income shifting, 106

K

***Knetsch v. U.S.*, 1102**

L

Leases
cancellation, and basis recovery, 503
sale-leaseback, 1401, 1402
substance over form, 1402

Legal judgment, issue-spotter exam question, Appendix B

Life annuity, 1102

Life insurance, 1402, Appendix A

Life interest, 1205

Lifelong Learning Tax Credit, 402.02

Like-kind exchanges, 606

Live-in jobs or live-out jobs, 203

Loans, losses on, 604. *See also* Borrowed funds

Lock-in, 1301

Long position, defined, Appendix A

Long-term capital gains, 1301

Losses. *See also* Gains and losses
capital. *See* Capital losses
defined, Appendix A
hobby losses, 1103
selective loss realization, 1105
tax. *See* Tax loss
unrealized, 604

Low-income housing tax credit, 402.01

***Lucas v. Earl*, 1203**

M

Machinery, depreciation of, 1003

Marginal tax rates
defined, 401, Appendix A
examples, 401
progressive rates, 401
regressive rates, 401
for tax planning, 401
value of tax breaks, 402
education, 402.02
real estate, 402.01

Mark-to-market gain measurement, 601

Marriage
income shifting and, 1201
marriage bonus, 1201
marriage penalty, 1201

Meals
as a business deduction, 901, 903
deduction at 50%, 901
fringe benefit valuation of, 203
tax lobbying and the restaurant industry, 903
valuation of, 901

Mortgage
defaults, 702
defined, Appendix A
interest deduction, 1101

Mortgagee, defined, Appendix A

Mortgagor, defined, Appendix A

***Moss v. Commissioner*, 901**

Motives for capital asset acquisition, 1304

N

Net income
business deductions, 800, 801
business vs. personal expenses, 102
deduction for losses, 501
defined, 102, Appendix A
gains and losses, 500
measuring over time, 1000
overview, 102

Netting rules for capital gains, 1301

***Nickerson v. Commissioner*, 1103**

Nonrecourse debt
defined, Appendix A
overvaluation shelters, 1401
underwater, 704

Notional principal contract, 1403

O

OID (original issue discount), 1305, Appendix A

***Old Colony Trust v. Commissioner*, 404**

Open transaction, 504

Options
defined, Appendix A
purchase, 1402
stock, 202

Ordinary income
converted to capital gains, 1306
defined, 1300

Original issue discount (OID), 1305, Appendix A

Overvaluation shelters, 1401

P

Parking, tax-free, 205

Partnership taxation, 1403

Personal consumption
- *Duberstein v. Commissioner*, 302
- hobby losses, 1103
- meals, 901, 903
- personal expenses vs. business deductions, 802
- valuation of, 203, 900

***Pevsner v. Commissioner*, 904**

Phantom income, Appendix A

Preferential rate, 1301, 1305, 1306

Pre-nuptial agreements, 507

Present value
- assignments of income from property, 1205
- borrowing and the time value of money, 706
- defined, Appendix A
- loans, 701
- realization and tax deferral, 1301
- tax deferral, 1001

Procter & Gamble Co., 502

Progressive tax rates, 106, 401, Appendix A

Property
- assignments of income from, 1205
- community property, 1201
- dividing, at divorce, 1202
- gifts of appreciated property, 506
- inherited property, 503
- overvalued, 1401
- taxes, 100

Public policy, income as tool for, 100

Purchase agreement, 701

Put options, Appendix A

Q

Quality of expression, issue-spotter exam question, Appendix B

R

Real estate
- basis recovery, 503
- as capital asset, 1304
- capital gains on sale of, 1304
- depreciation of, 1003
- inherited property, 503
- like-kind exchanges, 606
- loans and leases, 1402
- overvaluation of property, 1401
- swaps, 606
- tax deduction for investments in, 402.01
- value of tax breaks for, 402.01
- value-for-value exchange, 704

Realization
- advantages of using, 601
- amount realized, 501
- cancellation of indebtedness, 702
- capital gains, 1301
- defined, 103, 600, 603, Appendix A
- incentives bad for the economy, 103
- overview, 103
- real estate swaps, 606
- realization requirement
  - defined, Appendix A
  - tax deferral, 104
- sale or other disposition, 604
- selective loss realization, 1105, 1302
- tax deferral and, 104, 601
- timing, 103
- timing of gain, 601
- valuation and, 601, 603
- windfalls, 602
- year-end stock trading, 605

Real-world transactions
- bonus depreciation and the Great Recession, 1004
- bonuses, tips, and business gifts, 303
- closely-held business, sale of, 1303
- company stock and stock options, 202
- corporate acquisitions, 502
- disguised dividends and gifts, 804
- divorce, dividing property and income at, 1202
- education, value of tax breaks for, 402.02
- employer-provided health insurance, 204
- estate planning and the income tax, 506
- real estate swaps, 606
- real estate, value of tax breaks for, 402.01
- signing bonuses and gross up for taxes, 405
- stocks and bonds, 1305
- tax lobbying and the restaurant industry, 903
- tax planning for bankruptcy and insolvency, 705
- wash sales and repos, 1104
- year-end stock trading, 605

Recession. *See* Great Recession

Recourse debt
- bifurcated treatment of, 704
- defined, Appendix A

Refund suit, 602

Regressive tax rates, 401, Appendix A

Remainderman, 1205

Repo (repurchase agreement), 1104

Repurchase agreement (repo), 1104

Restaurant industry and tax lobbying, 903

Roadmaps to major casebooks, Appendix C

S

Salary
bonuses, 303, 405
deductibility of, 803
substance over form, 404
unreasonable compensation, 803
valuation, 200

Sale or other disposition
allocation of the purchase price, 1303
barter vs. cash, 103, 104
closely-held business, 1303
contingent installment sale, 1403
defined, 604
installment sale rules, 1403
wash sale, 605

Sale-leasebacks, 1401, 1402

Sales taxes, 100

Savings and Loan, loan losses, 604

Security wash sales and repos, 1104

Selective loss realization, 1105, 1302

Seller financing
defined, Appendix A
tax shelters, 1401
valuation and, 701, 703

Separate asset test, 1002

Shareholder, defined, Appendix A. *See also* Stockholder

Shifting income. *See* Income shifting

Short position, defined, Appendix A

Short-term capital gains, 1301

Signing bonus, 405

***Simon v. Commissioner*, 1003**

Sixteenth Amendment, 603

***Smith v. Commissioner*, 905**

Social Security payroll tax, 100

Stepped-down basis, 505

Stepped-up basis, 505, 506

Stock
basis recovery, 503
capital gains rate preference, 1305
capital loss limitation, 1302, 1305
corporate stock, 103, 502, Appendix A
dividing, at divorce, 1202
loss deduction, 501
options, 202
pre-nuptial agreements, 507
realization of dividends, 603
short-term capital gains on sale of, 1301
stock dividends, 603, Appendix A. *See also* Dividends
valuation of, 202
wash sales, 1104
year-end stock trading, 605

Stockholder
corporate acquisitions and, 502
defined, Appendix A
income upon realization of profits, 603

***Storey v. Commissioner*, 1103**

Straight-line depreciation, 1003, Appendix A

Stripped bond, 1205

Structure, issue-spotter exam, Appendix B

Student loan interest deduction, 402.02

Substance over form
conversion of ordinary income to capital gains, 1306
defined, Appendix A
disguised dividends and gifts, 804
Old Colony Trust v. Commissioner, 404
overvaluation shelters, 1401
overview, 105
owner vs. tenant, 1402
purpose of, 105
repurchase agreement (repo), 1104
salary vs. dividends, 803
selective loss realization, 1105
tax arbitrage, 1102
tax deferral and, 104
tax rates, 400
tax shelters, 1402, 1403

Substitution doctrine, 503

T

TANF (Temporary Assistance for Needy Families), 402.01

Tax arbitrage, 1102

Tax base, 400

Tax credit
American Opportunity Credit, 402.02
defined, Appendix A
earned income tax credit, 402.01
Lifelong Learning Tax Credit, 402.02
low-income housing, 402.01

to reduce tax owed, 402.01

Tax deductions
business
child care, 905
commuting, 902
disguised dividends and gifts, 804
double tax on corporate income, 803
Exacto Spring Corporation v. Commissioner, 803
exclusions, 801
meals, 901, 903
net income, 801
overview, 800
personal expenses vs., 802
Welch v. Helvering, 802
work clothing, 904
defined, 401, Appendix A
exclusions vs., 801
for income reduction, 402.01
interest, borrowing and the time value of money, 706
for losses, 501
marginal tax rate to evaluate, 401
mortgage interest, 1101
student loan interest, 402.02

Tax deferral
annuities, 1102
basis allocation, 504
basis recovery, 503
bonus depreciation, 104
capital gains, 1301
defined, 104, Appendix A
depreciation and, 1003. *See also* Depreciation
depreciation deductions and capital gains, 1401
gifts and bequests, 505
overview, 104
realization and, 601
selective loss realization, 1105
tax arbitrage, 1102
tax shelters, 1403
value of, 1001
year-end stock trading, 605

Tax forgiveness, 505, 605

Tax fraud vs. tax planning, 804

Tax goodie
basis, 503
business meals, 903
business trips, 203
cancellation of indebtedness, 705
deductible losses on sales, 604
depreciated assets, 506, 605
depreciation, 1402
losses, 604, 606
tax deferral, 605

Tax lobbying and the restaurant industry, 903

Tax loss. ***See also*** **Losses**
capital loss limitation, 1302
defined, Appendix A
gifts and bequests, basis rules for, 505, 506
real estate swaps, 606
from sales or other dispositions, 604
wash sales and repos, 1104, 1105
year-end stock trading, 605

Tax planning
bankruptcy and insolvency, 705
estate planning, 506
marginal tax rates used for, 401
value of tax deferral, 1001

Tax rates
average. *See* Average tax rates
marginal. *See* Marginal tax rates
overview, 400
preferential rate, 1301, 1305, 1306
progressive rates, 106, 401, Appendix A
regressive rates, 401, Appendix A

Tax Reform Act of 1986, 901

Tax shelters
overvaluation (*Estate of Franklin*), 1401
substance over form (*Frank Lyon Co. v. U.S.*), 1402
tax deferral (*ACM Partnership v. Commissioner*), 1403

"Tax upon a tax," 404, 405

Taxes
double tax on corporate income, 803
gross up for, 405
income tax
equality of, 200
estate planning and, 506
overview, 100
Sixteenth Amendment, 603
international, 1403
partnership, 1403
payroll, 100
property, 100
sales tax, 100

Tax-exempt entities, income shifting, 106

Tax-free compensation, fringe benefits, 203

Temporary Assistance for Needy Families (TANF), 402.01

Time value of money, 706

Timing
basis recovery, 503
business deductions, 802
capital expenditures, 1002
measuring net income over time, 1000
realization and, 103
realization and timing of gain, 601

Tips as taxable compensation, 303

Torts, defined, 100

Trust, life interests, 1205

***Tufts; Commissioner v.*, 704**

U

Underwater nonrecourse debt, 704

Uniforms, 904

***U.S. v. Kirby Lumber Co.*, 702**

Uses approach to defining income. *See* Haig-Simons (uses approach) definition of income

V

Valuation. *See also* Depreciation
- basis allocation, 504
- borrowed funds
  - exclusion of, 701
  - time value of money, 706
  - value of cancelled debt, 703
- business deductions, 800, 900
- business vs. personal expenses, 802
- capital expenditures, 1002
- capital gains, 1301
- child care expenses, 905
- conventions
  - categories of income, 201, 202
  - dollar measurement, 201, 202
  - Haig-Simons (uses approach) definition of income, 201, 202
- defined, Appendix A
- fringe benefits, 203, Appendix 2-1
- gifts and bequests, 505
- hobby losses, 1103
- income measurement problem, 201
- income tax, 200
- live-in jobs or live-out jobs, 203
- meals, 901
- overvaluation shelters, 1401
- overview, 101
- problem in measuring individual's gain in well-being, 101
- realization and, 601, 603
- stock and stock options, 202
- subjective, 203
- tax deferral, 1001, 1403
- tax shelters, 1401
- uncertainties to reduce taxes, 101
- underwater nonrecourse debt, 704
- windfalls, 602
- work clothing, 904

Value-for-value exchange, 704

Vehicles
- depreciation of, 1003
- valuation for business deductions, 802

W

Wash sales
- securities, 1104
- selective loss realization, 1105
- year-end stock trading, 605

***Welch v. Helvering*, 802**

Whipsaw, 507

Windfalls and realization, 602

Work clothing, deduction for, 904

Y

Year-by-year gain measurement, 601

Year-end stock trading, 605

Z

***Zarin v. Commissioner*, 703**